CGP — the only rational solution...

OK, so GCSE Maths can be seriously challenging — but the Higher Tier exams aren't as scary as they sound. Whichever units you're doing, help is at hand...

This life-saving CGP book is packed with no-nonsense explanations, worked examples and exam practice questions to prepare you for M3, M4, M7 & M8. There's just no better guide to GCSE Maths.

How to access your free Online Edition

This book includes a free Online Edition to read on your PC, Mac or tablet. To access it, just go to **cgpbooks.co.uk/extras** and enter this code...

0111 8277 0419 7469

By the way, this code only works for one person. If somebody else has used this book before you, they might have already claimed the Online Edition.

CGP — still the best! ☺

Our sole aim here at CGP is to produce the highest quality books — carefully written, immaculately presented and dangerously close to being funny.

Then we work our socks off to get them out to you — at the cheapest possible prices.

Contents

About the Exams
The Exams 1

Section One — Number
Types of Number and BODMAS [M3, M8] 2
Multiples, Factors and Prime Factors [M3] 3
LCM and HCF [M3] 4
Fractions [M3] 5
Fractions, Decimals and Percentages [M3] 7
Fractions and Recurring Decimals [M3] 8
Fractions and Recurring Decimals [M8] 9
Rounding Numbers [M3] 10
Estimating [M7] 11
Bounds [M3] 12
Bounds [M4] 13
Standard Form [M7] 14
Different Number Systems [M7] 16
Revision Questions for Section One 17

Section Two — Ratio, Proportion and Percentages
Ratios [M7] 18
Direct Proportion Problems [M7] 20
Inverse Proportion Problems [M8] 22
Harder Proportion Problems [M7, M8] 23
Percentages [M3] 24
Repeated Percentage Change [M3, M8] 27
Revision Questions for Section Two 28

Section Three — Algebra
Algebra Basics [M3] 29
Multiplying Out Brackets [M3] 30
Factorising [M3] 31
Powers [M7] 32
Powers and Roots [M8] 33
Manipulating Surds [M8] 34
Solving Equations [M3] 35
Expressions and Formulas [M3] 37
Expressions, Formulas and Functions [M3] 38
Trial and Improvement [M7] 39
Rearranging Formulas [M7] 40
Factorising Quadratics [M3] 42
Factorising Quadratics [M4] 43
The Quadratic Formula [M4] 44
Algebraic Fractions [M3] 45
Algebraic Fractions [M3, M4] 46
Simultaneous Equations [M7] 47
Simultaneous Equations [M8] 48
Inequalities [M7] 49
Graphical Inequalities [M7] 50
Sequences [M7] 51
Revision Questions for Section Three 53

Section Four — Graphs
Straight Lines and Gradients [M3] 54
Line Segments [M3] 55
$y = mx + c$ [M3] 56
Parallel and Perpendicular Lines [M3, M4] 57
Quadratic Graphs [M7] 58
Harder Graphs [M7] 59
Harder Graphs [M8] 60
Solving Equations Using Graphs [M7, M8] 61
Real-Life Graphs [M3, M7] 62
Distance-Time Graphs [M7] 63
Gradients of Real-Life Graphs [M8] 64
Revision Questions for Section Four 65

Section Five — Measures and Angles

Unit Conversions [M3, M7] 66
Speed, Density and Pressure [M3] 67
Five Angle Rules [M3] 68
Parallel Lines [M3] 69
Geometry Problems [M3] 70
Angles in Shapes [M7] 71
Bearings [M7] 72
Circle Geometry [M4] 73
Pythagoras' Theorem [M3] 75
Trigonometry [M3] 76
The Sine and Cosine Rules [M8] 78
3D Pythagoras [M8] 80
3D Trigonometry [M8] 81
Revision Questions for Section Five 82

Section Six — Shapes and Area

Properties of 2D Shapes [M3] 83
Similar Shapes [M7] 85
Area — Triangles and Quadrilaterals [M3] 86
Area — Circles [M3] 87
Plans and Elevations [M3] 88
3D Shapes — Surface Area [M3] 89
3D Shapes — Volume [M3] 90
3D Shapes — Volume [M4] 91
Construction [M7] 92
Loci and Construction [M7] 94
Loci and Construction — Examples [M7] 95
Translation, Rotation and Reflection [M7] 96
Enlargement [M7, M8] 97
Enlargement — Area and Volume [M7, M8] 98
Revision Questions for Section Six 99

Section Seven — Statistics and Probability

Planning an Investigation [M3] 100
Sampling and Data Collection [M3] 101
Sampling and Data Collection [M3, M4] 102
Sampling and Data Collection [M3] 103
Venn Diagrams [M3] 104
Other Charts and Graphs [M3] 105
Scatter Graphs [M3] 107
Mean, Mode, Median and Range [M3] 108
Frequency Tables — Finding Averages [M3] 109
Grouped Frequency Tables [M3] 110
Averages and Spread [M3] 111
Cumulative Frequency [M3] 113
Histograms and Frequency Density [M4] 114
Probability Basics [M7] 116
Counting Outcomes [M7] 117
Expected Frequency [M7] 118
Probability Experiments [M7] 119
The AND / OR Rules [M7] 120
Tree Diagrams [M7] 121
Tree Diagrams [M8] 122
Revision Questions for Section Seven 123

Answers 124
Index 131

Published by CGP

Written by Richard Parsons

Editors: Luke Bennett, Rob Hayman, Luke Molloy, Caroline Purvis, Rachael Rogers and George Wright

With thanks to Mona Allen, Paul Jordin and Glenn Rogers for the proofreading.

ISBN: 978 1 78908 562 4

Clipart from Corel®
Printed by Bell and Bain Ltd, Glasgow

Text, design, layout and original illustrations © Richard Parsons 2020
All rights reserved.

Photocopying more than one section of this book is not permitted, even if you have a CLA licence.
Extra copies are available from CGP with next day delivery • 0800 1712 712 • www.cgpbooks.co.uk

About the Exams

The Exams

This page has all the info about the exams along with a few tips to help you ace them.

There Are Different Unit Exams

1) CCEA Higher GCSE maths is split into different units. Each unit covers different bits of maths and some units build on what you learn in others.
2) You will only take exams in two units — either M3 or M4 AND either M7 or M8. The two most common combinations are 'M3 and M7' and 'M4 and M8'.
3) The combination you take will depend on the grade you're hoping to get. M3 and M7 are targeted at grades B-E, while M4 and M8 are targeted at grades A*-C (grade D is also allowable).
4) Every page in this book has been stamped with one of these stamps so you know which bits you need to learn, depending on which exams you plan to take. You'll find most stamps at the top of the page but if a page covers more than one unit, each separate bit will be stamped.
5) Below is a summary of the Higher exams.

You could also get your GCSE by sitting a combination of Foundation and Higher unit exams — your teacher should be able to tell you more about this.

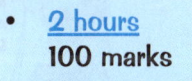

← You'll take one of these unit exams... →

M3
- 2 hours
- 100 marks
- 45% of the total GCSE.

M4
- 2 hours
- 100 marks
- 45% of the total GCSE.
- Could test anything marked up as M3 or M4.

The stuff marked up as M3 in this book crops up in the other unit exams, so you need to learn it whatever combination you're taking.

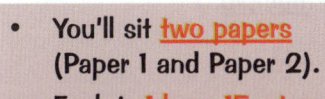

...and then one of these unit exams.

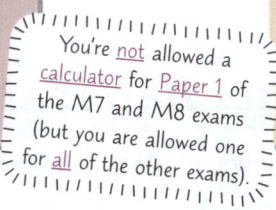

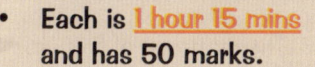

M7
- You'll sit two papers (Paper 1 and Paper 2).
- Each is 1 hour 15 mins and has 50 marks.
- Together they make up 55% of the total GCSE.
- Both papers could test anything marked up as M3 or M7.

M8
- You'll sit two papers (Paper 1 and Paper 2).
- Each is 1 hour 15 mins and has 50 marks.
- Together they make up 55% of the total GCSE.
- Both papers could test anything marked up as M3, M4, M7 or M8.

You're not allowed a calculator for Paper 1 of the M7 and M8 exams (but you are allowed one for all of the other exams).

So if you're doing M8, you'll need to know everything in this book. Sorry.

These Top Tips Will Help in the Exams

1) Always make sure you read the question properly. For example, if the question asks you to give your answer in metres, don't give it in centimetres.
2) Show each step in your working. You're less likely to make a mistake if you write things out in stages. And even if your final answer's wrong, you'll probably pick up some marks if the examiner can see that your method is right.
3) Check that your answer is sensible. Worked out an angle of 450° or 0.045° in a triangle? You've probably gone wrong somewhere...
4) If you have any time left at the end of the exam, check all your answers. Look back through your answers and make sure you haven't made any silly mistakes. Don't just stare at the hottie in front.

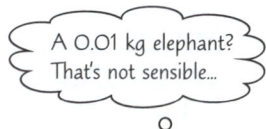

A 0.01 kg elephant? That's not sensible...

Types of Number and BODMAS

Ah, the glorious world of GCSE Maths. OK, maybe it's more like whiffy socks at times, but learn it you must. Here are some handy definitions of different types of number, and a bit about what order to do things in.

Integers:

You need to make sure you know the meaning of this word — it'll come up all the time in GCSE Maths. An integer is another name for a whole number — either a positive or negative number, or zero.

Examples:
- Integers: −365, 0, 1, 17, 989, 1 234 567 890
- Not integers: 0.5, $\frac{2}{3}$, $\sqrt{7}$, $13\frac{3}{4}$, −1000.1, 66.66, π

BODMAS

Brackets, **O**ther, **D**ivision, **M**ultiplication, **A**ddition, **S**ubtraction

BODMAS tells you the ORDER in which these operations should be done: Work out Brackets first, then Other things like squaring, then Divide / Multiply groups of numbers before Adding or Subtracting them.

You can use BODMAS when it's not clear what to do next, or if there's more than one thing you could do.

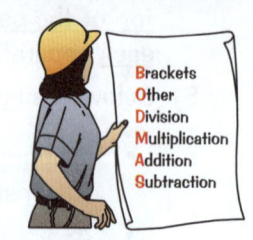

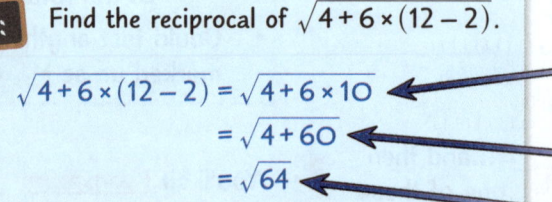

EXAMPLE: Find the reciprocal of $\sqrt{4 + 6 \times (12 - 2)}$.

$\sqrt{4 + 6 \times (12 - 2)} = \sqrt{4 + 6 \times 10}$ ← It's not obvious what to do inside the square root — so use BODMAS. Brackets first...

$= \sqrt{4 + 60}$ ← ... then multiply...

$= \sqrt{64}$ ← ... then add.

$= 8$ ← Take the square root

The reciprocal of 8 is $\frac{1}{8}$. ← Finally, take the reciprocal (the reciprocal of a number is just 1 ÷ the number).

All Numbers are Either Rational or Irrational

Rational numbers can be written as fractions. Most numbers you deal with are rational.

Rational numbers come in 3 different forms:

1) Integers e.g. 4 $(=\frac{4}{1})$, −5 $(=\frac{-5}{1})$, −12 $(=\frac{-12}{1})$
2) Fractions p/q, where p and q are (non-zero) integers, e.g. $\frac{1}{4}$, $-\frac{1}{2}$, $\frac{7}{4}$
3) Terminating or recurring decimals e.g. 0.125 $(=\frac{1}{8})$, 0.33333333... $(=\frac{1}{3})$, 0.143143143... $(=\frac{143}{999})$

Irrational numbers are messy. They can't be written as fractions — they're never-ending, non-repeating decimals. Square roots of positive integers are either integers or irrational (e.g. $\sqrt{2}$ and $\sqrt{3}$ are irrational, but $\sqrt{4} = 2$ isn't). Surds (see p.34) are numbers or expressions containing irrational roots. π is also irrational.

What's your BODMAS? About 50 kg, dude...

It's really important to check your working on BODMAS questions. You might be certain you did it right, but it's surprisingly easy to make a slip. Try this Exam Practice Question and see how you do.

Q1   Without using a calculator, find the value of $3 + 22 \times 3 - 14$.   [2 marks]

Multiples, Factors and Prime Factors

If you think '<u>factor</u>' is short for 'fat actor', you should give this page a read. Stop thinking about fat actors.

Multiples and *Factors*

The **MULTIPLES** of a number are just its <u>times table</u>.

EXAMPLE: Find the first 8 multiples of 13.
You just need to find the first 8 numbers in the 13 times table:
13   26   39   52   65   78   91   104

The **FACTORS** of a number are all the numbers that <u>divide into it</u>.

There's a method that guarantees you'll find them all:
1) Start off with 1 × the number itself, then try 2 ×, then 3 × and so on, listing the pairs in rows.
2) Try each one in turn. Cross out the row if it doesn't divide exactly.
3) Eventually, when you get a number <u>repeated</u>, <u>stop</u>.
4) The numbers in the rows you haven't crossed out make up the list of factors.

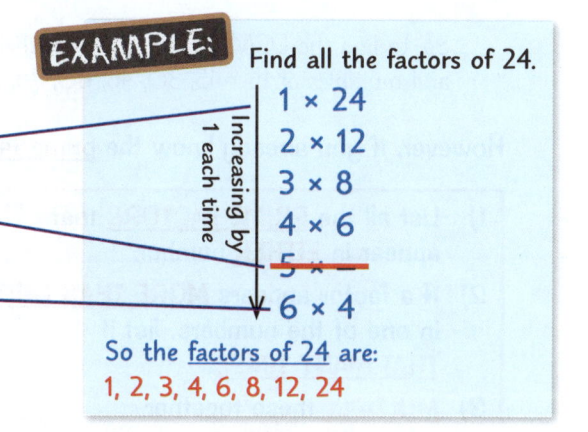

EXAMPLE: Find all the factors of 24.
(Increasing by 1 each time)
1 × 24
2 × 12
3 × 8
4 × 6
~~5 ×~~
6 × 4
So the <u>factors of 24</u> are:
1, 2, 3, 4, 6, 8, 12, 24

Prime Numbers:

2   3   5   7   11   13   17   19   23   29   31   37   41   43...

A <u>prime number</u> is a number which <u>doesn't divide by anything</u>, apart from itself and 1 — i.e. its only <u>factors</u> are itself and 1. (The only exception is <u>1</u>, which is <u>NOT</u> a prime number.)

Finding Prime Factors — *The Factor Tree*

<u>Any integer bigger than 1</u> can be broken down into a string of prime factors all multiplied together — this is called '<u>prime factor decomposition</u>' or '<u>prime factorisation</u>'.

EXAMPLE: Express 420 as a product of prime factors.

```
       420
      /    \
    42      10
   /  \    /  \
  (7)  6  (2) (5)
      / \
    (2) (3)
```

So 420 = 2 × 2 × 3 × 5 × 7
      = 2^2 × 3 × 5 × 7

To write a number as a product of its prime factors, use the <u>Factor Tree</u> method:
1) Start with the number at the top, and <u>split</u> it into <u>factors</u> as shown.
2) Every time you get a prime, <u>ring it</u>.
3) Keep going until you can't go further (i.e. you're just left with primes), then write the primes out <u>in order</u>. If there's more than one of the <u>same factor</u>, you can write them as <u>powers</u>.

No matter which numbers you choose at each step, you'll find that the prime factorisation is exactly the same. Each number has a <u>unique</u> set of prime factors.

Takes me back, scrumping prime factors from the orchard...

Make sure you know the Factor Tree method inside out, then give this Exam Practice Question a go...

Q1   Express as products of their prime factors: a) 990   [2 marks]   b) 160   [2 marks]

Section One — Number

LCM and HCF

As if the previous page wasn't enough excitement, here's some more factors and multiples fun...

LCM — 'Least Common Multiple'

LCM can also stand for 'lowest common multiple' — it means the same thing.

The SMALLEST number that will DIVIDE BY ALL the numbers in question.

If you're given two numbers and asked to find their LCM, just LIST the MULTIPLES of BOTH numbers and find the SMALLEST one that's in BOTH lists.

So, to find the LCM of 12 and 15, list their multiples (multiples of 12 = 12, 24, 36, 48, 60, 72, ... and multiples of 15 = 15, 30, 45, 60, 75, ...) and find the smallest one that's in both lists — so LCM = 60.

However, if you already know the prime factors of the numbers, you can use this method instead:

1) List all the PRIME FACTORS that appear in EITHER number.
2) If a factor appears MORE THAN ONCE in one of the numbers, list it THAT MANY TIMES.
3) MULTIPLY these together to give the LCM.

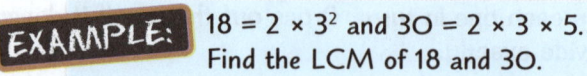

EXAMPLE: $18 = 2 \times 3^2$ and $30 = 2 \times 3 \times 5$. Find the LCM of 18 and 30.

$18 = 2 \times 3 \times 3$ $30 = 2 \times 3 \times 5$

So all the prime factors that appear in either number are: 2, 3, 3, 5 — List 3 twice as it appears twice in 18.

LCM = $2 \times 3 \times 3 \times 5 = $ **90**

HCF — 'Highest Common Factor'

The BIGGEST number that will DIVIDE INTO ALL the numbers in question.

If you're given two numbers and asked to find their HCF, just LIST the FACTORS of BOTH numbers and find the BIGGEST one that's in BOTH lists.

Take care listing the factors — make sure you use the proper method (as shown on the previous page).

So, to find the HCF of 36 and 54, list their factors (factors of 36 = 1, 2, 3, 4, 6, 9, 12, 18 and 36 and factors of 54 = 1, 2, 3, 6, 9, 18, 27 and 54) and find the biggest one that's in both lists — so HCF = 18.

Again, there's a different method you can use if you already know the prime factors of the numbers:

1) List all the PRIME FACTORS that appear in BOTH numbers.
2) MULTIPLY these together to find the HCF.

EXAMPLE: $180 = 2^2 \times 3^2 \times 5$ and $84 = 2^2 \times 3 \times 7$. Use this to find the HCF of 180 and 84.

$180 = ②\times②\times③\times 3 \times 5$ $84 = ②\times②\times③\times 7$

2, 2 and 3 are prime factors of both numbers, so HCF = $2 \times 2 \times 3 = $ **12**

2 appears twice in both lists, so it's listed twice for working out the HCF.

LCM and HCF live together — it's a House of Commons...

The first method is much simpler in both cases, but make sure you learn the second method as well — just in case the exam question specifically tells you to use prime factors, or the numbers are really big.

Q1 a) Find the least common multiple (LCM) of 9 and 12.
    b) Given that $28 = 2^2 \times 7$ and $8 = 2^3$, find the LCM of 28 and 8. [4 marks]

Q2 a) Find the highest common factor (HCF) of 36 and 84.
    b) Given that $150 = 2 \times 3 \times 5^2$ and $60 = 2^2 \times 3 \times 5$, find the HCF of 150 and 60. [4 marks]

Section One — Number

Fractions

One of your exams will be a non-calculator paper — so you need to be able to do fraction calculations without your beloved calculator. These two pages will show you all the tricks you need to work with fractions.

1) Cancelling Down

To cancel down or simplify a fraction, divide top and bottom by the same number, till they won't go further:

EXAMPLE: Simplify $\frac{18}{24}$.

Cancel down in a series of easy steps — keep going till the top and bottom don't have any common factors.

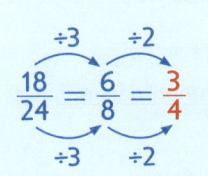

$$\frac{18}{24} = \frac{6}{8} = \frac{3}{4}$$
(÷3, ÷2 top; ÷3, ÷2 bottom)

The number on the top of the fraction is the numerator, and the number on the bottom is the denominator.

2) Mixed Numbers

Mixed numbers are things like $3\frac{1}{3}$, with an integer part and a fraction part. Improper fractions are ones where the top number is larger than the bottom number. You need to be able to convert between the two.

EXAMPLES:

1. Write $4\frac{2}{3}$ as an improper fraction.

1) Think of the mixed number as an addition:
$$4\frac{2}{3} = 4 + \frac{2}{3}$$

2) Turn the integer part into a fraction:
$$4 + \frac{2}{3} = \frac{12}{3} + \frac{2}{3} = \frac{12 + 2}{3} = \frac{14}{3}$$

2. Write $\frac{31}{4}$ as a mixed number.

Divide the top number by the bottom.
1) The answer gives the whole number part.
2) The remainder goes on top of the fraction.

$31 ÷ 4 = 7$ remainder 3 so $\frac{31}{4} = 7\frac{3}{4}$

3) Multiplying

Multiply top and bottom separately. It usually helps to cancel down first if you can.

EXAMPLE: Find $\frac{8}{15} \times \frac{5}{12}$.

Cancel down by dividing top and bottom by any common factors you find in either fraction:

Now multiply the top and bottom numbers separately:

8 and 12 both divide by 4
15 and 5 both divide by 5

$$\frac{8}{15} \times \frac{5}{12} = \frac{2}{15} \times \frac{5}{3} = \frac{2}{3} \times \frac{1}{3} = \frac{2 \times 1}{3 \times 3} = \frac{2}{9}$$

4) Dividing

Turn the 2nd fraction UPSIDE DOWN and then multiply:

When you're multiplying or dividing with mixed numbers, always turn them into improper fractions first.

EXAMPLE: Find $2\frac{1}{3} \div 3\frac{1}{2}$.

Rewrite the mixed numbers as fractions:
$$2\frac{1}{3} \div 3\frac{1}{2} = \frac{7}{3} \div \frac{7}{2}$$

Turn $\frac{7}{2}$ upside down and multiply:
$$= \frac{7}{3} \times \frac{2}{7}$$

Simplify by cancelling the 7s:
$$= \frac{1}{3} \times \frac{2}{1} = \frac{2}{3}$$

Section One — Number

Fractions

5) Common Denominators

This comes in handy for ordering fractions by size, and for adding or subtracting fractions. You need to find a number that all the denominators divide into — this will be your common denominator. The simplest way is to find the lowest common multiple of the denominators:

EXAMPLE: Put these fractions in ascending order of size: $\frac{8}{3}, \frac{5}{4}, \frac{12}{5}$

The LCM of 3, 4 and 5 is 60, so make 60 the common denominator:

$\frac{8}{3} = \frac{160}{60}$ (×20) $\frac{5}{4} = \frac{75}{60}$ (×15) $\frac{12}{5} = \frac{144}{60}$ (×12)

So the correct order is $\frac{75}{60}, \frac{144}{60}, \frac{160}{60}$ i.e. $\frac{5}{4}, \frac{12}{5}, \frac{8}{3}$

Don't forget to use the original fractions in the final answer.

6) Adding, Subtracting — Sort the Denominators First

1) Make sure the denominators are the same (see above).
2) Add (or subtract) the top lines (numerators) only.

If you're adding or subtracting mixed numbers, it usually helps to convert them to improper fractions first.

EXAMPLE: Calculate $2\frac{1}{5} - 1\frac{1}{2}$.

Rewrite the mixed numbers as fractions: $2\frac{1}{5} - 1\frac{1}{2} = \frac{11}{5} - \frac{3}{2}$

Find a common denominator: $= \frac{22}{10} - \frac{15}{10}$

Combine the top lines: $= \frac{22-15}{10} = \frac{7}{10}$

7) Fractions of Something

EXAMPLE: What is $\frac{9}{20}$ of £360?

'$\frac{9}{20}$ of' means '$\frac{9}{20}$ ×', so multiply the 'something' by the top of the fraction, and divide it by the bottom.

$\frac{9}{20}$ of £360 = (£360 ÷ 20) × 9
= £18 × 9 = **£162**

It doesn't matter which order you do those two steps in — just start with whatever's easiest.

8) Expressing as a Fraction

EXAMPLE: Write 180 as a fraction of 80.

Just write the first number over the second and cancel down.

$\frac{180}{80} = \frac{9}{4}$

No fractions were harmed in the making of these pages...

...although one was slightly frightened for a while, and several were tickled.
When you think you've learnt all this, try all of these Exam Practice Questions without a calculator.

Q1 Calculate, giving your answers in their simplest form: a) $\frac{3}{8} \times 1\frac{5}{12}$ [3 marks]

b) $1\frac{7}{9} \div 2\frac{2}{3}$ [3 marks] c) $4\frac{1}{9} + 2\frac{2}{27}$ [3 marks] d) $5\frac{2}{3} - 9\frac{1}{4}$ [3 marks]

Q2 Dean has made 30 sandwiches. $\frac{7}{15}$ of the sandwiches he has made are vegetarian, and $\frac{3}{7}$ of the vegetarian sandwiches are cheese sandwiches.
How many cheese sandwiches has he made? [2 marks]

Section One — Number

Fractions, Decimals and Percentages

The one word that describes all these three is PROPORTION. Fractions, decimals and percentages are simply three different ways of expressing a proportion of something — you should understand that they're closely related and completely interchangeable with each other. The tables below show some really common conversions — you should know these straight off without having to work them out:

Fraction	Decimal	Percentage
$\frac{1}{2}$	0.5	50%
$\frac{1}{4}$	0.25	25%
$\frac{3}{4}$	0.75	75%
$\frac{1}{3}$	0.333333...	$33\frac{1}{3}$%
$\frac{2}{3}$	0.666666...	$66\frac{2}{3}$%
$\frac{1}{10}$	0.1	10%
$\frac{2}{10}$	0.2	20%

Fraction	Decimal	Percentage
$\frac{1}{5}$	0.2	20%
$\frac{2}{5}$	0.4	40%
$\frac{1}{8}$	0.125	12.5%
$\frac{3}{8}$	0.375	37.5%
$\frac{5}{2}$	2.5	250%
$\frac{7}{2}$	3.5	350%
$\frac{9}{4}$	2.25	225%

The more of those conversions you learn, the better — but for those that you don't know, you must also learn how to convert between the three types. These are the methods:

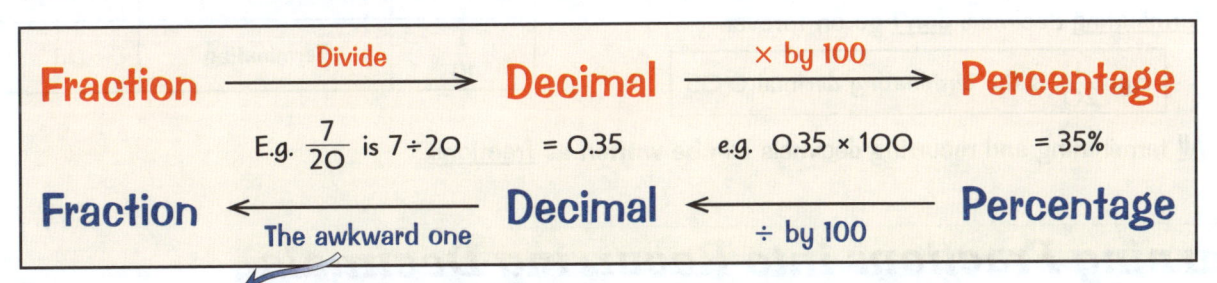

Fraction —Divide→ Decimal —× by 100→ Percentage

E.g. $\frac{7}{20}$ is 7 ÷ 20   = 0.35   e.g. 0.35 × 100   = 35%

Fraction ←The awkward one— Decimal ←÷ by 100— Percentage

Converting decimals to fractions is awkward, because it's different for different types of decimal. There are two different methods you need to learn:

1) Terminating decimals to fractions — this is fairly easy. The digits after the decimal point go on the top, and a power of 10 on the bottom — with the same number of zeros as there were decimal places.

Terminating decimals are ones where the digits don't go on forever — see the next page. Recurring decimals are ones where the digits do go on forever.

$0.6 = \frac{6}{10}$ $0.3 = \frac{3}{10}$ $0.7 = \frac{7}{10}$ etc.

$0.12 = \frac{12}{100}$ $0.78 = \frac{78}{100}$ $0.05 = \frac{5}{100}$ etc.

$0.345 = \frac{345}{1000}$ $0.908 = \frac{908}{1000}$ $0.024 = \frac{24}{1000}$ etc.

These can often be cancelled down — see p.5.

2) Recurring decimals to fractions — this is trickier. See page 9...

Eight out of ten cats prefer the perfume Eighty Purr Scent...

Learn the top tables and the 4 conversion processes. Then it's time to break into a mild sweat...

Q1 Turn the following decimals into fractions and reduce them to their simplest form.
    a) 0.4   b) 0.02   c) 0.77   d) 0.555   e) 5.6   [5 marks]

Q2 Which is greater: a) 57% or $\frac{5}{9}$, b) 0.2 or $\frac{6}{25}$, c) $\frac{7}{8}$ or 90%?   [3 marks]

Q3 A farm produces 120 eggs per week. The farmers use 18 eggs per week and sell the rest. What percentage of the eggs produced each week is sold?   [2 marks]

Section One — Number

Fractions and Recurring Decimals

You might think that a decimal is just a decimal. But oh no — things get a lot more juicy than that...

Recurring or Terminating...

1) <u>Recurring</u> decimals have a <u>pattern</u> of numbers which repeats forever.

> For example, $\frac{1}{3}$ is the decimal 0.333333...

2) It doesn't have to be a single digit that repeats.

> E.g. You could have 0.143143143...

3) The <u>repeating part</u> is usually marked with <u>dots</u> on top of the number.

4) If there's <u>one dot</u>, only <u>one digit</u> is repeated. If there are <u>two dots</u>, then <u>everything from the first dot to the second dot</u> is the repeating bit.

> E.g. $0.2\dot{5} = 0.2555555...$
> $0.\dot{2}\dot{5} = 0.25252525...$
> $0.\dot{2}6\dot{5} = 0.265265265...$

5) <u>Terminating</u> decimals <u>don't</u> go on forever.

> E.g. $\frac{1}{20}$ is the terminating decimal 0.05

6) <u>All</u> terminating and recurring decimals can be written as <u>fractions</u>.

Fraction	Recurring decimal or terminating decimal?	Decimal
$\frac{1}{2}$	Terminating	0.5
$\frac{1}{3}$	Recurring	$0.\dot{3}$
$\frac{1}{4}$	Terminating	0.25
$\frac{1}{5}$	Terminating	0.2
$\frac{1}{6}$	Recurring	$0.1\dot{6}$
$\frac{1}{7}$	Recurring	$0.\dot{1}4285\dot{7}$
$\frac{1}{8}$	Terminating	0.125
$\frac{1}{9}$	Recurring	$0.\dot{1}$
$\frac{1}{10}$	Terminating	0.1

Turning Fractions into Recurring Decimals

This isn't so different from turning a fraction into a terminating decimal, but you need to make sure you've found the whole <u>repeating pattern</u> before you write your final answer.

EXAMPLE: Without using a calculator, write $\frac{5}{11}$ as a recurring decimal.

1) Remember, $\frac{5}{11}$ means 5 ÷ 11, so you can just <u>do the division</u>. The trick is to treat the 5 as a decimal — write it as 5.000...

> 11 into 50 goes 4 times...
>
> 0.4
> 11) 5.⁵0⁶0 0 0 0
> ...and carry the 6
>
> 11 into 60 goes 5 times...
>
> 0.4 5
> 11) 5.⁵0⁶0⁵0 0 0
> ...and carry the 5
>
> 0.4 5 4 5
> 11) 5.⁵0⁶0⁵0⁶0⁵0

2) Keep going until you can see the <u>repeating pattern</u>. Write the recurring decimal using dots above the repeating part.

> 5 ÷ 11 = 0.454545...
> so $\frac{5}{11} = 0.\dot{4}\dot{5}$

Oh, what's recurrin'?...

This seems pretty tricky, I admit, but you'll be on the right track if you know what those dots on top of a decimal mean, and how to turn a fraction into a decimal by dividing — even without a calculator.

Q1 Without a calculator, use division to show that $\frac{1}{6} = 0.1\dot{6}$. [3 marks]

Section One — Number

Fractions and Recurring Decimals

...and juiciest of all, here's the method for changing recurring decimals into fractions.

Changing Recurring Decimals into Fractions

1) Basic Ones

Turning a recurring decimal into a fraction uses a really clever trick. Just watch this...

EXAMPLE: Write $0.2\dot{3}\dot{4}$ as a fraction.

1) Name your decimal — I've called it r.
   Let r = $0.2\dot{3}\dot{4}$

2) Multiply r by a power of ten to move it past the decimal point by one full repeated lump — here that's 1000:
   1000r = $234.2\dot{3}\dot{4}$

3) Now you can subtract to get rid of the decimal part:
   1000r = $234.2\dot{3}\dot{4}$
   − r = $0.2\dot{3}\dot{4}$
   999r = 234

4) Then just divide to leave r, and cancel if possible:
   r = $\frac{234}{999} = \frac{26}{111}$

The 'Just Learning the Result' Method:

1) For converting recurring decimals to fractions, you could just learn the result that the fraction always has the repeating unit on the top and the same number of nines on the bottom...
2) BUT this only works if the repeating bit starts straight after the decimal point — see below.
3) If you get asked to 'show that' or 'prove' that a fraction and a recurring decimal are equivalent, make sure you use the proper method.

2) The Trickier Type

If the recurring bit doesn't come right after the decimal point, things are just slightly trickier.

EXAMPLE: Write $0.1\dot{6}$ as a fraction.

1) Name your decimal.
   Let r = $0.1\dot{6}$

2) Multiply r by a power of ten to move the non-repeating part past the decimal point.
   10r = $1.\dot{6}$

3) Now multiply again to move one full repeated lump past the decimal point.
   100r = $16.\dot{6}$

4) Subtract to get rid of the decimal part:
   100r = $16.\dot{6}$
   − 10r = $1.\dot{6}$
   90r = 15

5) Divide to leave r, and cancel if possible:
   r = $\frac{15}{90} = \frac{1}{6}$

I used to name my recurring decimals after types of cheese...

...but writing 'Gorgonzola' out loads of times for every exam question was a bit much. This isn't an easy page — make sure you learn the full method then try applying it to these questions...

Q1   Express $0.\dot{1}2\dot{6}$ as a fraction in its simplest form. [2 marks]

Q2   Show that $0.\dot{0}\dot{7} = \frac{7}{99}$. [2 marks]

Section One — Number

Rounding Numbers

Two different ways of specifying how a number can be rounded are 'decimal places' and 'significant figures'.

Decimal Places (d.p.)

To round to a given number of decimal places:

1) IDENTIFY the position of the 'LAST DIGIT' from the number of decimal places.
2) Then look at the next digit to the RIGHT — called THE DECIDER.
3) If the DECIDER is 5 OR MORE, then ROUND UP the LAST DIGIT.
   If the DECIDER is 4 OR LESS, then LEAVE the LAST DIGIT as it is.
4) There must be NO MORE DIGITS after the last digit (not even zeros).

'Last digit' = last one in the rounded version, not the original number.

EXAMPLE: What is 7.45839 to 2 decimal places?

7.4**5**8**3**9 = 7.46 ← The LAST DIGIT rounds UP because the DECIDER is 5 or more.

LAST DIGIT   DECIDER

If you have to round up a 9 (to 10), replace the 9 with 0, and carry 1 to the left. Remember to keep enough zeros to fill the right number of decimal places — so to 2 d.p. 45.699 would be rounded to 45.70, and 64.996 would be rounded to 65.00.

65 has the same value as 65.00, but 65 isn't expressed to 2 d.p. so it would be marked wrong.

Significant Figures (s.f.)

The method for significant figures is identical to that for decimal places except that locating the last digit is more difficult — it wouldn't be so bad, but for the zeros...

1) The 1st significant figure of any number is simply the first digit which isn't a zero.

2) The 2nd, 3rd, 4th, etc. significant figures follow on immediately after the 1st, regardless of being zeros or not zeros.

      0.002309   2.03070

SIG. FIGS: 1st 2nd 3rd 4th   1st 2nd 3rd 4th

(If we're rounding to say, 3 s.f., then the LAST DIGIT is simply the 3rd sig. fig.)

3) After rounding the last digit, end zeros must be filled in up to, but not beyond, the decimal point.

No extra zeros must ever be put in after the decimal point.

EXAMPLES:

	to 3 s.f.	to 2 s.f.	to 1 s.f.
1) 54.7651	54.8	55	50
2) 0.0045902	0.00459	0.0046	0.005
3) 30895.4	30900	31000	30000

Well, I think that's put those decimals in their place...

Rounding is a really useful skill, so get some practice in by having a go at these questions:

Q1   Give 21.435 correct to: a) 1 d.p.   b) 2 d.p.   [2 marks]

Q2   Round 76.841 to: a) 2 s.f.   b) 3 s.f.   c) 4 s.f.   [3 marks]

Section One — Number

Estimating

'Estimating' doesn't mean 'take a wild guess' — it means 'look at the numbers, make them a bit easier, then do the calculation'. Your answer won't be as accurate as the real thing but hey, it's easier on your brain.

Estimating Calculations

It's time to put your rounding skills to use and do some estimating.

EXAMPLE: Estimate the value of $\frac{127.8 + 41.9}{56.5 \times 3.2}$, showing all your working.

≈ means 'approximately equal to'.

1) Round all the numbers to easier ones — 1 or 2 s.f. usually does the trick.
2) You can round again to make later steps easier if you need to.

$$\frac{127.8 + 41.9}{56.5 \times 3.2} \approx \frac{130 + 40}{60 \times 3} = \frac{170}{180} \approx 1$$

EXAMPLE: A cylindrical glass has a height of 18 cm and a radius of 3 cm.
a) Find an estimate in cm³ for the volume of the glass.

The formula for the volume of a cylinder is $V = \pi r^2 h$ (see p.90).
Round the numbers to 1 s.f.:
$\pi = 3.14159... = 3$ (1 s.f.), height = 20 cm (1 s.f.) and radius = 3 cm (1 s.f.).
Now just put the numbers into the formula:
$V = \pi r^2 h \approx 3 \times 3^2 \times 20 = 3 \times 9 \times 20 \approx 540$ cm³

b) Use your answer to part a) to estimate the number of glasses that could be filled from a 2.5 litre bottle of lemonade.

2.5 litres = 2500 cm³
2500 ÷ 540 ≈ 2500 ÷ 500 = **5 glasses**

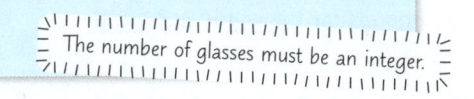

The number of glasses must be an integer.

Estimating Square Roots

Estimating square roots can be a bit tricky, but there are only 2 steps:
1) Find two square numbers, one either side of the number you're given.
2) Decide which number it's closer to, and make a sensible estimate of the digit after the decimal point.

EXAMPLE: Estimate the value of $\sqrt{87}$ to 1 d.p.

87 is between 81 (= 9²) and 100 (= 10²).
It's closer to 81, so its square root will be closer to 9 than 10: $\sqrt{87} \approx 9.3$
(the actual value of $\sqrt{87}$ is 9.32737..., so this is a reasonable estimate).

By my estimate, it's time to go home...

If you're asked to estimate something in the exam, make sure you show all your steps (including what each number is rounded to). That way the examiner will be able to tell that you didn't just use a calculator to work out the exact answer. That would be naughty.

Q1 Estimate the value of: a) $\frac{4.23 \times 11.8}{7.7}$ [2 marks] b) $\sqrt{136}$ [2 marks]

Q2 The volume of a sphere is given by the formula $V = \frac{4}{3}\pi r^3$.
a) Use this formula to estimate the volume of a sphere of radius 9 cm. [2 marks]
b) Will your estimate be bigger or smaller than the actual value? Explain why. [1 mark]

Section One — Number

Bounds

Finding *upper and lower bounds* is pretty easy, but using them in *calculations* is a bit trickier.

Upper and *Lower* Bounds

> When a measurement is ROUNDED to a given UNIT, the actual measurement can be anything up to HALF A UNIT bigger or smaller.

EXAMPLE: The mass of a cake is given as 2.4 kg to the nearest 0.1 kg.
Find the interval within which m, the actual mass of the cake, lies.

lower bound = 2.4 − 0.05 = 2.35 kg
upper bound = 2.4 + 0.05 = 2.45 kg

So the interval is 2.35 kg ≤ m < 2.45 kg

The interval is written as an inequality. There's more about inequalities on page 49.

The actual value is *greater than or equal to* the *lower bound* but *strictly less than* the *upper bound*. The actual mass of the cake could be *exactly* 2.35 kg, but if it was exactly 2.45 kg it would *round up* to 2.5 kg instead.

Maximum and *Minimum* Values for Calculations

When a calculation is done using rounded values there will be a DISCREPANCY between the CALCULATED VALUE and the ACTUAL VALUE. You can use the *bounds* of the *rounded values* to work out the bounds of the *result* of the calculation.

EXAMPLE: A rectangular pinboard is measured as being 0.89 m wide and 1.23 m long, to the nearest cm.
a) Calculate the minimum and maximum possible values for the area of the pinboard.

Find the *bounds* for the *width* and *length*:

0.885 m ≤ width < 0.895 m
1.225 m ≤ length < 1.235 m

Find the *minimum* area by multiplying the *lower bounds*, and the *maximum* by multiplying the *upper bounds*:

minimum possible area = 0.885 × 1.225
= 1.084125 m²

maximum possible area = 0.895 × 1.235
= 1.105325 m²

b) Use your answers to part a) to give the area of the pinboard to an appropriate degree of accuracy.

The area of the pinboard lies in the interval 1.084125 m² ≤ a < 1.105325 m². Both the *upper bound* and the *lower bound* round to 1.1 m² to 1 d.p. so the area of the pinboard is **1.1 m² to 1 d.p.**

c) Find the interval which contains the possible values for the perimeter of the pinboard.

Find the *perimeter* by adding the sides together.
Find the *upper bound* by adding together all the *upper bounds*,
and the *lower bound* by adding together all the *lower bounds*:

upper bound = 0.895 + 0.895 + 1.235 + 1.235
= 4.26 m

lower bound = 0.885 + 0.885 + 1.225 + 1.225
= 4.22 m

So the interval is 4.22 m ≤ perimeter < 4.26 m

You're bound to find this page tricky...

Be careful with bounds if the quantity has to be a whole number. For example, the maximum value of the bound 145 ≤ x < 155 is 154 for a number of people but 154.99999... for the height of a person.

Q1 Anisha is painting the walls in her living room. She works out that it costs £1.20 to the nearest 10p to buy enough paint to cover 1 m² of wall. The area of the walls in the room is 31 m² to the nearest m². Calculate the maximum and minimum amounts Anisha could spend. [4 marks]

Section One — Number

Bounds

Another page on bounds, so soon? I'm afraid so. There's more to learn about using bounds in calculations — they're a little harder if you have to divide or subtract, so read on...

Dividing and Subtracting Bounds

The examples on the previous page showed you how to work out the bounds of a calculation if you need to multiply or add values — you use the biggest possible values to get the maximum value, and the smallest possible values to get the minimum value.

But you need to use a different rule when dividing or subtracting, because the bigger the number you divide or subtract by, the smaller the result:

> For Division: Upper bound = Maximum ÷ Minimum
> Lower bound = Minimum ÷ Maximum
>
> For Subtraction: Upper bound = Maximum − Minimum
> Lower bound = Minimum − Maximum

EXAMPLES:

1. $a = 5.3$ and $b = 4.2$, both given to 1 d.p.
   What are the maximum and minimum values of $a \div b$?

   First find the bounds for a and b. → $5.25 \leq a < 5.35$, $4.15 \leq b < 4.25$

   The bigger the number you divide by, the smaller the answer, so:

   maximum value = $5.35 \div 4.15$
   = 1.289 (to 3 d.p.)

   $\max(a \div b) = \max(a) \div \min(b)$

   minimum value = $5.25 \div 4.25$
   = 1.235 (to 3 d.p.)

   and $\min(a \div b) = \min(a) \div \max(b)$

2. Baako is making custard. He pours 800 ml of milk into a measuring jug.
   He pours some milk from the jug into a saucepan, leaving 210 ml of milk in the jug.
   The recipe called for him to add 610 ml of milk to the saucepan. If both measurements were correct to the nearest 10 ml, is it possible that Baako added exactly 610 ml of milk to the saucepan?

   Find the bounds for both measurements.
   795 ml ≤ amount poured into jug < 805 ml,
   205 ml ≤ amount left in jug < 215 ml

   Then find the bounds of the amount added to the saucepan, making sure to subtract the largest from the smallest value and vice versa.

   upper bound = 805 − 205 = 600 ml
   lower bound = 795 − 215 = 580 ml

   It is not possible as 610 ml is not within the bounds of the amount added.

Whenever I crack a joke, laughter a-bounds...

...or maybe it doesn't. Once you've learnt the rules on this page, you'll be able to tackle any bounds question. Make sure you double-check which operation you're using and what degree of accuracy values have been rounded to — those are places where it's easy to slip up.

Q1 The diagram on the right shows a rectangular field, with the length of one side given to the nearest m. The area of the field is 21 000 m² to three significant figures. Find, to the nearest m, the upper and lower bounds for the length of the side labelled x.

98 m

x [4 marks]

Q2 Naya runs 200 m (to the nearest m) in a time of 32.2 seconds (to the nearest 0.1 second). By considering bounds, find her speed in m/s to an appropriate degree of accuracy. [5 marks]

Section One — Number

Standard Form

Standard form is useful for writing **VERY BIG** or **VERY SMALL** numbers in a more convenient way.

A number written in standard form must *always* be in *exactly* this form:

This *number* must *always* be *between 1 and 10*.
(The fancy way of saying this is $1 \leq A < 10$)

$$A \times 10^n$$

This number is just the *number of places* the *decimal point* moves.

Learn the Three Rules:

1) The *front number* must always be *between 1 and 10*.
2) The power of 10, n, is *how far the decimal point moves*.
3) n is *positive for BIG numbers*, n is *negative for SMALL numbers*.
(This is much better than rules based on which way the decimal point moves.)

Five Important Examples:

1 Express 35 600 in standard form.

1) Move the decimal point until 35 600 becomes 3.56 ($1 \leq A < 10$)
2) The decimal point has moved 4 places so n = 4, giving: 10^4
3) 35 600 is a big number so n is +4, not –4

35600.0
= 3.56×10^4

2 Express 0.0000623 in standard form.

1) The decimal point must move 5 places to give 6.23 ($1 \leq A < 10$). So the power of 10 is 5.
2) Since 0.0000623 is a small number it must be 10^{-5} not 10^{+5}

0.0000623
= 6.23×10^{-5}

3 Express 4.95×10^{-3} as an ordinary number.

1) The power of 10 is negative, so it's a small number — the answer will be less than 1.
2) The power is –3, so the decimal point moves 3 places.

0004.95 × 10^{-3}
= 0.00495

4 What is 146.3 million in standard form?

Too many people get this type of question wrong. Just take your time and do it in two stages:

146.3 million = 146.3 × 1 000 000
= 146 300 000 ——— 1) Write the number out in full.
= 1.463×10^8 ——— 2) Convert to standard form.

The two favourite wrong answers for this are:
146.3×10^6 — which is kind of right but it's not in standard form because 146.3 is not between 1 and 10
1.463×10^6 — this one is in standard form but it's not big enough

5 Put the following numbers in size order, from biggest to smallest:
4.21×10^2, 4.22×10^{-2}, 6.00×10^6, 1.35×10^6.

Make sure that all of the numbers are actually in standard form before you use Steps 1 and 2 to compare them.

1) Look at the powers of 10 first — the bigger the power, the bigger the number, so put the numbers with the biggest powers of 10 first.
2) If any numbers have the same power of 10, just look at the numbers themselves and order them biggest to smallest.

1 — 6.00×10^6
2 — 1.35×10^6
3 — 4.21×10^2
4 — 4.22×10^{-2}

Section One — Number

Standard Form

Calculations with Standard Form

Now that you've met numbers in standard form, it's time to do some calculations with them. In the exam, you might be asked to add, subtract, multiply or divide in standard form without using a calculator.

Multiplying and Dividing — not too bad

1) Rearrange to put the front numbers and the powers of 10 together.
2) Multiply or divide the front numbers, and use the power rules (see p.32) to multiply or divide the powers of 10.
3) Make sure your answer is still in standard form.

EXAMPLES:

1. Find $(2 \times 10^3) \times (6.75 \times 10^5)$ without using a calculator. Give your answer in standard form.

   Multiply front numbers and powers separately:
   $(2 \times 10^3) \times (6.75 \times 10^5)$
   $= (2 \times 6.75) \times (10^3 \times 10^5)$
   $= 13.5 \times 10^{3+5}$ — Add the powers (see p.32)
   $= 13.5 \times 10^8$

   Not in standard form — convert it:
   $= 1.35 \times 10 \times 10^8$
   $= 1.35 \times 10^9$

2. Calculate $240\,000 \div (4.8 \times 10^{10})$ without using a calculator. Give your answer in standard form.

   Convert 240 000 to standard form:
   $240\,000 \div (4.8 \times 10^{10})$
   $= \dfrac{2.4 \times 10^5}{4.8 \times 10^{10}}$

   Divide front numbers and powers separately:
   $= \dfrac{2.4}{4.8} \times \dfrac{10^5}{10^{10}}$

   Subtract the powers (see p.32):
   $= 0.5 \times 10^{5-10}$
   $= 0.5 \times 10^{-5}$

   Not in standard form — convert it:
   $= 5 \times 10^{-1} \times 10^{-5}$
   $= 5 \times 10^{-6}$

Adding and Subtracting — a bit trickier

1) Make sure the powers of 10 are the same — you'll probably need to rewrite one of them.
2) Add or subtract the front numbers.
3) Convert the answer to standard form if necessary.

EXAMPLE: Calculate $(9.8 \times 10^4) + (6.6 \times 10^3)$ without using a calculator. Give your answer in standard form.

1) Rewrite one number so both powers of 10 are equal:
2) Now add the front numbers:
3) 10.46×10^4 isn't in standard form, so convert it:

$(9.8 \times 10^4) + (6.6 \times 10^3)$
$= (9.8 \times 10^4) + (0.66 \times 10^4)$
$= (9.8 + 0.66) \times 10^4$
$= 10.46 \times 10^4 = 1.046 \times 10^5$

To put standard form numbers into your calculator, use the [EXP] or the [×10ˣ] button. E.g. enter 2.67×10^{15} by pressing [2.67] [EXP] [15] [=] or [2.67] [×10ˣ] [15] [=].

Or for just £25, you can upgrade to luxury form...

Make sure you understand all the examples on these pages. Then answer these Exam Practice Questions:

Q1 Express 0.854 million and 0.00018 in standard form. [2 marks]

Q2 Work out the following without using a calculator. Give your answers in standard form.
   a) $(3.2 \times 10^7) \div (1.6 \times 10^{-4})$ [2 marks]   b) $(6.7 \times 10^{10}) + (5.8 \times 10^{11})$ [2 marks]

Section One — Number

Different Number Systems

There are lots of different number systems, such as decimal (the system you usually use) and Roman numerals. This page covers another you need to know for your exam — binary.

The Binary Number System Uses Two Digits

1) Our standard number system uses ten different digits (0-9) and is called decimal or base-10. The place value in decimal numbers increases from right to left in powers of 10 (1, 10, 100, 1000 etc). So 101 = (1 × 100) + (0 × 10) + (1 × 1)

2) Binary (or base-2) is a different number system which only uses two different digits (0 and 1). The place value in binary numbers increases each time in powers of 2 (1, 2, 4, 8 etc).

3) For example, the binary number 101 ("one zero one" — DEFINITELY NOT "one hundred and one") has a 1 in the place value 1 (on the right), a 0 in the place value 2 and a 1 in the place value 4 (on the left). So as a decimal number, 101 = (1 × 4) + (0 × 2) + (1 × 1) = 5.

4) This table shows the binary equivalents of the decimal numbers 0-15:

0 = 0	4 = 100	8 = 1000	12 = 1100
1 = 1	5 = 101	9 = 1001	13 = 1101
2 = 10	6 = 110	10 = 1010	14 = 1110
3 = 11	7 = 111	11 = 1011	15 = 1111

Binary Numbers are easier to Convert using Tables

Drawing a table with binary place values in the first row makes binary to decimal conversion easier.

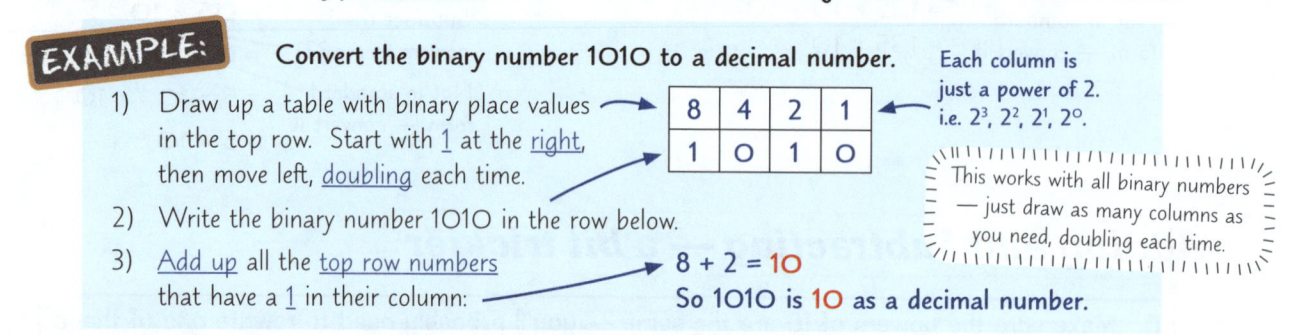

EXAMPLE: Convert the binary number 1010 to a decimal number.

1) Draw up a table with binary place values in the top row. Start with 1 at the right, then move left, doubling each time.

8	4	2	1
1	0	1	0

Each column is just a power of 2. i.e. $2^3, 2^2, 2^1, 2^0$.

2) Write the binary number 1010 in the row below.

3) Add up all the top row numbers that have a 1 in their column: 8 + 2 = 10
So 1010 is 10 as a decimal number.

This works with all binary numbers — just draw as many columns as you need, doubling each time.

Convert Decimal to Binary by Subtracting

When converting from decimal to binary, it's easier to draw a table of binary place values, then subtract them from largest to smallest. Have a look at this example:

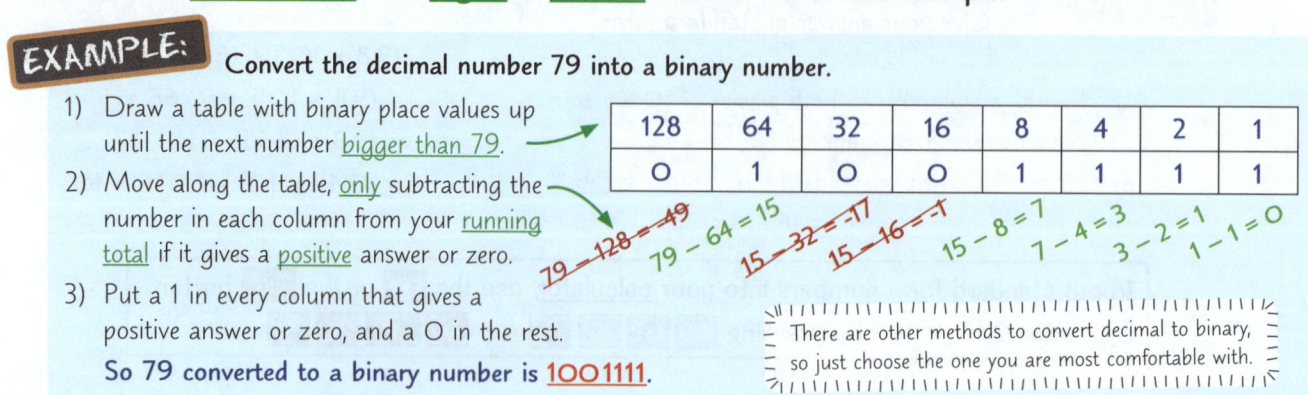

EXAMPLE: Convert the decimal number 79 into a binary number.

1) Draw a table with binary place values up until the next number bigger than 79.

128	64	32	16	8	4	2	1
0	1	0	0	1	1	1	1

79 − 128 = −49   79 − 64 = 15   15 − 32 = −17   15 − 16 = −1   15 − 8 = 7   7 − 4 = 3   3 − 2 = 1   1 − 1 = 0

2) Move along the table, only subtracting the number in each column from your running total if it gives a positive answer or zero.

3) Put a 1 in every column that gives a positive answer or zero, and a 0 in the rest.

So 79 converted to a binary number is **1001111**.

There are other methods to convert decimal to binary, so just choose the one you are most comfortable with.

There are 10 types of people in this world...

... those who understand binary, and those who don't. Go over the page again, then try these:

Q1 Convert these to decimal numbers: a) 111   b) 100010   c) 1101100   [3 marks]

Q2 Convert these to binary numbers: a) 22   b) 40   c) 63   [3 marks]

Section One — Number

Revision Questions for Section One

Well, that wraps up Section One — time to put yourself to the test and find out how much you really know.
- Try these questions and tick off each one when you get it right.
- When you've done all the questions for a topic and are completely happy with it, tick off the topic.

Types of Number, Factors and Multiples (p2-4) ☐

1) What are: a) integers   b) rational numbers   c) prime numbers?
2) Use BODMAS to answer these questions: a) $7 + 8 \div 2$ b) $7 \div (5 + 9)$ c) $(2 - 5 \times 3)^2$
3) Buns are sold in packs of 6, cheese slices are sold in packs of 16 and hot dogs are sold in packs of 12. Noah wants to buy the same number of each item. What is the smallest number of packs of buns, cheese slices and hot dogs he can buy?
4) a) Write 320 and 880 as products of their prime factors.
   b) Use the prime factorisations to find the LCM and HCF of 320 and 880.

Fractions (p5-6) ☐

5) How do you simplify a fraction?
6) a) Write $\frac{74}{9}$ as a mixed number.   b) Write $4\frac{5}{7}$ as an improper fraction.
7) What are the rules for multiplying, dividing and adding/subtracting fractions?
8) Calculate: a) $\frac{2}{11} \times \frac{7}{9}$ b) $5\frac{1}{2} \div 1\frac{3}{4}$ c) $\frac{5}{8} - \frac{1}{6}$ d) $3\frac{3}{10} + 4\frac{1}{4}$
9) a) Find $\frac{7}{9}$ of 270 kg.   b) Write 88 as a fraction of 56.
10) Which of $\frac{5}{8}$ and $\frac{7}{10}$ is closer in value to $\frac{3}{4}$?

You're not allowed to use a calculator for q5-16 and 22-24. Sorry.

Fractions, Decimals and Percentages (p7-9) ☐

11) How do you convert: a) a fraction to a decimal? b) a terminating decimal to a fraction?
12) Write: a) 0.04 as: (i) a fraction, (ii) a percentage.   b) 65% as: (i) a fraction, (ii) a decimal.
13) 25 litres of fruit punch is made up of 50% orange juice, $\frac{2}{5}$ lemonade and $\frac{1}{10}$ cranberry juice. How many litres of orange juice, lemonade and cranberry juice are there in the punch?
14) Show that $0.5\dot{1} = \frac{17}{33}$

Rounding, Estimating and Bounds (p10-13) ☐

15) Round 427.963 to: a) 2 d.p.   b) 1 d.p.   c) 2 s.f.   d) 4 s.f.
16) Estimate the value of: a) $(104.6 + 56.8) \div 8.4$ b) $\sqrt{45}$ to 1 d.p.
17) The volume of water in a jug is given as 2.4 litres to the nearest 100 ml. Find the upper and lower bounds for the volume of the jug. Give your answer as an inequality.
18) A rectangle measures 15.6 m by 8.4 m, to the nearest 0.1 m. Find its maximum possible area.
19) A car uses 9 gallons of fuel to the nearest gallon on a 410 mile journey. If the distance travelled is accurate to 2 significant figures, find the lowest possible fuel economy in miles per gallon.
20) Roisin buys 500 g of chocolate. She eats 200 g of the chocolate. If both of these weights are correct to 10 g, what is the maximum amount of chocolate Roisin could have left over?

Standard Form and Different Number Systems (p14-16) ☐

21) What are the three rules for writing numbers in standard form?
22) Write these numbers in standard form: a) 970 000   b) 3 560 000 000   c) 0.00000275
23) Express 4.56×10^{-3} and 2.7×10^5 as ordinary numbers.
24) Calculate: a) $(3.2 \times 10^6) \div (1.6 \times 10^3)$ b) $(1.75 \times 10^{12}) + (9.89 \times 10^{11})$
    Give your answers in standard form.
25) Convert the following: a) 10101 from binary to decimal,   b) 29 from decimal to binary.

Section One — Number

Ratios

Ratios are a pretty important topic — they can crop up in all sorts of questions, so you need to be prepared. Make sure you understand the examples on the next two pages, then get practising.

Reducing Ratios to their Simplest Form

1) To reduce a ratio to a simpler form, divide all the numbers in the ratio by the same thing (a bit like simplifying a fraction — see p.5).
It's in its simplest form when there's nothing left you can divide by.

> **EXAMPLE:** Write the ratio 15:18 in its simplest form.
>
> For the ratio 15:18, both numbers have a factor of 3, so divide them by 3.
> ÷3 (15:18) ÷3 = 5:6
> We can't reduce this any further. So the simplest form of 15:18 is **5:6**.

A handy trick for the calculator papers — use the fraction button

If you enter a fraction with the ▭ or a^b_c button, the calculator automatically cancels it down when you press =.
So for the ratio 8:12, just enter $\frac{8}{12}$ as a fraction, and you'll get the reduced fraction $\frac{2}{3}$.
Now you just change it back to ratio form, i.e. **2 : 3**. Ace.

2) If the ratio has mixed units — convert to the smaller unit then simplify.

> **EXAMPLE:** Reduce the ratio 24 mm : 7.2 cm to its simplest form.
>
> 1) Convert 7.2 cm to millimetres.
> 2) Simplify the resulting ratio. Once the units on both sides are the same, get rid of them for the final answer.
>
> 24 mm : 7.2 cm
> = 24 mm : 72 mm
> ÷24 ↘ ↙ ÷24
> = 1 : 3

Writing Ratios as Fractions

1) To write one part as a fraction of another part — put one number over the other.

E.g. if apples and oranges are in the ratio **2 : 9** then we say there are
$\frac{2}{9}$ as many apples as oranges or $\frac{9}{2}$ times as many oranges as apples.

2) To write one part as a fraction of the total — add up the parts to find the total, then put the part you want over the total.

E.g. a pie dough is made by mixing flour, butter and water in the ratio **3 : 2 : 1**.
The total number of parts is 3 + 2 + 1 = **6**.
So $\frac{3}{6} = \frac{1}{2}$ of the dough is flour, $\frac{2}{6} = \frac{1}{3}$ is butter and $\frac{1}{6}$ is water.

The simpler the ratio the better as far as I'm concerned...

Whole number ratios are easy to simplify, but you need to make sure you can do the awkward cases too.

Q1 Simplify: a) 25 : 35   b) 2.5 kg : 750 g   c) 40 s : 4 min   [5 marks]

Q2 Niamh mixes red paint, blue paint and white paint in the ratio 2:3:5 to make some lilac paint.

   a) Write the amount of blue paint Niamh uses as a fraction of the amount of red paint she uses. [1 mark]

   b) What fraction of the lilac paint is made up of white paint? [2 marks]

Section Two — Ratio, Proportion and Percentages

Ratios

I'm afraid you're not done with ratios just yet. There are some more examples to get your head around here...

Scaling Up Ratios

If you know the ratio between parts and the actual size of one part, you can scale the ratio up to find the other parts.

EXAMPLE: Mortar is made from mixing sand and cement in the ratio 7:2. How many buckets of mortar will be made if 21 buckets of sand are used in the mixture?

You need to multiply by 3 to go from 7 to 21 on the left-hand side (LHS) — so do that to both sides:

So 21 buckets of sand and 6 buckets of cement are used.

sand : cement
×3 (7 : 2) ×3
    21 : 6

Amount of mortar made = 21 + 6 = **27 buckets**

The two parts of a ratio are always in direct proportion (see p.20-21). So in the example above, sand and cement are in direct proportion, e.g. if the amount of sand doubles, the amount of cement doubles.

Proportional Division

In a proportional division question a TOTAL AMOUNT is split into parts in a certain ratio. The key word here is PARTS — concentrate on 'parts' and it all becomes quite painless:

EXAMPLE: Jess, Mo and Greg share £9100 in the ratio 2:4:7. How much does Mo get?

1) **ADD UP THE PARTS:**
   The ratio 2:4:7 means there will be a total of 13 parts: 2 + 4 + 7 = 13 parts

2) **DIVIDE TO FIND ONE "PART":**
   Just divide the total amount by the number of parts: £9100 ÷ 13 = £700 (= 1 part)

3) **MULTIPLY TO FIND THE AMOUNTS:**
   We want to know Mo's share, which is 4 parts: 4 parts = 4 × £700 = **£2800**

EXAMPLE: In an office, the ratio of people who drink tea to people who drink coffee is 8:5. 18 more people drink tea than coffee. How many people drink coffee?

You know how many more people drink tea than coffee, so work out how many more parts drink tea than coffee.   8 − 5 = 3 parts

Then divide to find how many people there are in one part.   1 part = 18 ÷ 3 = 6 people

The ratio tells you that 5 parts of the people drink coffee, so multiply by 5 to calculate the number that drink coffee.   Coffee = 5 parts = 5 × 6 = **30 people**

I always divide sweets in the ratio me:you = 3:1...

There's loads of stuff to learn about ratios, so have another look over it and then try these questions:

Q1   Orange squash is made of water and concentrate in the ratio 11:2.
     a) What fraction of the squash is made up from concentrate?   [1 mark]
     b) How many litres of water are needed if 6 litres of concentrate are used?   [1 mark]

Q2   The ages of Ben, Tanvi and Pam are in the ratio 5:3:1.
    Their combined age is 108. How old is Tanvi?   [2 marks]

Section Two — Ratio, Proportion and Percentages

Direct Proportion Problems

Direct proportion problems all involve amounts that increase or decrease together. Awww.

Learn the Golden Rule for Proportion Questions

There are lots of exam questions which at first sight seem completely different but can all be done using the GOLDEN RULE...

DIVIDE FOR ONE, THEN TIMES FOR ALL

EXAMPLE: Emma is handing out some leaflets. She gets paid per leaflet she hands out. If she hands out 300 leaflets she gets £12.00. How many leaflets will she have to hand out to earn £28.50?

Divide by 12.00 to find how many leaflets she has to hand out to earn £1.
Multiply by 28.50 to find how many leaflets she has to hand out to earn £28.50.

To earn £1: 300 ÷ 12.00 = 25 leaflets
To earn £28.50: 25 × 28.50 = 712.5
So she'll need to hand out 713 leaflets.

You need to round your answer up because 712 wouldn't be enough.

Scaling Recipes Up or Down

EXAMPLE: Judy is making orange and pineapple punch using the recipe shown below. She wants to make enough to serve 20 people. How much of each ingredient will Judy need?

The GOLDEN RULE tells you to divide each amount by 8 to find how much FOR ONE PERSON, then multiply by 20 to find how much FOR 20 PEOPLE.

Fruit Punch (serves 8)
800 ml orange juice
140 g fresh pineapple

So for 1 person you need:
800 ml ÷ 8 = 100 ml orange juice
140 g ÷ 8 = 17.5 g pineapple

And for 20 people you need:
⇒ 20 × 100 ml = 2000 ml orange juice
⇒ 20 × 17.5 g = 350 g pineapple

Exchange Rates

1) An exchange rate tells you what one unit of one currency is worth in another currency. For example, £1 = $1.25 means that for every £1, you'd get 1.25 US dollars.

2) If the exchange rate is in the form £1 = ..., then to go from pounds to the other currency you'll need to multiply by the exchange rate, or divide to go from the other currency to pounds.

Because the exchange rate already tells you how much you'll get for one unit, you won't usually need to do the 'divide for one' step when answering questions.

EXAMPLE: Josh changes £200 into euro for his holiday to Italy. The exchange rate is £1 = €1.11. How much, in euro, does Josh receive?

£1 is €1.11, so to find out what £200 is in euro, multiply by 1.11.   200 × 1.11 = €222

The hotel room Josh stays in costs €75 a night. How much does the room cost in pounds?

Divide by 1.11 to work out how many pounds there are in 75 euro.   75 ÷ 1.11 = 67.5675...
Then round to 2 d.p. to give an answer in pounds and pence.   = £67.57

The Three Mathsketeers say "divide for one, then times for all"...

Ah, real-life maths. I love a quick currency conversion calculation on my holidays, so I do.

Q1 Seven pencils cost £1.40. How much will four pencils cost? [2 marks]

Q2 It costs £43.20 for 8 people to go on a rollercoaster 6 times.
    How much will it cost for 15 people to go on the rollercoaster 5 times? [4 marks]

Q3 Ayida changes £600 into dollars for a trip to America.
    The exchange rate is £1 = $1.25. How many dollars will she receive? [1 mark]

Section Two — Ratio, Proportion and Percentages

Direct Proportion Problems

Hang on, more direct proportion? That's right — there are more types of problem you need to know about.

Best Buy Questions

A slightly different type of direct proportion question is comparing the 'value for money' of 2 or 3 similar items. For these, follow the second GOLDEN RULE...

Divide by the PRICE in pence (to get the amount per penny)

EXAMPLE: The local 'Supplies 'n' Vittals' stocks two sizes of Jamaican Gooseberry Jam, as shown on the right. Which of these represents better value for money?

Follow the GOLDEN RULE —
divide by the price in pence to get the amount per penny.

In the 350 g jar you get   350 g ÷ 80p = 4.38 g per penny
In the 100 g jar you get   100 g ÷ 42p = 2.38 g per penny

The 350 g jar is better value for money, because you get more jam per penny.

350 g at 80p   100 g at 42p

In some cases it might be easier to divide by the weight to get the cost per gram.
If you're feeling confident then you can do it this way — if not, the golden rule always works.

Graphing Direct Proportion

Two things are in direct proportion if, when you plot them on a graph, you get a straight line through the origin.

The general equation for a straight line through the origin is $y = kx$, where k is a number (see p.54 for more on straight line graphs).
All direct proportions can be written as an equation in this form.

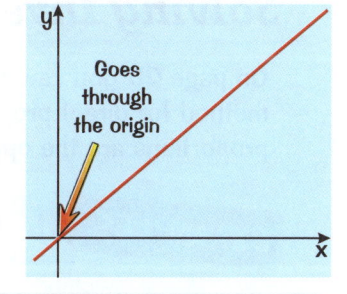

Goes through the origin

EXAMPLE: The amount of petrol, p litres, a car uses is directly proportional to the distance, d km, that the car travels. The car used 12 litres of petrol on a 160 km journey.

a) Write an equation in the form $p = kd$ to represent this direct proportion.

1) Put the values of $p = 12$ and $d = 160$ into the equation to find the value of k.

$12 = k \times 160$
$k = \dfrac{12}{160}$
$k = 0.075$

2) Put the value of k back into the equation.

$p = 0.075d$

b) Sketch the graph of this direct proportion, marking two points on the line.

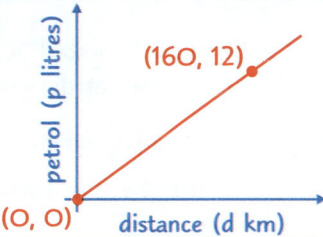

(160, 12)
(0, 0)
petrol (p litres)
distance (d km)

Calm down, you're blowing this page all out of proportion...

A mixed bag on this page — soak it all in and then have a crack at these questions.

Q1   Tomato ketchup comes in bottles of three sizes: 250 g for 50p, 770 g for £1.40 and 1600 g for £3.20. Which bottle represents the best value for money? [3 marks]

Q2   Brass is made by mixing copper and zinc in the ratio 3 : 2 by weight.
  a) Sketch a graph showing the weight of copper against the weight of zinc in a sample of brass. Mark two points on the graph with their coordinates. [3 marks]
  b) What aspects of the graph show that copper and zinc are in direct proportion? [1 mark]

Section Two — Ratio, Proportion and Percentages

Inverse Proportion Problems

Here's a **trickier type of proportion** — but once you've learnt this page you'll be an expert. Well, almost.

Graphing Inverse Proportion

Inverse proportion can also be called 'indirect proportion'.

When two things are in inverse proportion, one increases as the other decreases.

On the graph you can see that as the value of x increases, the value of y decreases. E.g. if x is doubled, y is halved, or if x is multiplied by 5, y is divided by 5.

The general equation for inverse proportion is $y = \frac{k}{x}$.

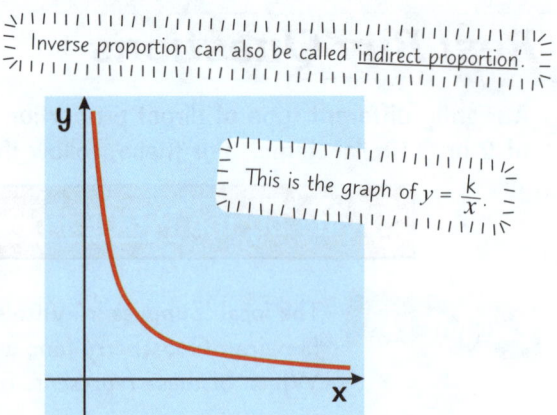

This is the graph of $y = \frac{k}{x}$.

EXAMPLE: Circle each of the equations below that show that s is inversely proportional to t.

$$s = \frac{3}{t} \quad 9s = t \quad t = \frac{1}{s} \quad s = \frac{3}{t^2} \quad s = \frac{3}{t} + 7 \quad \frac{s}{5} = \frac{1}{t}$$

$$s = \frac{3}{t} \qquad s = \frac{1}{t} \qquad s = \frac{5}{t}$$

Check which equations can be written in the form $s = \frac{k}{t}$.

Solving Inverse Proportion Questions

On page 20 you saw the 'divide and times' method for direct proportions. Well, inverse proportions are the opposite so you have to:

TIMES for ONE, then DIVIDE for ALL

EXAMPLES:

1. It takes 3 farmers 10 hours to plough a field. How long would it take 6 farmers?

Multiply by 3 to find how long it would take 1 farmer.   10 × 3 = 30 hours for 1 farmer

Divide by 6 to find how long it would take 6 farmers.   30 ÷ 6 = 5 hours for 6 farmers

Note: Another way of looking at this question is that there are twice as many farmers, so it will take half as long (10 ÷ 2 = 5 hours).

2. 4 bakers can decorate 100 cakes in 5 hours. If 5 bakers work at the same rate, how much quicker would they decorate 100 cakes?

Multiply by 4 to find how long it would take 1 baker.   5 hours × 4 = 20 hours for 1 baker

Divide by 5 to find how long it would take 5 bakers.   20 ÷ 5 = 4 hours for 5 bakers

So 5 bakers are 5 − 4 = **1 hour quicker** than 4.

noitroporp — it's an inverse proportion...

Here's a fun fact for you — if you get the same number each time you multiply any x-value on a graph by its y-value, then you know that x and y are inversely proportional with each other. What joy.

Q1 It takes 2 painters 6 hours to paint a fence.
How long would it take 8 painters to paint a fence? [2 marks]

Q2 It takes 2 carpenters 4 hours to make 3 bookcases.
How long would it take 5 carpenters to make 10 bookcases? [4 marks]

Section Two — Ratio, Proportion and Percentages

Harder Proportion Problems

Oooh — a whole page on proportion questions and algebra mixed together, what a treat.

Handling Algebraic Direct Proportion Questions

1) The simplest direct proportion is 'y is proportional to x' ($y \propto x$). $\propto$ means 'is proportional to'.
2) Trickier direct proportions involve y varying according to some function of x, e.g. x^2, x^3, $\sqrt{x}$ etc.
3) In any proportion question, you can always turn the proportion statement into an equation by replacing '$\propto$' with '$= k$' like this:

	Proportionality	Equation
'y is proportional to x'	$y \propto x$	$y = kx$
'y is proportional to the square of x'	$y \propto x^2$	$y = kx^2$
't is proportional to the square root of h'	$t \propto \sqrt{h}$	$t = k\sqrt{h}$

k is just some constant (unknown number)

4) Once you've turned your statement into an equation, find a pair of values (x and y) somewhere in the question and substitute them into the equation to find k.
5) Put the value of k into the equation and it's now ready to use, e.g. $y = 3x^2$.
6) Inevitably, they'll ask you to find y, having given you a value for x (or vice versa).

EXAMPLE: In a computer game, the number of points scored, P, is proportional to the cube of the time in minutes, T, that the game lasts for. When P = 32, T = 4. Find an equation for P in terms of T, and use it to work out the number of points scored in a game that lasts for 6 minutes.

1) Write a proportionality and replace $\propto$ with '$= k$'. $P \propto T^3$ so $P = kT^3$
2) Use the values of P and T (32 and 4) to find k. $32 = k(4^3) = 64k \Rightarrow k = 32 \div 64 = \frac{1}{2}$
3) Put the value of k into the equation. $P = \frac{1}{2}T^3$ ← This is the equation for P in terms of T.
4) Use your equation to find the value of P when T = 6. $P = \frac{1}{2}(6^3) = 216 \div 2 = 108$

Inverse Proportion Problems are Similar

Answering questions for inverse proportion uses the same steps as described above. Start by turning the proportion statement into an equation:

	Proportionality	Equation
'y is inversely proportional to x'	$y \propto \frac{1}{x}$	$y = \frac{k}{x}$
'V is inversely proportional to r cubed'	$V \propto \frac{1}{r^3}$	$V = \frac{k}{r^3}$

EXAMPLE: G is inversely proportional to the square root of H. When G = 2, H = 16. Find an equation for G in terms of H, and use it to work out the value of G when H = 36.

1) Convert to a proportionality and replace $\propto$ with '$= k$' to form an equation. $G \propto \frac{1}{\sqrt{H}}$ $G = \frac{k}{\sqrt{H}}$
2) Use the values of G and H (2 and 16) to find k. $2 = \frac{k}{\sqrt{16}} = \frac{k}{4} \Rightarrow k = 8$
3) Put the value of k back into the equation. $G = \frac{8}{\sqrt{H}}$
4) Use your equation to find the value of G.   When H = 36, $G = \frac{8}{\sqrt{36}} = \frac{8}{6} = \frac{4}{3}$

Joy $\propto$ 1/algebra...

Q1 An object is moving with a velocity that changes proportionally with time. After 5 seconds its velocity is 105 m/s. How fast will it be travelling after 13 seconds? [3 marks]

Q2 P is inversely proportional to the square of Q (where Q is positive). When P = 3, Q = 4. Find an equation for P in terms of Q and find the value of Q to 2 d.p. when P = 8. [4 marks]

Section Two — Ratio, Proportion and Percentages

Percentages

'Per cent' means 'out of 100' — remember this and you'll easily be able to convert percentages into fractions and decimals (p.7). Then you're ready to tackle the first three simple types of percentage question.

Three Simple Question Types

Type 1 — "Find x% of y"

Turn the percentage into a decimal/fraction, then multiply. E.g. 15% of £46 = $\frac{15}{100}$ × £46 = £6.90.

EXAMPLE: A shopkeeper had a box of 140 chocolate bars. He sold 60% of the chocolate bars for 62p each and he sold the other 40% at 2 for £1. How much did the box of chocolate bars sell for in total?

1) Find 60% and 40% of 140:
   60% of 140 bars = 0.6 × 140 = 84 bars
   40% of 140 bars = 0.4 × 140 = 56 bars

2) So he sold 84 bars for 62p each and 56 bars at 2 for £1.
   Total sales = (84 × 0.62) + (56 ÷ 2) = **£80.08**

Type 2 — "Find the new amount after a % increase/decrease"

This time, you first need to find the multiplier — the decimal that represents the percentage change.
E.g. 5% increase is 1.05 (= 1 + 0.05)
    26% decrease is 0.74 (= 1 − 0.26)

Then you just multiply the original value by the multiplier and voilà — you have the answer.

A % increase has a multiplier greater than 1, a % decrease has a multiplier less than 1.

EXAMPLE: A toaster is £38 excluding VAT. VAT is paid at 20%. What is the price of the toaster including VAT?

1) Find the multiplier: 20% increase = 1 + 0.2 = 1.2
2) Multiply the original value by the multiplier: £38 × 1.2 = **£45.60**

If you prefer, you can work out the percentage, then add it to or subtract it from the original value:
20% of £38 = 0.2 × 38 = £7.60
£38 + £7.60 = **£45.60**

Type 3 — "Express x as a percentage of y"

Divide x by y, then multiply by 100. E.g. 209 as a percentage of 400 = $\frac{209}{400}$ × 100 = 52.25%.
N.B. if x is bigger than y you'll get a percentage that's bigger than 100.

EXAMPLE: There are 480 pupils in a school. 55% of them are girls and 59 of the girls have blonde hair. What percentage of the girls have blonde hair?

1) Find the number of girls in the school:
   55% = 55 ÷ 100 = 0.55
   55% of 480 = 0.55 × 480 = 264 girls

2) Divide the number of blonde-haired girls by the number of girls and multiply by 100.
   $\frac{59}{264}$ × 100 = 22.348...% = **22.3% (1 d.p.)**

Fact: 70% of people understand percentages, the other 40% don't...

Learn the details for the three simple types of percentage question, then try this Practice Question:

Q1 A cricket team scored 250 runs in their first innings. One player scored 30% of these runs. In the second innings, the same player scored 105 runs.
Express his second innings score as a percentage of his first innings score. [3 marks]

Section Two — Ratio, Proportion and Percentages

Percentages

Watch out for these <u>trickier types</u> of percentage question — they'll often include lots of real-life context. Just make sure you know the <u>proper method</u> for each of them and you'll be fine.

Two *Trickier* Question Types

Type 1 — Finding the percentage change

1) This is the formula for giving a <u>change in value</u> as a <u>percentage</u> — **LEARN IT, AND USE IT**:

$$\text{PERCENTAGE 'CHANGE'} = \frac{\text{'CHANGE'}}{\text{ORIGINAL}} \times 100$$

2) You end up with a <u>percentage</u> rather than an amount, as you did for Type 3 on the previous page.

3) Typical questions will ask 'Find the percentage <u>increase</u>/<u>profit</u>/<u>error</u>' or 'Calculate the percentage <u>decrease</u>/<u>loss</u>/<u>discount</u>', etc.

EXAMPLE: A trader buys 6 watches at £25 each. He scratches one of them, so he sells that one for £11. He sells the other five for £38 each. Find his profit as a percentage.

1) Here the 'change' is <u>profit</u>, so the formula looks like this: $\text{percentage profit} = \frac{\text{profit}}{\text{original}} \times 100$

2) Work out the <u>actual</u> profit (amount made − amount spent): $\text{profit} = (£38 \times 5) + £11 - (6 \times £25) = £51$

3) Calculate the <u>percentage</u> profit: $\text{percentage profit} = \frac{51}{6 \times 25} \times 100 = \mathbf{34\%}$

Type 2 — Finding the original value

This is the type that <u>most people get wrong</u> — but only because they <u>don't recognise</u> it as this type and don't apply this simple method:

1) Write the amount in the question as a <u>percentage of the original value</u>.
2) <u>Divide</u> to find <u>1%</u> of the original value.
3) <u>Multiply by 100</u> to give the original value (= 100%).

EXAMPLE: A house increases in value by 10.5% to £132 600. Find what it was worth before the rise.

Note — the new, not the original value is given.

1) An <u>increase</u> of 10.5% means £132 600 represents <u>110.5% of the original</u> value.

2) Divide by 110.5 to find <u>1%</u> of the original value.

3) Then multiply by 100.

£132 600 = 110.5%
÷110.5 ↓
£1200 = 1%
×100 ↓
£120 000 = 100%

So the original value was **£120 000**

If it was a <u>decrease</u> of 10.5%, then you'd put '£132 600 = <u>89.5%</u>' and divide by 89.5 instead of 110.5.

Always set them out <u>exactly like this example</u>. The trickiest bit is deciding the top % figure on the right-hand side — the 2nd and 3rd rows are <u>always</u> 1% and 100%.

The % change in my understanding of this topic is 100%...

The methods above are easy to follow but the questions can be a bit tricky — practise on these ones:

Q1 A cereal company has decreased the amount of cereal in a box from 1.2 kg to 900 g. What is the percentage decrease in the amount of cereal per box? [3 marks]

Q2 A shop sells kebabs for a 20% loss. The kebabs sell for £4.88 each. The shop wants to reduce its loss on kebabs to 10%. How much should the shop charge per kebab? [3 marks]

Section Two — Ratio, Proportion and Percentages

Percentages

Percentages are almost certainly going to come up in your exam, but they could crop up in lots of different contexts. Here are some more examples of where you might see them.

Simple Interest

Compound interest is covered on the next page.

Simple interest means a certain percentage of the original amount only is paid at regular intervals (usually once a year). So the amount of interest is the same every time it's paid.

EXAMPLE: Regina invests £380 in an account which pays 3% simple interest each year. How much interest will she earn in 4 years?

1) Work out the amount of interest earned in one year:
   3% = 3 ÷ 100 = 0.03
   3% of £380 = 0.03 × £380 = £11.40

2) Multiply by 4 to get the total interest for 4 years:
   4 × £11.40 = £45.60

AER is Used for Savings and APR is Used for Borrowing

1) AER (Annual Equivalent Rate) is a rate used to work out how much interest a savings account pays over a full year.

2) It's used to compare savings accounts which pay interest at different intervals (e.g. annually, monthly).

EXAMPLE: Erin's savings account has an AER of 6.5%. She deposits £3000 in the account. How much interest will she earn in a year?

Calculate 6.5% of £3000.   0.065 × £3000 = £195

3) APR (Annual Percentage Rate) is a rate used to work out how much it costs you to borrow money — e.g. when you take out a loan, get a mortgage to buy a house or pay for something on a credit card.

4) It takes into account both the interest charged on what you borrowed, and any extra charges that you might have to pay (e.g. the fee you pay the bank for arranging a mortgage).

5) It allows you to make meaningful comparisons between lenders.

EXAMPLE: Ivor wants to take out a £200 loan. He goes to two lenders with different rates:
• Mako Money offers him a loan with 14% APR.
• Great White Loans offers an annual interest rate of 10% with a £5 initial fee.
If Ivor pays the loan back in full after one year, which is the better offer?

Work out how much he'll have to pay at the end of the year with each lender:

Mako Money: £200 plus 14% = £200 × 1.14 = £228
Great White Loans: £200 plus 10%, plus £5 fees
= (£200 × 1.1) + £5 = £225
So Great White Loans is offering the better deal.

Simple Interest — it's simple, but it's not that interesting...

The only difference between AER and APR is what they refer to — either the interest on saving or the interest on borrowing money. You'll need to find a way to remember which way round they go — I like to match the E in AER with 'earning', and the P in APR with 'price'.

Q1 Faheem invests some money for 5 years in an account at 4% simple interest per annum. What is the percentage increase of the investment at the end of the 5 years? [1 mark]

Q2 Rebecca borrows £3500 from a bank. She is charged interest with a 7% APR for the first year of the loan and 12% APR after the first year. How much would Rebecca pay back if she settles the debt after three years? (Assume that both interest rates refer to simple interest.) [3 marks]

Section Two — Ratio, Proportion and Percentages

Repeated Percentage Change

One more sneaky % type for you... In a repeated percentage change, the amount added on/taken away changes each time — it's a percentage of the new amount, rather than the original amount.

Repeated Percentage Increase (Compound Growth)

Compound interest is a good example of repeated percentage change — it means the interest is added on each time, and the next lot of interest is calculated using the new total rather than the original amount.

EXAMPLE: Daniel invests £10 000 in a savings account which pays 4% compound interest per annum. How much money will there be in his account after 3 years?

1) Work out the multiplier: Multiplier = 4% increase = 1.04
2) Find the amount in the savings account each year until you get to 3 years.
   After 1 year: £10 000 × 1.04 = £10 400
   After 2 years: £10 400 × 1.04 = £10 816
   After 3 years: £10 816 × 1.04 = **£11 248.64**

'Per annum' just means 'each year'.

Repeated Percentage Decrease (Compound Decay)

Some questions are about things that decrease in value or number over time.

EXAMPLE: Susan has just bought a car for £6500. The car depreciates by 16% each year. How many years will it be before the car is worth less than £5000?

1) Work out the multiplier: 16% decrease = 1 − 0.16 = 0.84
2) Calculate the value of the car each year — stop when the value drops below £5000.
   After 1 year: £6500 × 0.84 = £5460
   After 2 years: £5460 × 0.84 = £4586.40

So it will be **2 years** before the car is worth less than £5000.

'Depreciates' means 'decreases in value'.

There's a Handy Formula You Can Use

You could get a tricky compound growth or decay question in the exam — this formula will help you out:
(In fact, it will help you out in easier questions too — use it as you wish.)

$$N = N_0 \times (\text{multiplier})^n$$

- Amount after n days/hours/years → N
- Initial amount → N_0
- Percentage change multiplier → multiplier
- Number of days/hours/years → n

EXAMPLES:

1. Saaed invests £1000 in a savings account which pays 8% compound interest per annum. How much will there be after 6 years?

   Use the formula: Amount = $1000(1.08)^6$ = **£1586.87**
   (initial amount, 8% increase, 6 years)

2. The number of bacteria in a sample increases at a rate of 30% each day. After 6 days the number of bacteria is 7500. How many bacteria were there in the original sample?

   Put the numbers you know into the formula, then rearrange to find the initial amount, N_0.

   $7500 = N_0(1.3)^6$
   $N_0 = 7500 \div (1.3)^6 = 1553.82...$

   Round the answer to the nearest whole number. So there were **1554** bacteria originally.

I thought you'd depreciate all the work I've put into this page...

Q1 Priya's bank account pays 2.5% compound interest per annum and her bank balance is £3200. If she doesn't pay in or withdraw money, what will Priya's balance be after 3 years? [3 marks]

Section Two — Ratio, Proportion and Percentages

Revision Questions for Section Two

Lots of things to remember in Section Two — there's only one way to find out what you've taken in...
- Try these questions and tick off each one when you get it right.
- When you've done all the questions for a topic and are completely happy with it, tick off the topic.

Ratios (p18-19)
1) Reduce: a) 18:22 to its simplest form   b) 4.9 kg : 1400 g to its simplest form
2) A pencil case contains pencils and rubbers. The ratio of pencils to rubbers is 7:2. What fraction of the items in the pencil case are pencils?
3) Sarah is in charge of ordering stock for a clothes shop. The shop usually sells red scarves and blue scarves in the ratio 5:8. Sarah orders 150 red scarves. How many blue scarves should she order?
4) Ryan, Joel and Yewande are delivering 800 newspapers. They split the newspapers in the ratio 5:8:12.
   a) What fraction of the newspapers does Ryan deliver?
   b) How many more newspapers does Yewande deliver than Joel?

Direct and Inverse Proportion (p20-23)
5) The recipe on the right shows CGP's secret pasta sauce recipe. The recipe serves 6 people. How much of each ingredient is needed to make enough for 17 servings?
   - 18 ml olive oil
   - 360 g tomatoes
   - 9 g garlic powder
   - 72 g onions
6) Maria is changing $130 of leftover holiday money back into pounds. The bank offers her an exchange rate of £1 = $1.45. How much money will she get back, in pounds and pence?
7) A DIY shop sells varnish in two different sized tins. A 500 ml tin costs £8 and a 1800 ml tin costs £30. Which tin represents the best value for money?
8) Which graph below (A-D) shows direct proportion?
9) 6 gardeners can plant 360 flowers in 3 hours.
   a) How many flowers could 8 gardeners plant in 6 hours?
   b) How many hours would it take for 15 gardeners to plant 1170 flowers?
10) 'y is proportional to the square of x'. Write the statement as an equation.
11) p is proportional to the cube of q. When p = 9, q = 3. Find the value of p when q = 6.
12) The pressure a cube exerts on the ground is inversely proportional to the square of its side length. When the side length is 3 cm the pressure is 17 Pa. Find the pressure when the side length is 13 cm.

Percentages (p24-27)
13) If x = 20 and y = 95: a) Find x% of y.   b) Find the new value after x is increased by y%.
    c) Express x as a percentage of y.   d) Express y as a percentage of x.
14) What's the formula for finding a change in value as a percentage?
15) An antique wardrobe decreased in value from £800 to £520. What was the percentage decrease?
16) A tree's height has increased by 15% in the last year to 20.24 m. What was its height a year ago?
17) Explain the meaning of the terms AER and APR.
18) Lily's farm is worth £300 000 but is expected to depreciate in value by 11% a year. How much will the farm be worth in three years time?
19) What's the formula for compound growth and decay?
20) Collectable baseball cards increase in value by 7% each year. A particular card is worth £80. How much will it be worth in 10 years?

Section Two — Ratio, Proportion and Percentages

Section Three — Algebra

Algebra Basics

Before you can really get your teeth into algebra, there are some basics you need to get your head around.

Negative Numbers

Negative numbers crop up everywhere so you need to learn these rules for dealing with them:

+ + makes +
+ − makes −
− + makes −
− − makes +

Use these rules when:
1) **Multiplying or dividing**.
   e.g. $-2 \times 3 = -6$, $-8 \div -2 = +4$, $-4p \times -2 = +8p$
2) **Two signs are together**.
   e.g. $5 - -4 = 5 + 4 = 9$, $x + -y - -z = x - y + z$

Letters Multiplied Together

Watch out for these combinations of letters in algebra that regularly catch people out:

1) abc means $a \times b \times c$. The ×'s are often left out to make it clearer.
2) gn^2 means $g \times n \times n$. Note that only the n is squared, not the g as well — e.g. πr^2 means $\pi \times r \times r$.
3) $(gn)^2$ means $g \times g \times n \times n$. The brackets mean that **BOTH** letters are squared.
4) $p(q - r)^3$ means $p \times (q - r) \times (q - r) \times (q - r)$. Only the brackets get cubed.
5) -3^2 is a bit ambiguous. It should either be written $(-3)^2 = 9$, or $-(3^2) = -9$ (you'd usually take -3^2 to be -9).

Terms

Before you can do anything else with algebra, you must understand what a term is:

A TERM IS A COLLECTION OF NUMBERS, LETTERS AND BRACKETS, ALL MULTIPLIED/DIVIDED TOGETHER

Terms are separated by + and − signs. Every term has a + or − attached to the front of it.

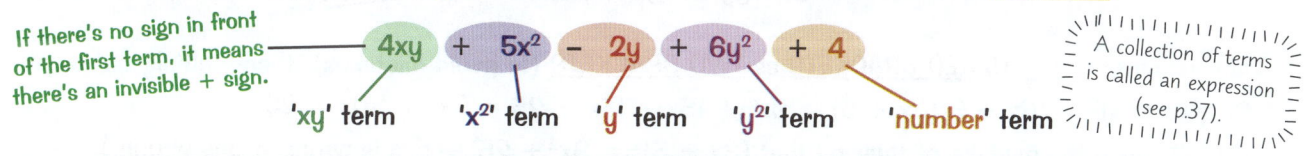

If there's no sign in front of the first term, it means there's an invisible + sign.

$4xy$ + $5x^2$ − $2y$ + $6y^2$ + 4

'xy' term   'x²' term   'y' term   'y²' term   'number' term

A collection of terms is called an expression (see p.37).

Simplifying or 'Collecting Like Terms'

To simplify an algebraic expression, you combine 'like terms' — terms that have the same combination of letters (e.g. all the x terms, all the y terms, all the number terms etc.).

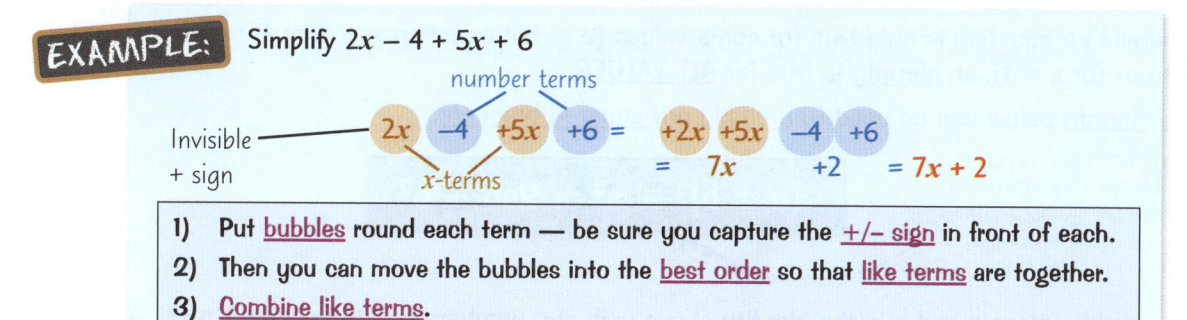

EXAMPLE: Simplify $2x - 4 + 5x + 6$

Invisible + sign

$2x$ -4 $+5x$ $+6$ = $+2x$ $+5x$ -4 $+6$
         x-terms   number terms   = $7x$ $+2$ = $7x + 2$

1) Put **bubbles** round each term — be sure you capture the **+/− sign** in front of each.
2) Then you can move the bubbles into the **best order** so that **like terms** are together.
3) **Combine like terms**.

Ahhh algebra, it's as easy as abc, or 2(ab) + c, or something...

Nothing too tricky on this page, but you'll have to simplify in the exam, so here's some practice:

Q1   A rectangle has sides measuring $5x$ cm and $(3y + 1)$ cm.
     Find an expression for its perimeter.
     [2 marks]

Multiplying Out Brackets

I usually use brackets to make witty comments (I'm very witty), but in algebra they're useful for simplifying things. First of all, you need to know how to expand brackets (multiply them out).

Single Brackets

The main thing to remember when multiplying out brackets is that the thing outside the bracket multiplies each separate term inside the bracket.

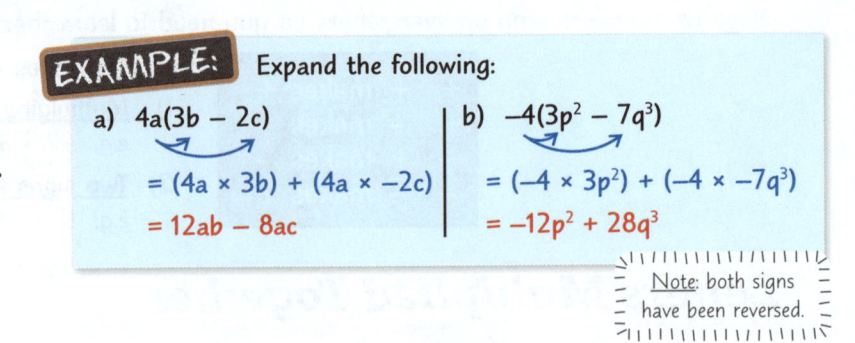

EXAMPLE: Expand the following:

a) $4a(3b - 2c)$
$= (4a \times 3b) + (4a \times -2c)$
$= 12ab - 8ac$

b) $-4(3p^2 - 7q^3)$
$= (-4 \times 3p^2) + (-4 \times -7q^3)$
$= -12p^2 + 28q^3$

Note: both signs have been reversed.

Double Brackets

Double brackets are trickier than single brackets — this time, you have to multiply everything in the first bracket by everything in the second bracket. You'll get 4 terms, and usually 2 of them will combine to leave 3 terms. There's a handy way to multiply out double brackets — it's called the FOIL method:

First — multiply the first term in each bracket together
Outside — multiply the outside terms (i.e. the first term in the first bracket by the second term in the second bracket)
Inside — multiply the inside terms (i.e. the second term in the first bracket by the first term in the second bracket)
Last — multiply the second term in each bracket together

EXAMPLE: Expand and simplify $(2p - 4)(3p + 1)$

$(2p - 4)(3p + 1) = (2p \times 3p) + (2p \times 1) + (-4 \times 3p) + (-4 \times 1)$
$= 6p^2 + 2p - 12p - 4$
$= 6p^2 - 10p - 4$

The two p terms combine together.

Always write out SQUARED BRACKETS as TWO BRACKETS (to avoid mistakes), then multiply out as above.
So $(3x + 5)^2 = (3x + 5)(3x + 5) = 9x^2 + 15x + 15x + 25 = 9x^2 + 30x + 25$.
(DON'T make the mistake of thinking that $(3x + 5)^2 = 9x^2 + 25$ — this is wrong wrong wrong.)

An Identity is Different to an Equation

Identities and equations look very similar, but they aren't quite the same thing...

1) Whereas an equation is only true for some values (e.g. the equation $x + 5 = 9$ is true for $x = 4$ but not for $x = 1$), an identity is true for ALL VALUES.

2) The identity below can be used to multiply out squared brackets.

Identities are shown by a triple line symbol, $\equiv$, rather than the equals sign.

$$(a \pm b)^2 \equiv a^2 \pm 2ab + b^2$$

3) You could replace a and b in the identity above with any numbers and it would still be true.

Go forth and multiply out brackets...

Remember the identity $(a \pm b)^2 \equiv a^2 \pm 2ab + b^2$. It can help multiply out those pesky squared brackets.

Q1 Expand and simplify: a) $(y + 4)(y - 5)$ [2 marks] b) $(2p - 3)^2$ [2 marks]

c) $(x - 2y)^2$ [2 marks] d) $(2t + \sqrt{2})(t - 3\sqrt{2})$ [3 marks]

Section Three — Algebra

Factorising

Right, now you know how to expand brackets, it's time to put them back in. This is known as factorising.

Factorising — Taking Out a Common Factor

This is the exact reverse of multiplying out brackets. Here's the method to follow:

1) Take out the biggest number that goes into all the terms.
2) For each letter in turn, take out the highest power (e.g. x, x² etc.) that will go into EVERY term.
3) Open the bracket and fill in all the bits needed to reproduce each term.
4) Check your answer by multiplying out the bracket and making sure it matches the original expression.

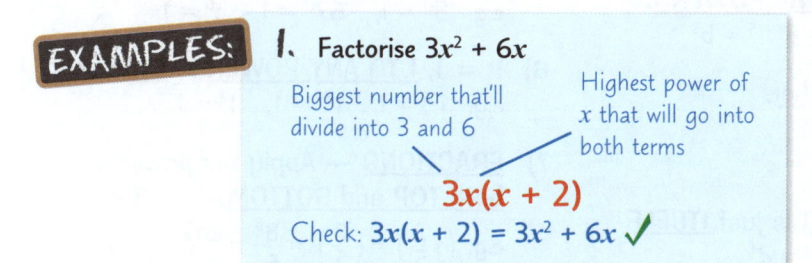

EXAMPLES:

1. Factorise $3x^2 + 6x$

   Biggest number that'll divide into 3 and 6
   Highest power of x that will go into both terms

   $3x(x + 2)$

   Check: $3x(x + 2) = 3x^2 + 6x$ ✓

2. Factorise $8x^2y + 2xy^2$

   Biggest number that'll divide into 8 and 2
   Highest powers of x and y that will go into both terms

   $2xy(4x + y)$

   Check: $2xy(4x + y) = 8x^2y + 2xy^2$ ✓

REMEMBER: The bits taken out and put at the front are the common factors. The bits inside the bracket are what's needed to get back to the original terms if you multiply the bracket out again.

D.O.T.S. — The Difference Of Two Squares

The 'difference of two squares' (D.O.T.S. for short) is where you have 'one thing squared' take away 'another thing squared'. There's a quick and easy way to factorise it — just use the rule below:

$$a^2 - b^2 = (a + b)(a - b)$$

EXAMPLE: Factorise:

a) $9p^2 - 16q^2$ Answer: $9p^2 - 16q^2 = (3p + 4q)(3p - 4q)$
   Here you had to spot that 9 and 16 are square numbers.

b) $3x^2 - 75y^2$ Answer: $3x^2 - 75y^2 = 3(x^2 - 25y^2) = 3(x + 5y)(x - 5y)$
   This time, you had to take out a factor of 3 first.

c) $x^2 - 5$ Answer: $x^2 - 5 = (x + \sqrt{5})(x - \sqrt{5})$
   Although 5 isn't a square number, you can write it as $(\sqrt{5})^2$.

Watch out — the difference of two squares can creep into other algebra questions.

You could be asked to simplify a fraction featuring a difference of two squares. There's more on algebraic fractions on p.45.

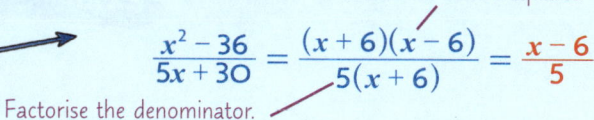

EXAMPLE: Simplify $\dfrac{x^2 - 36}{5x + 30}$

The numerator is a difference of two squares.

$$\dfrac{x^2 - 36}{5x + 30} = \dfrac{(x + 6)(x - 6)}{5(x + 6)} = \dfrac{x - 6}{5}$$

Factorise the denominator.

Well, one's blue and one's yellow...

As factorising is the reverse process of expanding brackets, you must check your answer by multiplying out the brackets. Make sure you can spot differences of two squares as well — they can be a bit sneaky.

Q1 Factorise $6xy + 15y^2$ [2 marks]

Q2 Factorise $x^2 - 16y^2$ [2 marks]

Q3 Factorise $x^2 - 11$ [2 marks]

Q4 Simplify $\dfrac{6x - 42}{x^2 - 49}$ [3 marks]

Section Three — Algebra

Powers

Powers are a very useful shorthand: $2 \times 2 \times 2 \times 2 \times 2 \times 2 \times 2 = 2^7$ ('two to the power 7')

That bit is easy to remember. Unfortunately, you also need to learn <u>seven rules</u> for positive and zero powers, and <u>one rule</u> for negative powers. Sad times.

Seven Basic Rules

Warning: Rules 1 & 2 don't work for things like $2^3 \times 3^7$, only for powers of the same number.

1) When **MULTIPLYING**, you **ADD THE POWERS**.
   e.g. $3^6 \times 3^4 = 3^{6+4} = 3^{10}$, $a^2 \times a^7 = a^{2+7} = a^9$

2) When **DIVIDING**, you **SUBTRACT THE POWERS**.
   e.g. $5^4 \div 5^2 = 5^{4-2} = 5^2$, $b^8 \div b^5 = b^{8-5} = b^3$

3) When **RAISING** one power to another, you **MULTIPLY THEM**.
   e.g. $(3^2)^4 = 3^{2 \times 4} = 3^8$, $(c^3)^6 = c^{3 \times 6} = c^{18}$

4) $x^1 = x$, **ANYTHING** to the **POWER 1** is just **ITSELF**.
   e.g. $3^1 = 3$, $d \times d^3 = d^1 \times d^3 = d^{1+3} = d^4$

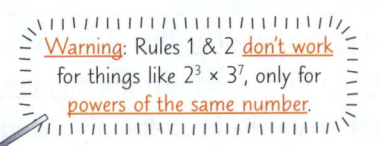

5) $x^0 = 1$, **ANYTHING** to the **POWER 0** is just **1**.
   e.g. $5^0 = 1$, $67^0 = 1$, $e^0 = 1$

6) $1^x = 1$, **1 TO ANY POWER** is **STILL JUST 1**.
   e.g. $1^{23} = 1$, $1^{89} = 1$, $1^2 = 1$

7) **FRACTIONS** — Apply the power to both **TOP** and **BOTTOM**.
   e.g. $\left(1\frac{3}{5}\right)^3 = \left(\frac{8}{5}\right)^3 = \frac{8^3}{5^3} = \frac{512}{125}$, $\left(\frac{u}{v}\right)^5 = \frac{u^5}{v^5}$

EXAMPLES:

1. Simplify $12x^4 \div 6x^3$

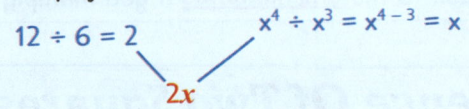

$12 \div 6 = 2$
$x^4 \div x^3 = x^{4-3} = x$
$= 2x$

2. Simplify $(y^3)^5 \times y^2$

$(y^3)^5 = y^{3 \times 5} = y^{15}$
$y^{15} \times y^2 = y^{15+2} = y^{17}$

3. What is $\left(\frac{2}{3}\right)^3$?

Top: $2^3 = 2 \times 2 \times 2 = 8$
Bottom: $3^3 = 3 \times 3 \times 3 = 27$
$\frac{8}{27}$

4. Simplify $(3a^2b^4c)^3$

Deal with each bit separately:
$(3a^2b^4c)^3 = (3)^3 \times (a^2)^3 \times (b^4)^3 \times (c)^3$
$= 27 \times a^{2 \times 3} \times b^{4 \times 3} \times c^3$
$= 27a^6b^{12}c^3$

The Negative Power Rule

The rule for <u>negative powers</u>...

Turn it Upside-Down

The reciprocal of a number is '1 divided by that number' — so it's another name for a power of –1.

People have real difficulty remembering this — whenever you see a negative power you need to immediately think: "Aha, that means turn it the other way up and make the power positive".

e.g. $7^{-2} = \frac{1}{7^2} = \frac{1}{49}$, $a^{-4} = \frac{1}{a^4}$

EXAMPLE: Evaluate $\left(\frac{3}{5}\right)^{-2}$ without a calculator.

$\left(\frac{3}{5}\right)^{-2} = \left(\frac{5}{3}\right)^{+2} = \frac{5^2}{3^2} = \frac{25}{9}$

Don't let the power go to your head...

Learn all the exciting rules on this page and then have a crack at these Exam Practice Questions.

Q1 Simplify: a) $e^4 \times e^7$ [1 mark]   b) $f^9 \div f^5$ [1 mark]
                  c) $(g^6)^0$ [1 mark]   d) $2h^5j^{-2} \times 3h^2j^4$ [2 marks]

Q2 Evaluate the following without a calculator:
        a) 613^{-1} [1 mark]   b) 5^{-2} [1 mark]   c) $\left(\frac{2}{3}\right)^{-3}$ [2 marks]

Section Three — Algebra

Powers and Roots

Imagine how hard things would get if your powers had fractions in them.
Bad news — you don't have to imagine...

Simple Fractional Powers

"Fractional powers are the root of all evil..."

When you see a FRACTIONAL POWER think ROOT.
This handy equation will help you convert fractional powers when the numerator is 1:

$$x^{\frac{1}{a}} = \sqrt[a]{x}$$

The denominator of a fractional power = the number of the root.

The power $\frac{1}{2}$ means Square Root ($\sqrt{}$),
The power $\frac{1}{3}$ means Cube Root ($\sqrt[3]{}$),
The power $\frac{1}{4}$ means Fourth Root ($\sqrt[4]{}$).

e.g. $25^{\frac{1}{2}} = \sqrt[2]{25} = \sqrt{25} = 5$, $64^{\frac{1}{3}} = \sqrt[3]{64} = 4$, $81^{\frac{1}{4}} = \sqrt[4]{81} = 3$, $z^{\frac{1}{5}} = \sqrt[5]{z}$

Negative Fractional Powers

For a negative fractional power: **turn upside-down** first, then **root**.

EXAMPLES:

1. Simplify $4^{-\frac{1}{2}}$.

You don't need to flip the power upside down — just make it positive.

1) Turn upside-down first and make the power positive: $4^{-\frac{1}{2}} = \left(\frac{1}{4}\right)^{\frac{1}{2}}$

2) Then root: $\left(\frac{1}{4}\right)^{\frac{1}{2}} = \sqrt{\frac{1}{4}} = \frac{\sqrt{1}}{\sqrt{4}} = \frac{1}{2}$

2. Simplify $(9x^4)^{-\frac{1}{2}}$.

1) $(9x^4)^{-\frac{1}{2}} = \left(\frac{1}{9x^4}\right)^{\frac{1}{2}}$

2) $\left(\frac{1}{9x^4}\right)^{\frac{1}{2}} = \sqrt{\frac{1}{9x^4}} = \frac{\sqrt{1}}{\sqrt{9x^4}} = \frac{1}{3x^2}$

Harder Fractional Powers

When the fraction doesn't have a 1 as its numerator, the equation for fractional powers changes.

$$x^{\frac{p}{a}} = (\sqrt[a]{x})^p$$

e.g. $64^{\frac{5}{6}} = (\sqrt[6]{64})^5 = (2)^5 = 32$, $k^{\frac{9}{8}} = (\sqrt[8]{k})^9$

Basically: split the fraction into a root and a power, and do them in that order: root first, then power.

EXAMPLE: Simplify $27^{\frac{2}{3}}$.

1) Split the fraction into a root and power: $27^{\frac{2}{3}} = (\sqrt[3]{27})^2$ 2) Root first: $(\sqrt[3]{27})^2 = (3)^2$ 3) Then power: $(3)^2 = 9$

I like cube-rooting everything — some say I'm power mad...

Don't forget — the denominator of a fractional power = the number of the root. Now try:

Q1 Evaluate without a calculator: a) $125^{\frac{1}{3}}$ [1 mark] b) $9^{-\frac{1}{2}}$ [1 mark] c) $16^{\frac{6}{4}}$ [1 mark]

Q2 Simplify: a) $(9x^2)^{\frac{3}{2}}$ [1 mark] b) $\left(\frac{1}{x}\right)^{-\frac{1}{3}}$ [1 mark]

Section Three — Algebra

Manipulating Surds

Surds are expressions with irrational square roots in them (remember from p.2 that irrational numbers are ones which can't be written as fractions, such as most square roots, cube roots and π).

Manipulating Surds — 6 Rules to Learn

There are 6 rules you need to learn for dealing with surds...

1. $\sqrt{a} \times \sqrt{b} = \sqrt{a \times b}$ e.g. $\sqrt{2} \times \sqrt{3} = \sqrt{2 \times 3} = \sqrt{6}$ — also $(\sqrt{b})^2 = \sqrt{b} \times \sqrt{b} = \sqrt{b \times b} = b$

2. $\dfrac{\sqrt{a}}{\sqrt{b}} = \sqrt{\dfrac{a}{b}}$ e.g. $\dfrac{\sqrt{8}}{\sqrt{2}} = \sqrt{\dfrac{8}{2}} = \sqrt{4} = 2$

3. $\sqrt{a} + \sqrt{b}$ — DO NOTHING — in other words it is definitely NOT $\sqrt{a+b}$

4. $(a + \sqrt{b})^2 = (a + \sqrt{b})(a + \sqrt{b}) = a^2 + 2a\sqrt{b} + b$ — NOT just $a^2 + (\sqrt{b})^2$ (see p.30)

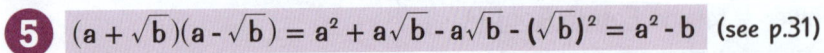

5. $(a + \sqrt{b})(a - \sqrt{b}) = a^2 + a\sqrt{b} - a\sqrt{b} - (\sqrt{b})^2 = a^2 - b$ (see p.31)

6. $\dfrac{a}{\sqrt{b}} = \dfrac{a}{\sqrt{b}} \times \dfrac{\sqrt{b}}{\sqrt{b}} = \dfrac{a\sqrt{b}}{b}$ e.g. $\dfrac{5}{3\sqrt{2}} = \dfrac{5}{3\sqrt{2}} \times \dfrac{3\sqrt{2}}{3\sqrt{2}} = \dfrac{15\sqrt{2}}{18} = \dfrac{5\sqrt{2}}{6}$

This is known as 'RATIONALISING the denominator' — it's where you get rid of the $\sqrt{}$ on the bottom of the fraction. For denominators of the form $a \pm \sqrt{b}$, you multiply by the denominator but change the sign in front of the root (see example 3 below).

Use the Rules to Simplify Expressions

EXAMPLES:

1. Write $\sqrt{300} + \sqrt{48} - 2\sqrt{75}$ in the form $a\sqrt{3}$, where a is an integer.

Write each surd in terms of $\sqrt{3}$:
$\sqrt{300} = \sqrt{100 \times 3} = \sqrt{100} \times \sqrt{3} = 10\sqrt{3}$
$\sqrt{48} = \sqrt{16 \times 3} = \sqrt{16} \times \sqrt{3} = 4\sqrt{3}$
$2\sqrt{75} = 2\sqrt{25 \times 3} = 2 \times \sqrt{25} \times \sqrt{3} = 10\sqrt{3}$

Then do the sum (leaving your answer in terms of $\sqrt{3}$):
$\sqrt{300} + \sqrt{48} - 2\sqrt{75} = 10\sqrt{3} + 4\sqrt{3} - 10\sqrt{3} = 4\sqrt{3}$

2. A rectangle with length $4x$ cm and width x cm has an area of 32 cm². Find the exact value of x, giving your answer in its simplest form.

Area of rectangle = length × width = $4x \times x = 4x^2$
So $4x^2 = 32$
$x^2 = 8$
$x = \pm\sqrt{8}$

You can ignore the negative square root (see p.36) as length must be positive.

'Exact value' means you have to leave your answer in surd form, so get $\sqrt{8}$ into its simplest form:
$\sqrt{8} = \sqrt{4 \times 2} = \sqrt{4}\sqrt{2}$
$= 2\sqrt{2}$ So $x = 2\sqrt{2}$

3. Write $\dfrac{3}{2 + \sqrt{5}}$ in the form $a + b\sqrt{5}$, where a and b are integers.

To rationalise the denominator, multiply top and bottom by $2 - \sqrt{5}$:

$\dfrac{3}{2 + \sqrt{5}} = \dfrac{3(2 - \sqrt{5})}{(2 + \sqrt{5})(2 - \sqrt{5})}$

$= \dfrac{6 - 3\sqrt{5}}{2^2 - 2\sqrt{5} + 2\sqrt{5} - (\sqrt{5})^2}$

$= \dfrac{6 - 3\sqrt{5}}{4 - 5} = \dfrac{6 - 3\sqrt{5}}{-1} = -6 + 3\sqrt{5}$

(so $a = -6$ and $b = 3$)

Rationalise the denominator? How absurd...

Learn the 6 rules for manipulating surds, then give these Exam Practice Questions a go...

Q1 Simplify $\sqrt{180} + \sqrt{20} + (\sqrt{5})^3$ [3 marks]

Q2 Write $\dfrac{2}{2 + \sqrt{3}}$ in the form $a + b\sqrt{3}$, where a and b are integers. [3 marks]

Section Three — Algebra

Solving Equations

The basic idea of solving equations is very simple — keep rearranging until you end up with x = number. The two most common methods for rearranging equations are: 1) 'same to both sides' and 2) do the opposite when you cross the '='. We'll use the 'same to both sides' method on these pages.

Rearrange Until You Have x = Number

The easiest ones to solve are where you just have a mixture of x's and numbers.

1) First, rearrange the equation so that all the x's are on one side and the numbers are on the other. Combine terms where you can.
2) Then divide both sides by the number multiplying x to find the value of x.

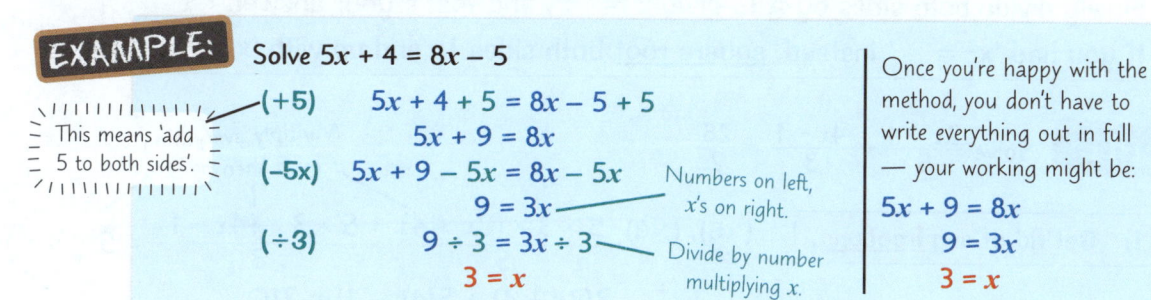

EXAMPLE: Solve $5x + 4 = 8x - 5$

(+5) $5x + 4 + 5 = 8x - 5 + 5$
        $5x + 9 = 8x$
(−5x) $5x + 9 - 5x = 8x - 5x$
        $9 = 3x$ — Numbers on left, x's on right.
(÷3) $9 ÷ 3 = 3x ÷ 3$ — Divide by number multiplying x.
        $3 = x$

This means 'add 5 to both sides'.

Once you're happy with the method, you don't have to write everything out in full — your working might be:

$5x + 9 = 8x$
$9 = 3x$
$3 = x$

Multiply Out Brackets First

If your equation has brackets in it...
1) Multiply them out before rearranging.
2) Solve it in the same way as above.

EXAMPLE: Solve $3(3x - 2) = 5x + 10$

        $9x - 6 = 5x + 10$
(−5x) $9x - 6 - 5x = 5x + 10 - 5x$
        $4x - 6 = 10$
(+6) $4x - 6 + 6 = 10 + 6$
        $4x = 16$
(÷4) $4x ÷ 4 = 16 ÷ 4$
        $x = 4$

Get Rid of Fractions (before they take over the world)

1) Fractions make everything more complicated — so you need to get rid of them before doing anything else (yep, even before multiplying out brackets).
2) To get rid of fractions, multiply every term of the equation by whatever's on the bottom of the fraction. If there are two fractions, you'll need to multiply by both denominators.

EXAMPLES:

1. Solve $\frac{x+2}{4} = 4x - 7$

(×4) $\frac{4(x+2)}{4} = 4(4x) - 4(7)$

Multiply every term by 4 to get rid of the fraction.

$x + 2 = 16x - 28$
$30 = 15x$ — And solve.
$2 = x$

2. Solve $\frac{3x+5}{2} = \frac{4x+10}{3}$ Multiply everything by 2 then by 3.

(×2), (×3) $\frac{2 \times 3 \times (3x+5)}{2} = \frac{2 \times 3 \times (4x+10)}{3}$

$3(3x+5) = 2(4x+10)$
And solve. $9x + 15 = 8x + 20$
$x = 5$

Solving equations — more fun than greasing a seal...

Here's a handy final tip — you can always check your answer by sticking it in both sides of the original equation. They should both give the same number. Now practise what you've learned on these beauts:

Q1   Solve $2x + 5 = 17 - 4x$ [2 marks]

Q2   Solve $4(y + 3) = 3y + 16$ [3 marks]

Q3   Solve $\frac{3x+2}{5} = \frac{5x+6}{9}$ [3 marks]

Section Three — Algebra

Solving Equations

Now you know the basics of solving equations, it's time to put it all together into a step-by-step method.

Solving Equations Using the 6-Step Method

1) Get rid of any fractions.
2) Multiply out any brackets.
3) Collect all the x-terms on one side and all number terms on the other.
4) Reduce it to the form 'Ax = B' (by combining like terms).
5) Finally divide both sides by A to give 'x =   ', and that's your answer.
6) If you had 'x^2 =   ' instead, square root both sides to end up with 'x = ±   '.

EXAMPLE: Solve $\frac{3x+4}{5} + \frac{4x-1}{3} = \frac{28}{2}$

Multiply everything by 5 then by 3.

1) Get rid of any fractions.   (×5), (×3) $\frac{5 \times 3 \times (3x+4)}{5} + \frac{5 \times 3 \times (4x-1)}{3} = 5 \times 3 \times 14$

$3(3x + 4) + 5(4x - 1) = 210$

simplify $\frac{28}{2}$ to 14

2) Multiply out any brackets. $9x + 12 + 20x - 5 = 210$

3) Collect all the x-terms on one side and all number terms on the other.
(−12), (+5) $9x + 20x = 210 - 12 + 5$

4) Reduce it to the form 'Ax = B' (by combining like terms). $29x = 203$

5) Finally divide both sides by A to give 'x =   ', and that's your answer.
(÷29) $x = 7$ (You're left with 'x = ' so you can ignore step 6.)

For an equation where the denominators contain algebra, see p.46.

Dealing with Squares

If you're unlucky, you might get an x^2 in an equation. If you do, you'll end up with 'x^2 = ...' at step 5 and have to do step 6 — take square roots. There's one important thing to remember: whenever you take the square root of a number, the answer can be positive or negative (unless there's a reason it can't be −ve).

EXAMPLE: There are 75 tiles on a roof. Each row contains three times the number of tiles as each column. How many tiles are there in one column?

Let the number of tiles in a column be x. Write an equation for the total number of tiles in terms of x.

$3x \times x = 75$
$3x^2 = 75$
(÷3) $x^2 = 25$
($\sqrt{}$) $x = \pm 5$

Ignore the negative square root — you can't have a negative number of tiles.

So there are 5 tiles in one column.

You always get a +ve and −ve version of the same number (your calculator only gives the +ve answer). This shows why: $5^2 = 5 \times 5 = 25$ but also $(-5)^2 = (-5) \times (-5) = 25$.

Some numbers have really messy square roots — e.g. $\sqrt{5} = 2.236067...$ If you get a question involving a square root step and you're asked to give the **EXACT** solution, leave the square root symbol in your answer (unless the root gives you a nice number).

$\sqrt{5}$ is a surd — see p.34.

Square Roots? Must be a geomer-tree...

The 6-step method won't work for every equation, but it's still an important method to learn and practise.

Q1 Solve $2x^2 + 8 = 80$ [2 marks]

Q2 Solve $\frac{3x-2}{2} - \frac{4x-5}{3} = 2$ [3 marks]

Section Three — Algebra

Expressions and Formulas

In the exam, you might be given a wordy question and have to make an expression or formula from the information. You just have to go through the information slowly and carefully and extract the maths from it.

Before we get started, make sure you know these definitions:

1) EXPRESSION — a collection of terms (see p.29). Expressions DON'T have an = sign in them.
2) EQUATION — an expression with an = sign in it (so you can solve it).
3) FORMULA — a rule that helps you work something out (it will also have an = sign in it).

Make Expressions or Formulas from Given Information

Here are some examples of how to use the information to write expressions and formulas.

EXAMPLE: Aoife is x years old. Leah is 5 years younger than Aoife. Martin is 4 times as old as Aoife. Find a simplified expression for the sum of their ages in terms of x.

Aoife's age is x
Leah's age is $x - 5$ (Leah is 5 years younger, so subtract 5)
Martin's age is $4 \times x = 4x$ (4 times older)

The sum of their ages is:
$x + (x - 5) + 4x = 6x - 5$

If you'd been told the sum of their ages, you'd have to set your expression equal to the sum and solve it to find x.

EXAMPLE: In rugby union, tries score 5 points and conversions score 2 points. A team scores a total of P points, made up of t tries and c conversions. Write a formula for P in terms of t and c.

Tries score 5 points — t tries will score $5 \times t = 5t$ points
Conversions score 2 points — c conversions will score $2 \times c = 2c$ points
So total points scored are $P = 5t + 2c$

Because you're asked for a formula, you must include the 'P = ' bit to get full marks (i.e. don't just put $5t + 2c$).

Use Your Expression to Solve Equations

Sometimes, you might be asked to use an expression to solve an equation.

EXAMPLE: Liên, Naveed and Camille give some books to charity. Naveed gives 6 more books than Liên, and Camille gives 7 more books than Naveed. Between them, they give away 46 books. How many books did they give each?

Let the number of books Liên gives be x.
Then Naveed gives $x + 6$ books
and Camille gives $(x + 6) + 7 = x + 13$ books
So in total they give $x + x + 6 + x + 13 = 3x + 19$ books

So $3x + 19 = 46$ — You're told this in the question.
$3x = 27$
$x = 9$

So Liên gives 9 books,
Naveed gives $9 + 6 = 15$ books and
Camille gives $15 + 7 = 22$ books.

I have the formula for the perfect cup of tea...

Some exam questions might not tell you to write an equation or a formula but you'll still have to come up with one so that you can answer it. Knowing this, have a go at the questions below:

Q1 Noah, Hellä and Joe sell 73 raffle tickets between them. Hellä sells twice as many tickets as Noah, and Joe sells 8 more tickets than Hellä. How many tickets does each person sell? [4 marks]

Q2 Three positive whole numbers have a sum of 48. The second number is five times the first, and the third number is double the second number. What are the three numbers? [3 marks]

Section Three — Algebra

M3 Expressions, Formulas and Functions

Containing all the fun of the previous page, but with added shapes...

Use Shape Properties to Find Formulas and Equations

In some questions, you'll need to use what you know about shapes (e.g. side lengths or areas) to come up with a formula or an equation to solve.

EXAMPLE:

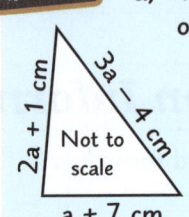

a) Write a formula for P, the perimeter of the triangle below, in terms of a.

Form an expression for the perimeter and set it equal to P:
P = (a + 7) + (2a + 1) + (3a − 4)
P = 6a + 4 cm

Triangle with sides $2a + 1$ cm, $3a - 4$ cm, $a + 7$ cm. Not to scale.

b) If the triangle has a perimeter of 58 cm, find the value of a.

P = 58, so set your formula equal to 58 and solve to find a:
6a + 4 = 58
6a = 54
a = 9

EXAMPLE: The area of the square is the same as the area of the triangle. Find the length of the base of the triangle.

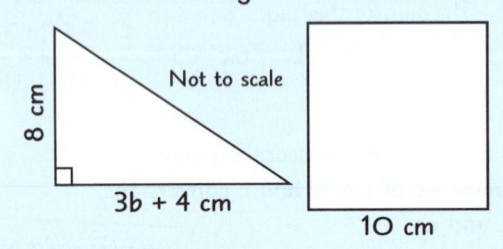

Right triangle with height 8 cm and base $3b + 4$ cm; square with side 10 cm. Not to scale.

Area of triangle: $\frac{1}{2} \times (3b + 4) \times 8 = 12b + 16$ cm²
Area of square: $10^2 = 100$ cm²

Set the areas equal to each other and solve:
12b + 16 = 100
12b = 84
b = 7
So base length = (3 × 7) + 4 = **25 cm**

Functions Produce Outputs from Inputs

1) A function takes an input, processes it (e.g. multiplies it by 5 and adds 2) and outputs a value.
2) If you're given a function machine, just put in the number, follow the steps and see what comes out.
3) If you're given the output and have to find the input, use the function machine in reverse.

EXAMPLE: The function machine below represents the function 'multiply by 5 and add 2'.

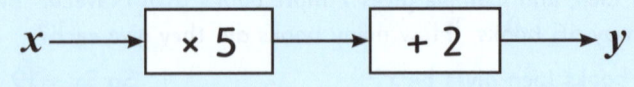

x → [× 5] → [+ 2] → y

If this was an equation, it'd be written as $y = 5x + 2$.

a) Find the value of y when x = 5.
Just put 5 into the machine: 5 —×5→ 25 —+2→ 27. So **y = 27**.

b) Find the value of x when y = 42.
This time, put y = 42 into the machine and work backwards:
42 —−2→ 40 —÷5→ 8. So **x = 8**.

Don't forget to reverse each step as well — so +2 becomes −2 and ×5 becomes ÷5.

Perimeter? Area? I thought this was an algebra section...

Don't be put off by the shapey words — once you've turned the information into an equation, it's just normal algebra (though I'm not sure if that makes it better or worse...). Anyway, try these questions.

Q1 Using the function machine above, find the value of x when y = 57. [2 marks]

Q2 A regular pentagon has sides of length x cm. A square with sides of length x + 4 cm has the same perimeter as the pentagon. Find the value of x. [3 marks]

Section Three — Algebra

Trial and Improvement

Trial and improvement is a way of finding an <u>approximate</u> solution to an equation that's too hard to be solved using normal methods. You'll be told <u>WHEN</u> to use trial and improvement — don't go using it <u>willy-nilly</u>.

Keep Trying *Different Values* in the Equation

The basic idea of trial and improvement is to keep trying <u>different values</u> of x that are getting <u>closer</u> and <u>closer</u> to the solution. Here's the <u>method</u> to follow:

1) **SUBSTITUTE TWO INITIAL VALUES** into the equation that give **OPPOSITE CASES**.
   These could be suggested in the question. 'Opposite cases' means <u>one answer too big, one too small</u>.

2) Now **CHOOSE YOUR NEXT VALUE IN BETWEEN THE PREVIOUS TWO**, and **SUBSTITUTE** it into the equation.
   <u>Continue this process</u>, always choosing a new value <u>between the two closest opposite cases</u> (and preferably nearer to the one that was closer to the answer).

3) **AFTER ONLY 3 OR 4 STEPS** you should have **2 numbers** which are to the <u>right degree of accuracy but DIFFER BY 1 IN THE LAST DIGIT</u>.
   For example, if you had to get your answer to 1 d.p. then you'd eventually end up with say 5.4 and 5.5, with these giving **OPPOSITE** results of course.

4) <u>At this point</u> you ALWAYS take the <u>exact middle value</u> to decide which is the answer you want.
   E.g. for 5.4 and 5.5 you'd try 5.45 to see if the real answer was between <u>5.4 and 5.45</u> (so 5.4 to 1 d.p.) or between <u>5.45 and 5.5</u> (so 5.5 to 1 d.p.).

You'll be asked for a certain level of accuracy (often 1 d.p.) in the question.

It's a good idea to keep track of your working in a <u>table</u> — see example below.

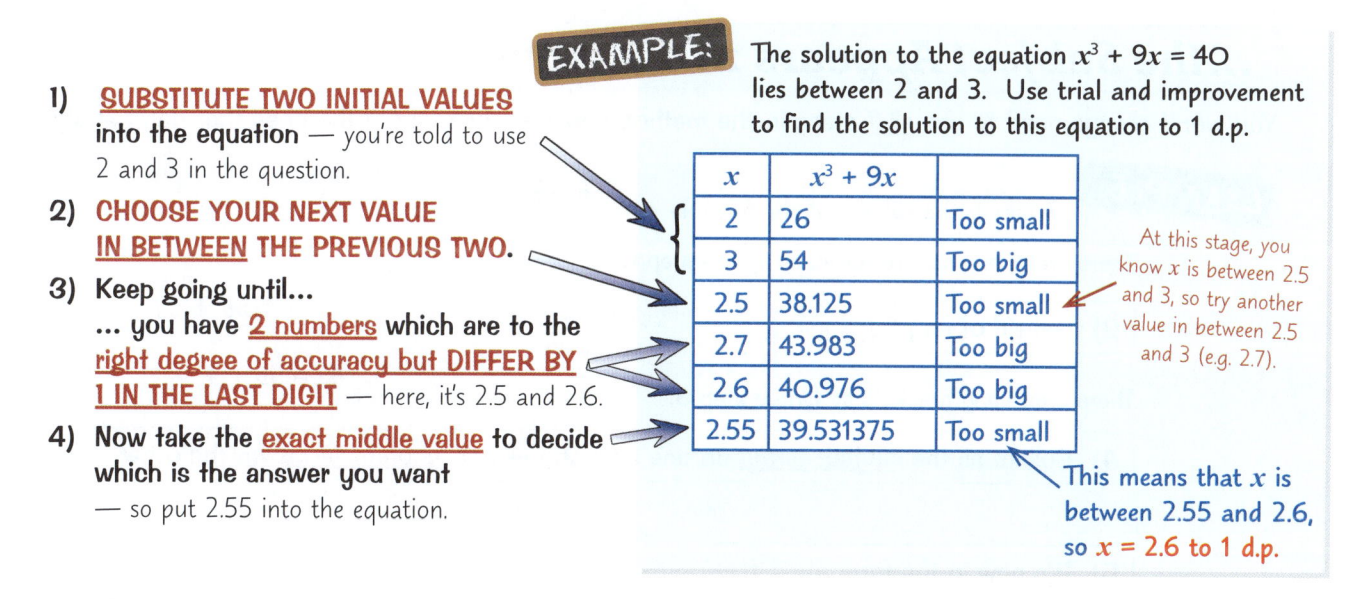

EXAMPLE: The solution to the equation $x^3 + 9x = 40$ lies between 2 and 3. Use trial and improvement to find the solution to this equation to 1 d.p.

1) **SUBSTITUTE TWO INITIAL VALUES** into the equation — you're told to use 2 and 3 in the question.

2) **CHOOSE YOUR NEXT VALUE IN BETWEEN THE PREVIOUS TWO.**

3) Keep going until...
   ... you have **2 numbers** which are to the <u>right degree of accuracy but DIFFER BY 1 IN THE LAST DIGIT</u> — here, it's 2.5 and 2.6.

4) Now take the <u>exact middle value</u> to decide which is the answer you want — so put 2.55 into the equation.

x	$x^3 + 9x$	
2	26	Too small
3	54	Too big
2.5	38.125	Too small
2.7	43.983	Too big
2.6	40.976	Too big
2.55	39.531375	Too small

At this stage, you know x is between 2.5 and 3, so try another value in between 2.5 and 3 (e.g. 2.7).

This means that x is between 2.55 and 2.6, so $x = 2.6$ to 1 d.p.

Make sure you show <u>all your working</u> — you could lose marks if it's not clear which method you've used.

Trial and improvement — not a good strategy for lion-taming...

Sorry, it's not the most exciting page in the world — but it is a good way of picking up easy marks in the exam just by putting some numbers into equations. Try it out on these Exam Practice Questions:

Q1 $x^3 + 6x = 69$ has a solution between 3 and 4.
   Use trial and improvement to find this solution to 1 d.p. [4 marks]

Q2 $x^3 - 12x = 100$ has a solution between 5 and 6.
   Use trial and improvement to find this solution to 1 d.p. [4 marks]

Section Three — Algebra

Rearranging Formulas

Rearranging formulas means making one letter the subject, e.g. getting 'y = ' from '2x + z = 3(y + 2p)' — you have to get the subject on its own.

Rearrange Formulas with the Solving Equations Method

Rearranging formulas is remarkably similar to solving equations (see p.35-36). The method below is identical to the method for solving equations, except that there is an extra step at the start.

1) Get rid of any square root signs by squaring both sides.
2) Get rid of any fractions.
3) Multiply out any brackets.
4) Collect all the subject terms on one side and all non-subject terms on the other.
5) Reduce it to the form '$Ax = B$' (by combining like terms). You might have to do some factorising here too.
6) Divide both sides by A to give '$x =$ '.
7) If you're left with '$x^2 =$ ', square root both sides to get '$x = \pm$ ' (don't forget the ±).

x is the subject term here. A and B could be numbers or letters (or a mix of both).

You might have to tweak step 1 or 7 if you get a trickier root or power. For example, if your formula has a cube root you'll have to cube both sides to get rid of it.

What To Do If...

...the Subject Appears in a Fraction

You won't always need to use all 7 steps in the method above — just ignore the ones that don't apply.

EXAMPLE: Make b the subject of the formula $a = \dfrac{5b + 3}{4}$.

There aren't any square roots, so ignore step 1.

2) Get rid of any fractions. (by multiplying every term by 4, the denominator)   (×4) $4a = \dfrac{4(5b+3)}{4}$
$4a = 5b + 3$

There aren't any brackets so ignore step 3.

4) Collect all the subject terms on one side and all non-subject terms on the other.
(remember that you're trying to make b the subject)   (−3) $5b = 4a - 3$

5) It's now in the form $Ab = B$. (where A = 5 and B = 4a − 3)

6) Divide both sides by 5 to give '$b =$ '.   (÷5) $b = \dfrac{4a - 3}{5}$

b isn't squared, so you don't need step 7.

If I could rearrange my subjects, I'd have maths all day...

Learn the 7 steps for rearranging formulas. Then get rearrangin' with these snazzy practice questions:

Q1 Make q the subject of the formula $p = \dfrac{q}{7} + 2r$ [2 marks]

Q2 Make v the subject of the formula $a = \dfrac{v - u}{t}$ [2 marks]

Section Three — Algebra

Rearranging Formulas

Carrying straight on from the previous page, now it's time for what to do if...

...there's a *Square* or *Square Root* Involved

If the subject appears as a square or in a square root, you'll have to use steps 1 and 7 (not necessarily both).

EXAMPLE: Make u the subject of the formula $v^2 = u^2 + 2as$.

There aren't any square roots, fractions or brackets so ignore steps 1-3 (this is pretty easy so far).

4) Collect all the subject terms on one side and all non-subject terms on the other.

$(-2as)$ $u^2 = v^2 - 2as$

5) It's now in the form $\underline{Au^2 = B}$ (where $A = 1$ and $B = v^2 - 2as$)

$A = 1$, which means it's already in the form '$u^2 =$ ', so ignore step 6.

7) Square root both sides to get '$u = \pm$ '. $(\sqrt{\ })$ $u = \pm\sqrt{v^2 - 2as}$

EXAMPLE: Make n the subject of the formula $2(m + 3) = \sqrt{n + 5}$.

1) Get rid of any square roots by squaring both sides.
$[2(m + 3)]^2 = (\sqrt{n + 5})^2$
$4(m^2 + 6m + 9) = n + 5$
$4m^2 + 24m + 36 = n + 5$

There aren't any fractions so ignore step 2.
The brackets were removed when squaring so ignore step 3.

4) Collect all the subject terms on one side and all non-subject terms on the other.

(-5) $n = 4m^2 + 24m + 31$ This is in the form '$n =$ ' so you don't need to do steps 5-7.

...the Subject Appears *Twice*

Go home and cry. No, not really — you'll just have to do some factorising, usually in step 5.

EXAMPLE: Make p the subject of the formula $q = \dfrac{p + 1}{p - 1}$.

There aren't any square roots so ignore step 1.

2) Get rid of any fractions. $q(p - 1) = p + 1$ 3) Multiply out any brackets. $pq - q = p + 1$

4) Collect all the subject terms on one side and all non-subject terms on the other.
$pq - p = q + 1$

5) Combine like terms on each side of the equation. $p(q - 1) = q + 1$

This is where you factorise — p was in both terms on the LHS so it comes out as a common factor.

6) Divide both sides by $(q - 1)$ to give '$p =$ '. $p = \dfrac{q + 1}{q - 1}$ (p isn't squared, so you don't need step 7.)

...there's a pirate invasion — hide in a cupboard...

Try this Exam Practice Question to have a go at rearranging more complicated formulas...

Q1 Make y the subject of: a) $x = \dfrac{y^2}{4}$ [2 marks]   b) $x = \dfrac{y}{y - z}$ [4 marks]

Section Three — Algebra

Factorising Quadratics

A <u>quadratic equation</u> is one where the <u>highest power</u> is <u>x^2</u>. There are several ways to solve one...

Factorising a Quadratic

1) '<u>Factorising a quadratic</u>' means '<u>putting it into 2 brackets</u>'.
2) The standard format for quadratic equations is: $ax^2 + bx + c = 0$.
3) If <u>a = 1</u>, the quadratic is <u>much easier</u> to deal with. E.g. $x^2 + 3x + 2 = 0$
4) As well as factorising a quadratic, you might be asked to <u>solve</u> the equation. This just means finding the values of x that make each bracket <u>0</u> (see example below).

See the next page for when 'a' is not 1.

Factorising Method when a = 1

1) <u>ALWAYS</u> rearrange into the <u>STANDARD FORMAT</u>: $x^2 + bx + c = 0$.
2) Write down the <u>TWO BRACKETS</u> with the x's in: (x   )(x   ) = 0.
3) Then <u>find 2 numbers</u> that <u>MULTIPLY to give 'c'</u> (the end number) but also <u>ADD/SUBTRACT to give 'b'</u> (the coefficient of x).
4) Fill in the +/− signs and make sure they work out properly.
5) As an <u>ESSENTIAL CHECK</u>, <u>expand</u> the brackets to make sure they give the original equation.
6) Finally, <u>SOLVE THE EQUATION</u> by <u>setting each bracket equal to 0</u>.

Ignore any minus signs at this stage.

You <u>only</u> need to do step 6) if the question asks you to <u>solve</u> the equation — if it just tells you to <u>factorise</u>, you can <u>stop</u> at step 5).

EXAMPLE: Solve $x^2 - x = 12$.

1) $x^2 - x - 12 = 0$ ← 1) <u>Rearrange</u> into the standard format.

2) (x   )(x   ) = 0 ← 2) Write down the <u>initial brackets</u>.

3)
1 × 12 Add/subtract to give:	13 or 11
2 × 6 Add/subtract to give:	8 or 4
3 × 4 Add/subtract to give:	7 or ⓵

3) Find the right <u>pairs of numbers</u> that <u>multiply to give c</u> (= 12), and <u>add or subtract to give b</u> (= 1) (remember, we're ignoring the +/− signs for now).

(x   3)(x   4) = 0 *This is what we want.*

4) $(x + 3)(x - 4) = 0$

4) <u>Now fill in the +/− signs</u> so that 3 and 4 add/subtract to give −1 (= b).

5) Check:
$(x + 3)(x - 4) = x^2 - 4x + 3x - 12$
$= x^2 - x - 12$ ✓

5) <u>ESSENTIAL check</u> — <u>EXPAND the brackets</u> to make sure they give the original expression.

But we're not finished yet — we've only factorised it, we still need to...

6) $(x + 3) = 0 \Rightarrow x = -3$
$(x - 4) = 0 \Rightarrow x = 4$

6) <u>SOLVE THE EQUATION</u> by setting each bracket <u>equal to 0</u>.

Bring me a biscuit or I'll factorise your quadratic...

Handy tip: to help you work out which signs you need, look at c. If c is positive, the signs will be the same (both positive or negative), but if c is negative the signs will be different (one positive and one negative).

Q1   Factorise $x^2 + 2x - 15$ [2 marks]   Q2   Solve $x^2 - 9x + 20 = 0$ [3 marks]

Section Three — Algebra

Factorising Quadratics

So far so good. It gets a bit more complicated when 'a' isn't 1, but it's all good fun, right? Right? Well, I think it's fun anyway.

When 'a' is Not 1

The basic method is still the same but it's a bit messier — the initial brackets are different as the first terms in each bracket have to multiply to give 'a'. This means finding the other numbers to go in the brackets is harder as there are more combinations to try. The best way to get to grips with it is to have a look at an example.

EXAMPLE: Solve $3x^2 + 7x - 6 = 0$.

1) $3x^2 + 7x - 6 = 0$
2) $(3x\ \ )(x\ \ ) = 0$
3) Number pairs: 1×6 and 2×3

$(3x\ \ 1)(x\ \ 6)$ multiplies to give $18x$ and $1x$ which add/subtract to give $17x$ or $19x$
$(3x\ \ 6)(x\ \ 1)$ multiplies to give $3x$ and $6x$ which add/subtract to give $9x$ or $3x$
$(3x\ \ 3)(x\ \ 2)$ multiplies to give $6x$ and $3x$ which add/subtract to give $9x$ or $3x$
$(3x\ \ 2)(x\ \ 3)$ multiplies to give $9x$ and $2x$ which add/subtract to give $11x$ or $7x$ ✓

$(3x\ \ 2)(x\ \ 3)$

4) $(3x - 2)(x + 3)$
5) $(3x - 2)(x + 3) = 3x^2 + 9x - 2x - 6$
   $= 3x^2 + 7x - 6$ ✓
6) $(3x - 2) = 0 \Rightarrow x = \frac{2}{3}$
   $(x + 3) = 0 \Rightarrow x = -3$

1) Rearrange into the standard format.
2) Write down the initial brackets — this time, one of the brackets will have a $3x$ in it.
3) The tricky part: first, find pairs of numbers that multiply to give c (= 6), ignoring the minus sign for now.

   Then, try out the number pairs you just found in the brackets until you find one that gives $7x$. But remember, each pair of numbers has to be tried in 2 positions (as the brackets are different — one has $3x$ in it).

4) Now fill in the +/− signs so that 9 and 2 add/subtract to give +7 (= b).
5) ESSENTIAL check — EXPAND the brackets.
6) SOLVE THE EQUATION by setting each bracket equal to 0 (if a isn't 1, one of your answers will be a fraction).

EXAMPLE: Solve $2x^2 - 9x = 5$.

1) Put in standard form: $2x^2 - 9x - 5 = 0$
2) Initial brackets: $(2x\ \ )(x\ \ ) = 0$
3) Number pairs: 1×5

$(2x\ \ 5)(x\ \ 1)$ multiplies to give $2x$ and $5x$ which add/subtract to give $3x$ or $7x$
$(2x\ \ 1)(x\ \ 5)$ multiplies to give $1x$ and $10x$ which add/subtract to give $9x$ or $11x$

$(2x\ \ 1)(x\ \ 5)$ ✓

4) Put in the signs: $(2x + 1)(x - 5)$
5) Check:
   $(2x + 1)(x - 5) = 2x^2 - 10x + x - 5$
   $= 2x^2 - 9x - 5$ ✓
6) Solve:
   $(2x + 1) = 0 \Rightarrow x = -\frac{1}{2}$
   $(x - 5) = 0 \Rightarrow x = 5$

It's not scary — just think of it as brackets giving algebra a hug...

Learn the step-by-step method above, then have a go at these nice practice questions.

Q1 Factorise $2x^2 - 5x - 12$ [2 marks]
Q2 Solve $3x^2 + 10x - 8 = 0$ [3 marks]
Q3 Factorise $3x^2 + 32x + 20$ [2 marks]
Q4 Solve $5x^2 - 13x = 6$ [3 marks]

Section Three — Algebra

The Quadratic Formula

The solutions to ANY quadratic equation $ax^2 + bx + c = 0$ are given by this formula:

$$x = \frac{-b \pm \sqrt{b^2 - 4ac}}{2a}$$

Learn how to use this formula. It's not too hard, but there are a few pitfalls — so TAKE HEED of these crucial details:

Quadratic Formula — Five Crucial Details

1) Take it nice and slowly — always write it down in stages as you go.
2) **WHENEVER YOU GET A MINUS SIGN, THE ALARM BELLS SHOULD ALWAYS RING!**
3) Remember it's '2a' on the bottom line, not just 'a' — and you divide ALL of the top line by 2a.
4) The ± sign means you end up with two solutions (by replacing it in the final step with '+' and '−').
5) If you get a negative number inside your square root, go back and check your working. Some quadratics do have a negative value in the square root, but they won't come up at GCSE.

If either 'a' or 'c' is negative, the −4ac effectively becomes +4ac, so watch out. Also, be careful if b is negative, as −b will be positive.

EXAMPLE:
Solve $3x^2 + 7x = 1$, giving your answers to 2 decimal places.

$3x^2 + 7x - 1 = 0$

$a = 3, \; b = 7, \; c = -1$

$x = \dfrac{-b \pm \sqrt{b^2 - 4ac}}{2a}$

$= \dfrac{-7 \pm \sqrt{7^2 - 4 \times 3 \times -1}}{2 \times 3}$

$= \dfrac{-7 \pm \sqrt{49 + 12}}{6}$

$= \dfrac{-7 \pm \sqrt{61}}{6}$

$= \dfrac{-7 + \sqrt{61}}{6}$ or $\dfrac{-7 - \sqrt{61}}{6}$

$= 0.1350...$ or $-2.468...$

So to 2 d.p. the solutions are: $x = 0.14$ or -2.47

1) First get it into the form $ax^2 + bx + c = 0$.
2) Then carefully identify a, b and c.
3) Put these values into the quadratic formula and write down each stage.
4) Finally, as a check put these values back into the original equation:
E.g. for x = 0.1350: $3 \times 0.135^2 + 7 \times 0.135 = 0.999675$, which is 1, as near as...

Notice that you do two calculations at the final stage — one + and one −.

When to use the quadratic formula:
- If you have a quadratic that won't easily factorise.
- If the question mentions decimal places or significant figures.
- If the question asks for exact answers or surds (see p.34).

Enough number crunches? Now it's time to work on your quads...

You might have to do a bit of fancy rearranging to get your quadratic into the form $ax^2 + bx + c$.
In Q2 below, it won't even look like a quadratic until you start rearranging it and get rid of the fraction.

Q1   Solve $x^2 + 10x - 4 = 0$, giving your answers to 2 decimal places.   [3 marks]

Q2   Find the exact solutions of $2x + \dfrac{3}{x-2} = -2$.   [4 marks]

Section Three — Algebra

Algebraic Fractions

Unfortunately, fractions aren't limited to numbers — you can get algebraic fractions too.
Fortunately, everything you learnt about fractions on p.5-6 can be applied to algebraic fractions as well.

Simplifying Algebraic Fractions

You can simplify algebraic fractions by cancelling terms on the top and bottom — just deal with each letter individually and cancel as much as you can. You might have to factorise first (see pages 31 and 42-43).

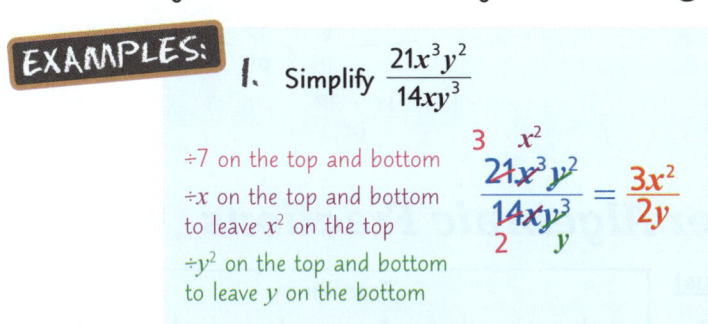

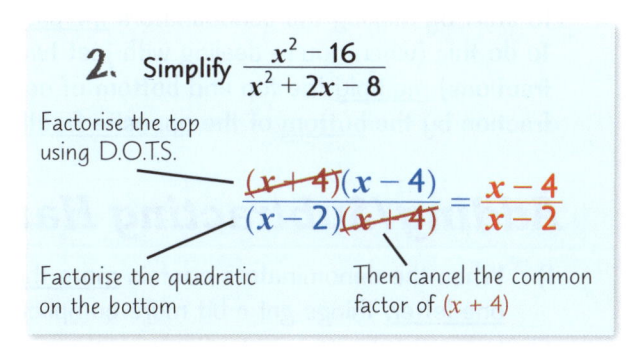

EXAMPLES:

1. Simplify $\dfrac{21x^3y^2}{14xy^3}$

   ÷7 on the top and bottom
   ÷x on the top and bottom to leave x^2 on the top
   ÷y^2 on the top and bottom to leave y on the bottom

   $\dfrac{21x^3y^2}{14xy^3} = \dfrac{3x^2}{2y}$

2. Simplify $\dfrac{x^2 - 16}{x^2 + 2x - 8}$

   Factorise the top using D.O.T.S.

   $\dfrac{(x+4)(x-4)}{(x-2)(x+4)} = \dfrac{x-4}{x-2}$

   Factorise the quadratic on the bottom. Then cancel the common factor of $(x + 4)$

Multiplying/Dividing Algebraic Fractions

1) To **multiply** two fractions, just multiply tops and bottoms **separately**.
2) To **divide**, turn the second fraction **upside down** then **multiply**.

EXAMPLE: Simplify $\dfrac{x^2-4}{x^2+x-12} \div \dfrac{2x+4}{x^2-3x}$

Turn the second fraction upside down — Factorise and cancel — Multiply tops and bottoms

$\dfrac{x^2-4}{x^2+x-12} \div \dfrac{2x+4}{x^2-3x} = \dfrac{x^2-4}{x^2+x-12} \times \dfrac{x^2-3x}{2x+4} = \dfrac{(x+2)(x-2)}{(x+4)(x-3)} \times \dfrac{x(x-3)}{2(x+2)} = \dfrac{x-2}{x+4} \times \dfrac{x}{2} = \dfrac{x(x-2)}{2(x+4)}$

Adding/Subtracting Algebraic Fractions

When you're adding or subtracting fractions, you need to start by giving them the **same denominator**:

1) Work out the **common denominator** by finding something all the denominators divide into (see p.6).
2) Multiply **top and bottom** of each fraction by whatever gives you the common denominator.
3) Add or subtract the **numerators** only.

There's more about adding and subtracting algebraic fractions on the next page.

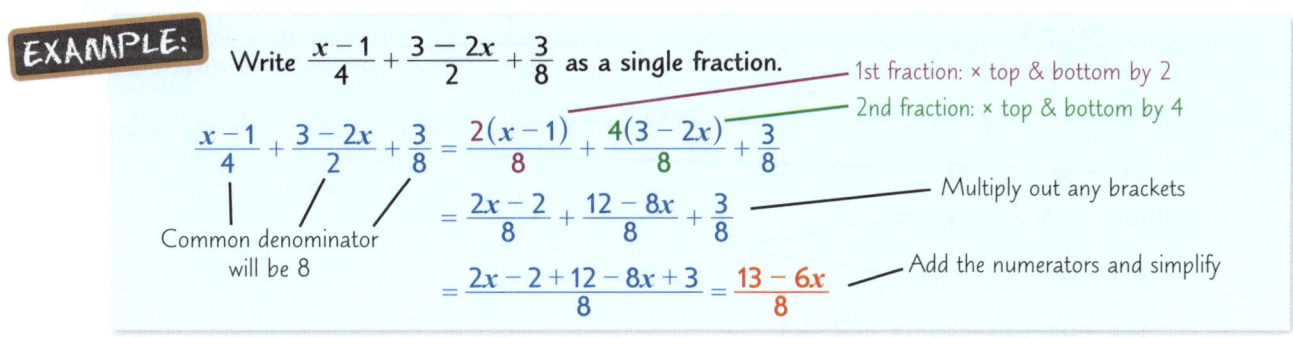

EXAMPLE: Write $\dfrac{x-1}{4} + \dfrac{3-2x}{2} + \dfrac{3}{8}$ as a single fraction.

1st fraction: × top & bottom by 2
2nd fraction: × top & bottom by 4

$\dfrac{x-1}{4} + \dfrac{3-2x}{2} + \dfrac{3}{8} = \dfrac{2(x-1)}{8} + \dfrac{4(3-2x)}{8} + \dfrac{3}{8}$

Common denominator will be 8

$= \dfrac{2x-2}{8} + \dfrac{12-8x}{8} + \dfrac{3}{8}$ — Multiply out any brackets

$= \dfrac{2x-2+12-8x+3}{8} = \dfrac{13-6x}{8}$ — Add the numerators and simplify

---

I'd like to cancel the Summer Term...

You'll have letters, numbers and lines all over the place with algebraic fractions, so keep your working neat.

Q1 Write $\dfrac{5x+4}{6} - \dfrac{x-5}{2}$ as a single fraction. [3 marks]

Q2 Simplify $\dfrac{x^2 + 2xy - 8y^2}{2x^2 - 5xy + 2y^2}$ [3 marks]

Q3 Write $\dfrac{x^2 - 3x - 10}{x - 2x^2} \div \dfrac{x^2 - 25}{6 - 12x}$ as a single fraction in its simplest form. [6 marks]

Section Three — Algebra

Algebraic Fractions

The previous page introduced you to algebraic fractions — everyone's favourite mash-up. This page shows what happens when you have to add and subtract with letters on the bottom. I bet you can't wait...

Adding/Subtracting with Algebraic Denominators

If you have to add or subtract fractions where the denominators are algebraic, you still need to start by making the denominators the same. To do this (when you're dealing with just two fractions) multiply the top and bottom of each fraction by the bottom of the opposite fraction.

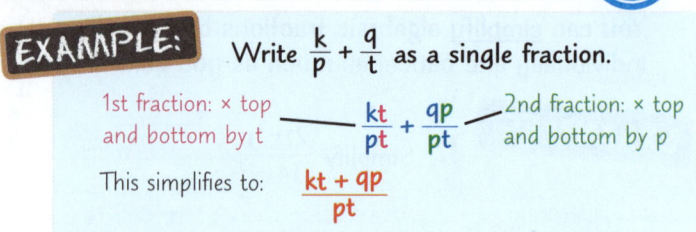

EXAMPLE: Write $\frac{k}{p} + \frac{q}{t}$ as a single fraction.

1st fraction: × top and bottom by t — $\frac{kt}{pt} + \frac{qp}{pt}$ — 2nd fraction: × top and bottom by p

This simplifies to: $\frac{kt + qp}{pt}$

Adding/Subtracting Harder Algebraic Fractions

1) When the denominators contain more than just one letter, things get a bit more complicated.
2) However, the idea is the same — you just need to work out the common denominator and then it's back to simple addition and subtraction.

Fractions		
$\frac{1}{x} + \frac{1}{3x}$	$\frac{1}{x+1} + \frac{1}{x-2}$	$\frac{1}{x} + \frac{1}{x(x+1)}$
$3x$	$(x+1)(x-2)$	$x(x+1)$
Common denominators		

EXAMPLE: Write $\frac{3}{(x+3)} + \frac{1}{(x-2)}$ as a single fraction.

— 1st fraction: × top & bottom by $(x-2)$
— 2nd fraction: × top & bottom by $(x+3)$

$\frac{3}{(x+3)} + \frac{1}{(x-2)} = \frac{3(x-2)}{(x+3)(x-2)} + \frac{(x+3)}{(x+3)(x-2)}$

Common denominator will be $(x+3)(x-2)$

$= \frac{3x-6}{(x+3)(x-2)} + \frac{x+3}{(x+3)(x-2)} = \frac{4x-3}{(x+3)(x-2)}$

— Add the numerators

Algebraic Fractions in Equations

Sometimes equations contain algebraic fractions. Don't panic if you have to solve one — just use what you know about working with algebraic fractions and take your time.

EXAMPLE: Solve the equation $\frac{2}{(x+2)} + \frac{3}{(2x-1)} = 1$.

$\frac{2(2x-1)}{(x+2)(2x-1)} + \frac{3(x+2)}{(x+2)(2x-1)} = \frac{4x-2+3x+6}{(x+2)(2x-1)} = \frac{7x+4}{(x+2)(2x-1)}$

Start by simplifying the fractions on the left-hand side of the equation.

$\frac{7x+4}{(x+2)(2x-1)} = 1$

Then put the simplified fraction back into the equation and solve.

$7x + 4 = (x+2)(2x-1) \Rightarrow 7x + 4 = 2x^2 + 3x - 2$

$2x^2 - 4x - 6 = 0$

As there is an x^2 term, this equation will be quadratic. So collect the terms and rearrange them into the form $ax^2 + bx + c$.

$(2x \quad)(x \quad) = 0$

$(2x - 6)(x + 1) = 0$

Number pairs: 1 × 6 and 2 × 3: $(2x \quad 6)(x \quad 1)$ multiplies to give $2x$ and $6x$, which add/subtract to give $8x$ or $4x$.

$(2x - 6) = 0 \Rightarrow x = \frac{6}{2} = 3$

$(x + 1) = 0 \Rightarrow x = -1$

The Common Denominator? Sounds like a new TV quiz show...

Well, that was a tough page. Have a go at this Exam Practice Question, then maybe go for a nice walk.

Q1 Write $\frac{2}{x+5} + \frac{3}{x-2}$ as a single fraction in its simplest form. [3 marks]

Section Three — Algebra

Simultaneous Equations

There are two types of simultaneous equations in the GCSE Maths world — first up, the easier type, where both equations are linear, e.g. $2x = 6 - 4y$ and $-3 - 3y = 4x$.

Six Steps for *Easy Simultaneous Equations*

EXAMPLE: Solve the simultaneous equations $2x = 6 - 4y$ and $-3 - 3y = 4x$

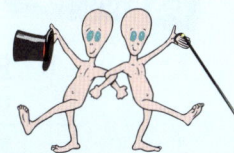

1. **Rearrange both equations** into the form $ax + by = c$, and label the two equations ① and ②.
   a, b and c are numbers (which can be negative)

   $2x + 4y = 6$ — ①
   $4x + 3y = -3$ — ②

2. **Match up the numbers in front** (the 'coefficients') of either the x's or y's in both equations. You may need to multiply one or both equations by a suitable number. Relabel them ③ and ④.

   ① × 2: $4x + 8y = 12$ — ③
   $4x + 3y = -3$ — ④

3. **Add or subtract the two equations** to eliminate the terms with the same coefficient.

   ③ − ④ $0x + 5y = 15$

   If the coefficients have the same sign (both +ve or both −ve) then subtract. If the coefficients have opposite signs (one +ve and one −ve) then add.

4. **Solve the resulting equation.**

   $5y = 15 \Rightarrow y = 3$

5. **Substitute** the value you've found back into equation ① and solve it.

   Sub $y = 3$ into ①: $2x + (4 \times 3) = 6 \Rightarrow 2x + 12 = 6 \Rightarrow 2x = -6 \Rightarrow x = -3$

6. **Substitute** both these values into equation ② to make sure it works. If it doesn't then you've done something wrong and you'll have to do it all again.

   Sub x and y into ②: $(4 \times -3) + (3 \times 3) = -12 + 9 = -3$, which is right, so it's worked.

   So the solutions are: $x = -3$, $y = 3$

   The solutions to simultaneous equations are the coordinates of the points where the graphs of the equations cross. There's more about this on p.61.

One small step for man, six giant leaps for solving equations...

You need to learn the 6 steps on this page. When you think you've got them, try them out on these Exam Practice Questions.

Q1 Issy buys two cups of tea and three slices of cake for £9.
    Rudy buys four cups of tea and one slice of cake from the same cafe for £8.
    Find the cost of one cup of tea and the cost of one slice of cake. [3 marks]

Q2 Find x and y given that $2x - 10 = 4y$ and $3y = 5x - 18$. [3 marks]

Section Three — Algebra

Simultaneous Equations

Now on to the second type of simultaneous equations, where one of them is a quadratic equation...

Seven Steps for TRICKY Simultaneous Equations

EXAMPLE: Solve these two equations simultaneously: $7x + y = 1$ and $2x^2 - y = 3$

1. **Rearrange the quadratic equation** so that you have the non-quadratic unknown on its own. Label the two equations ① and ②.

    $7x + y = 1$ — ① $y = 2x^2 - 3$ — ②

    You could also rearrange the linear equation and substitute it into the quadratic.

2. **Substitute** the quadratic expression into the other equation. You'll get another equation — label it ③.

    $7x + y = 1$ — ①
    $y = 2x^2 - 3$ — ② $\Rightarrow 7x + (2x^2 - 3) = 1$ — ③

    Put the expression for y into equation ① in place of y.

3. **Rearrange** to get a **quadratic equation**. And guess what... You've got to **solve** it.

    $2x^2 + 7x - 4 = 0$
    $(2x - 1)(x + 4) = 0$
    So $2x - 1 = 0$ OR $x + 4 = 0$
    $x = 0.5$ OR $x = -4$

    Remember — if it won't factorise, you'll have to use the quadratic formula on p.44.

4. Stick the **first value** back in one of the **original equations** (pick the easy one).

    ① $7x + y = 1$
    Substitute in $x = 0.5$: $3.5 + y = 1$, so $y = 1 - 3.5 = -2.5$

5. Stick the **second value** back in the **same original equation** (the easy one again).

    ① $7x + y = 1$
    Substitute in $x = -4$: $-28 + y = 1$, so $y = 1 + 28 = 29$

6. Substitute **both pairs** of answers back into the **other original equation** to check they work.

    ② $y = 2x^2 - 3$
    Substitute in $x = 0.5$: $y = (2 \times 0.25) - 3 = -2.5$ — beezer.
    Substitute in $x = -4$: $y = (2 \times 16) - 3 = 29$ — smashing.

7. Write the **pairs of answers** out again, clearly, at the bottom of your working.

    The two pairs of solutions are: $x = 0.5, y = -2.5$ and $x = -4, y = 29$

The graphs of $7x + y = 1$ and $2x^2 - y = 3$ cross at $(0.5, -2.5)$ and $(-4, 29)$ — just like the solutions in the example.

Simultaneous pain and pleasure — it must be algebra...

Don't get confused and think that there are 4 separate solutions — you end up with 2 pairs of solutions.

Q1   Solve the simultaneous equations $y = 2 - 3x$ and $y + 2 = x^2$. [4 marks]

Q2   Find the coordinates of A and B, the points where the graphs of $y = x^2 + 4$ and $y - 6x - 4 = 0$ intersect. [4 marks]

Section Three — Algebra

Inequalities

Inequalities aren't <u>half as difficult as they look</u>. Once you've learned the tricks involved, most of the algebra for them is <u>identical to ordinary equations</u> (have a look back at p.35-36 if you need a reminder).

The Inequality Symbols

> means '<u>Greater than</u>'   ≥ means '<u>Greater than or equal to</u>'
< means '<u>Less than</u>'   ≤ means '<u>Less than or equal to</u>'

I > All of you.

Algebra with Inequalities

The key thing about inequalities — solve them <u>just like regular equations</u> but WITH ONE BIG EXCEPTION:

Whenever you MULTIPLY OR DIVIDE by a NEGATIVE NUMBER, you must FLIP THE INEQUALITY SIGN.

EXAMPLES:

1. x is an integer such that $-4 < x \leq 3$. Find all the possible values of x.

Work out what each bit of the inequality is telling you:

$-4 < x$ means 'x is greater than -4',
$x \leq 3$ means 'x is less than or equal to 3'.

Now just write down all the values that x can take. (Remember, integers are just +ve or –ve whole numbers)

$-3, -2, -1, 0, 1, 2, 3$

2. Solve $6x + 7 > x + 22$.

Just solve it like an equation:

(-7) $6x + 7 - 7 > x + 22 - 7$
           $6x > x + 15$
$(-x)$ $6x - x > x + 15 - x$
           $5x > 15$
$(\div 5)$ $5x \div 5 > 15 \div 5$
           $x > 3$

3. Solve $-2 \leq \frac{x}{4} + 3 \leq 5$.

Don't be put off because there are two inequality signs — just do the same thing to each bit of the inequality:

(-3) $-2 - 3 \leq \frac{x}{4} + 3 - 3 \leq 5 - 3$
          $-5 \leq \frac{x}{4} \leq 2$
$(\times 4)$ $4 \times -5 \leq \frac{4 \times x}{4} \leq 4 \times 2$
          $-20 \leq x \leq 8$

4. Solve $9 - 2x > 15$.

Again, solve it like an equation:

(-9) $9 - 2x - 9 > 15 - 9$
           $-2x > 6$
$(\div -2)$ $-2x \div -2 < 6 \div -2$
           $x < -3$

The > has turned into a <, because we divided by a <u>negative number</u>.

You Can Show Inequalities on Number Lines

Drawing inequalities on a <u>number line</u> is dead easy — all you have to remember is that you use an <u>open circle</u> (○) for > or < and a <u>coloured-in circle</u> (●) for ≥ or ≤.

EXAMPLE: Show the inequality $-4 < x \leq 3$ on a number line.

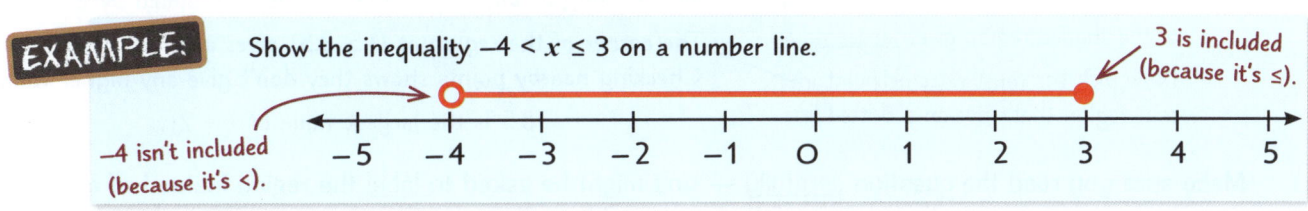

-4 isn't included (because it's <).
3 is included (because it's ≤).

I saw you flip the inequality sign — how rude...

To check you've got the inequality sign right, pop in a value for x and check the inequality's true.

Q1 Solve: a) $11x + 3 < 42 - 2x$ [2 marks]   b) $6 - 4x \geq 18$ [2 marks]

Q2 Solve the inequality $-8 \leq 5x + 2 \leq 22$ and represent the solution on a number line. [3 marks]

Section Three — Algebra

Graphical Inequalities

These questions usually involve <u>shading a region on a graph</u>. The method sounds very complicated, but once you've seen it in action with an example, you'll see that it's OK...

Showing Inequalities on a Graph

Here's the method to follow:

1) <u>CONVERT each INEQUALITY to an EQUATION</u> by simply putting an '=' in place of the inequality sign.
2) <u>DRAW THE GRAPH FOR EACH EQUATION</u> — if the inequality sign is < or > draw a <u>dotted line</u>, but if it's ≥ or ≤ draw a <u>solid line</u>.
3) <u>Work out WHICH SIDE of each line you want</u> — put a point (usually the origin) into the inequality to see if it's on the correct side of the line.
4) <u>SHADE THE REGION this gives you</u>.

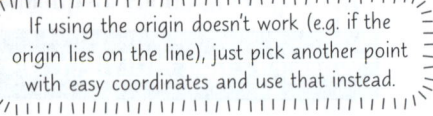

If using the origin doesn't work (e.g. if the origin lies on the line), just pick another point with easy coordinates and use that instead.

EXAMPLE: a) Shade the region that satisfies all three of the following inequalities:
$x + y \leq 5 \qquad y \leq x + 2 \qquad y > 1$.

1) **CONVERT EACH INEQUALITY TO AN EQUATION:**
$x + y = 5$, $y = x + 2$ and $y = 1$

2) **DRAW THE GRAPH FOR EACH EQUATION** (see p.54)
You'll need a <u>dotted</u> line for $y = 1$ and a <u>solid</u> line for $x + y = 5$ and $y = x + 2$.

3) **WORK OUT WHICH SIDE OF EACH LINE YOU WANT**
This is the fiddly bit. Put $x = 0$ and $y = 0$ (the origin) into each inequality and see if this makes the inequality <u>true</u> or <u>false</u>.
$x + y \leq 5$: $x = 0$, $y = 0$ gives $0 \leq 5$ which is <u>true</u>.
This means the <u>origin</u> is on the <u>correct</u> side of the line.

$y \leq x + 2$: $x = 0$, $y = 0$ gives $0 \leq 2$ which is <u>true</u>.
So the origin is on the <u>correct</u> side of this line.

$y > 1$: $x = 0$, $y = 0$ gives $0 > 1$ which is <u>false</u>.
So the origin is on the <u>wrong side</u> of this line.

A <u>dotted line</u> means the region <u>doesn't</u> include the points on the line.

A <u>solid line</u> means the region <u>does</u> include the points on the line

4) **SHADE THE REGION**
You want the region that satisfies all of these:
— below $x + y = 5$ (because the origin <u>is</u> on this side)
— right of $y = x + 2$ (because the origin <u>is</u> on this side)
— above $y = 1$ (because the origin <u>isn't</u> on this side).

b) Hence find the largest value of $x + 2y$ that satisfies these inequalities.

The trick here is to work out which part of the shaded region gives <u>larger values</u>. Now pick the <u>most extreme</u> point in that region that's <u>not</u> on a dotted line.

To give large values, both x and y should be large and positive, with y being as big as possible since it's multiplied by 2.
The corner of the region at (1.5, 3.5) gives a value of 8.5. Checking nearby points shows they don't give any higher values.
8.5 is the largest value of $x + 2y$.

Make sure you read the question <u>carefully</u> — you might be asked to <u>label</u> the region instead of shade it, or just <u>mark on points</u> that satisfy all three inequalities. No point throwing away marks because you didn't read the question properly.

Graphical inequalities — it's a shady business...

Once you've found the region, it's a good idea to pick a point inside it and check that it satisfies ALL the inequalities. Try it out on this Exam Practice Question:

Q1 On a grid, shade the region that satisfies $x \leq 5$, $y > -1$ and $y < x + 1$. [3 marks]

Section Three — Algebra

Sequences

Sequences are lists of numbers (or shapes) that follow a rule. You need to be able to spot what the rule is.

Finding the Rule for Number Sequences

The trick to finding the rule for number sequences is to write down what you have to do to get from one number to the next in the gaps between the numbers. There are 2 main types to look out for:

1) Add or subtract the same number

E.g. 2   5   8   11   14   ...
       +3 +3 +3 +3

The RULE: 'Add 3 to the previous term'

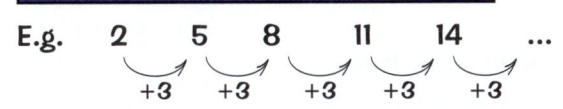

These are known as arithmetic sequences.

2) Multiply or divide by the same number each time

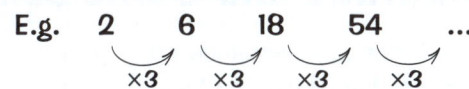

E.g. 2   6   18   54   ...
       ×3 ×3 ×3

The RULE: 'Multiply the previous term by 3'

These are known as geometric sequences.

Sometimes you might get sequences that follow a different rule — e.g. you might have to add or subtract a changing number each time, or add together the two previous terms. The triangular numbers are an example of this — you add 1, then 2, then 3, etc... This gives the sequence 1, 3, 6, 10, 15, ...

Find Any Term with the nth Term Formula

The nth term formula can be used to find any term in the sequence. It contains an n, which is the position of the term you want — e.g. to find the third term, use n = 3.

EXAMPLE: The nth term of a sequence is given by $4n - 5$. Find:

a) the first term,
Substitute n = 1 into the formula:
$(4 \times 1) - 5 = 4 - 5 = -1$

b) the eighth term,
Substitute n = 8 into the formula:
$(4 \times 8) - 5 = 32 - 5 = 27$

c) the ninety-ninth term.
Substitute n = 99 into the formula:
$(4 \times 99) - 5 = 396 - 5 = 391$

Finding the nth Term of a Linear Sequence

This method works for sequences with a common difference — where you add or subtract the same number each time.

EXAMPLE: Find an expression for the nth term of the sequence that starts 5, 8, 11, 14, ...

n: 1   2   3   4
term: 5   8   11 14
            +3 +3 +3

3n: 3   6   9   12
        +2 +2 +2 +2
term: 5   8   11 14

So the expression for the nth term is $3n + 2$

① Find the common difference. It's 3, so this tells you '3n' is in the formula.
② List the values of 3n.
③ Work out what you have to add or subtract to get from 3n to the term. So it's +2.
④ Put '3n' and '+2' together.

Always check your expression by putting the first few values of n back in, e.g. putting n = 1 into $3n + 2$ gives 5, n = 2 gives 8, etc. which is the original sequence you were given — hooray!

Knitting patterns follow the rule knit one, purl one...

Try out this Exam Practice Question to see how you're getting on with sequences.

Q1 A sequence starts 3, 6, 12, ... There are two possible rules for this sequence. Write down both possible rules and find the next two terms of the sequence in each case.   [2 marks]

Section Three — Algebra

Sequences

On the previous page you were introduced to the nth term of linear sequences. Now it's time to look at <u>non-linear sequences</u>. Excited? No? Well, better crack on with it anyway.

Finding the nth Term of a Non-Linear Sequence

Non-linear sequences <u>DON'T</u> increase by the same amount each time.
Quadratic and cubic sequences are non-linear and some (not all) fractional sequences are non-linear too.

Quadratic and Cubic Sequences

If the terms in a sequence are <u>increasing</u> by a greater amount each time, it's more than likely you have a <u>quadratic or cubic</u> sequence on your hands.
In this case, <u>compare</u> the sequence to the list of square or cube numbers (shown below) and add/subtract what you need.

> Quadratic means the nth term will contain an n^2. Cubic means the nth term will contain an n^3.

Square numbers: 1, 4, 9, 16, 25, 36, 49, 64, 81, 100, ... ⟶ nth term = n^2

Cube numbers: 1, 8, 27, 64, 125, ... ⟶ nth term = n^3

EXAMPLE: Find an expression for the nth term of the sequence 2, 5, 10, 17, ...

n: 1   2   3   4
term: 2   5   10 17
        +3   +5   +7

The sequence increases by a <u>larger amount</u> each time. Looking at the sequence, it looks very similar to n^2. So the next step is to <u>compare</u> the sequence to n^2.

n^2:   1   4   9   16
         +1 +1 +1 +1 — To get from n^2 to each term you <u>add 1</u>.
term: 2   5   10 17

So the expression for the nth term is $n^2 + 1$

Non-Linear Fractional Sequences

To find the nth term of a non-linear <u>fractional</u> sequence:
1) Find the nth term for the sequence of <u>numerators</u>.
2) Do the same for the sequence of <u>denominators</u>.
3) Put the nth terms into a <u>fraction</u>.

> Some fractional sequences are linear as the terms increase by the same amount each time e.g. $\frac{1}{4}, \frac{1}{2}, \frac{3}{4}, ...$

EXAMPLE: Find an expression for the nth term of the sequence $\frac{5}{7}, \frac{7}{10}, \frac{9}{13}, \frac{11}{16}, ...$

① Numerator — n: 1   2   3   4
          term: 5   7   9   11
                    +2   +2   +2

The common difference between the terms is <u>2</u>, so the nth term <u>must contain 2n</u>. To get from 2n to the sequence, you must <u>add 3</u>. So the rule is <u>2n + 3</u>.

② Denominator — n: 1   2   3   4
            term: 7   10 13 16
                      +3   +3   +3

The common difference between the terms is <u>3</u>, so the nth term <u>must contain 3n</u>. To get from 3n to the sequence, you must <u>add 4</u>. So the rule is <u>3n + 4</u>.

③ So the expression for the nth term is $\frac{2n + 3}{3n + 4}$

> The sequence of numerators is linear, as is the sequence of denominators. However, the fractional sequence itself is non-linear.

Warning: The sequence 1, 4, 9, 16, ... can give you square eyes...

Here are a couple of Exam Practice Questions to make sure you're a sequences whizz...

Q1 Find an expression for the *n*th term of the sequence 3, 10, 29, 66, ... [2 marks]

Q2 Find an expression for the *n*th term of the sequence $\frac{1}{5}, \frac{2}{9}, \frac{3}{13}, \frac{4}{17}, ...$ [2 marks]

Section Three — Algebra

Revision Questions for Section Three

That's all we've got time for in Section Three — I know, I'm relieved too. Time to see how much you've learned.
- Try these questions and tick off each one when you get it right.
- When you've done all the questions for a topic and are completely happy with it, tick off the topic.

Algebra Basics, Multiplying Out Brackets and Factorising (p29-31)

1) Simplify by collecting like terms: $3x + 2y - 5 - 6y + 2x$
2) Multiply out these brackets: a) $3(2x + 1)$ b) $(x + 2)(x - 3)$ c) $(x + 5)^2$
3) Factorise: a) $8x^2 - 2y^2$ b) $49 - 81p^2q^2$ c) $12x^2 - 48y^2$

Powers, Roots and Surds (p32-34)

4) Simplify the following: a) $x^3 \times x^6$ b) $y^7 \div y^5$ c) z^{-3}
5) Evaluate without a calculator: a) $27^{\frac{1}{3}}$ b) $25^{-\frac{1}{2}}$ c) $4^{\frac{3}{2}}$
6) Simplify the following: a) $\sqrt{27}$ b) $\sqrt{125} \div \sqrt{5}$
7) Write $\sqrt{98} + 3\sqrt{8} - \sqrt{200}$ in the form $a\sqrt{2}$, where a is an integer.

Solving Equations, Expressions, Formulas and Functions (p35-38)

8) Solve these equations: a) $5(x + 2) = 8 + 4(5 - x)$
   b) $\frac{x + 2}{3} = 5x - 18$ c) $4x^2 + 1 = 257$
9) Tony and Robbie have the same number of marbles. Nadia has 26 marbles. Between them, they have 100 marbles. How many marbles does Tony have?
10) A rectangle measures $2x$ cm by $7x$ cm. An equilateral triangle has the same perimeter as the rectangle. Find the length of one side of the triangle in terms of x.
11) A function machine takes a number, doubles it and subtracts 8. What is the result when 11 is put in the machine?

Trial and Improvement and Rearranging Formulas (p39-41)

12) Given that $x^3 + 8x = 103$ has a solution between 4 and 5, use trial and improvement to find this solution to 1 d.p.
13) Make p the subject of: a) $\frac{p}{s+1} = 4$ b) $p^2 + u^2 = 4v$ c) $\frac{p}{p-w} = 4$

Factorising Quadratics and the Quadratic Equation (p42-44)

14) Solve the following by factorising them first: a) $x^2 + 9x + 18 = 0$ b) $5x^2 - 17x - 12 = 0$
15) Find the solutions of these equations (to 2 d.p.) using the quadratic formula:
    a) $x^2 + x - 4 = 0$ b) $5x^2 + 6x = 2$ c) $3x^2 - 3x = 2$ d) $(2x + 3)^2 = 15$

Algebraic Fractions and Simultaneous Equations (p45-48)

16) Simplify the following fractions: a) $\frac{2a^2b^2}{4ab}$ b) $\frac{c-1}{c+2} \div \frac{d+5}{c^2+2c}$
17) Write the following as a single fraction: a) $\frac{f}{8} - \frac{2g}{4}$ b) $\frac{x}{z} - \frac{y}{w}$ c) $\frac{2}{x+3} + \frac{1}{x-1}$
18) Solve the following pair of simultaneous equations: $4x + 5y = 23$ and $3y - x = 7$
19) Solve these simultaneous equations: $y = 3x + 4$ and $x^2 + 2y = 0$

Inequalities and Sequences (p49-52)

20) Solve the following inequalities: a) $4x + 3 \leq 6x + 7$ b) $5x^2 > 180$
21) Show on a graph the region described by these conditions: $x + y \leq 6$, $y > 0.5$, $y \leq 2x - 2$
22) The nth term of a sequence is $5n + 1$. Find the first four terms of this sequence.
23) Find an expression for the nth term of the sequences: a) $-1, 2, 7, 14, \ldots$ b) $\frac{1}{3}, \frac{1}{10}, \frac{1}{17}, \frac{1}{24}, \ldots$

Section Three — Algebra

Straight Lines and Gradients

If you thought I-spy was a fun game, wait 'til you play 'recognise the straight-line graph from the equation'.

Learn to Spot These Straight Line Equations

If an equation has a y and/or x but no higher powers (like x^2 or x^3), then it's a straight line equation.

Vertical and horizontal lines: 'x = a' and 'y = a'

'x = a' is a vertical line through 'a' on the x-axis.
'y = a' is a horizontal line through 'a' on the y-axis.

The equation of the x-axis is $y = 0$.
The equation of the y-axis is $x = 0$.

The main diagonal through the origin: 'y = x'

'y = x' is the main diagonal that goes UPHILL from left to right.

Other sloping lines through the origin: 'y = ax'

The value of 'a' is the gradient — see below.

$y = -x$ is the main diagonal sloping downhill.

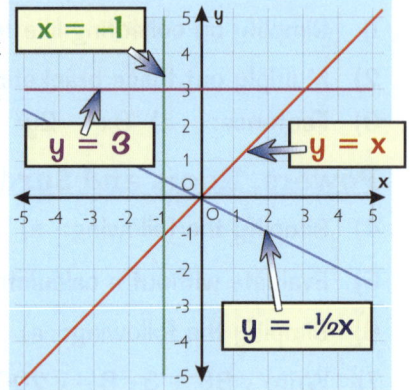

Drawing Straight Line Graphs

If you're given an equation and asked to plot the graph, this 'drawing a table of values' method works every time:

EXAMPLE: Draw the graph of $y = -2x + 4$ for values of x from –1 to 4.

1) Draw up a table with three suitable values of x.

x	0	2	4
y			

2) Find the y-values by putting each x-value into the equation:
E.g. when $x = 4$, $y = -2x + 4 = (-2 \times 4) + 4 = -4$

x	0	2	4
y	4	0	-4

3) Plot the points and draw the line from x = –1 to x = 4. Table gives the points (0, 4), (2, 0), (4, –4)

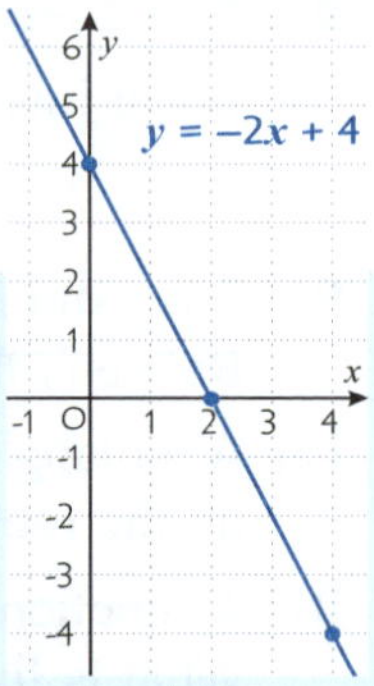

The Gradient is the Steepness of the Line

The gradient of the line is how steep it is — the larger the gradient, the steeper the slope. A negative gradient tells you it slopes downhill. You find it by dividing the change in y by the change in x.

EXAMPLE: Find the gradient of the straight line to the right.

1) Choose two accurate points on the line. A: (6, 50) B: (1, 10)

2) Find the change in y and change in x.
Change in y = 50 – 10 = 40   Change in x = 6 – 1 = 5
Make sure you subtract the y and x-coordinates in the same order. E.g. $y_A - y_B$ and $x_A - x_B$

3) Use this formula:
$$\text{GRADIENT} = \frac{\text{CHANGE IN Y}}{\text{CHANGE IN X}}$$
Gradient = $\frac{40}{5}$ = 8

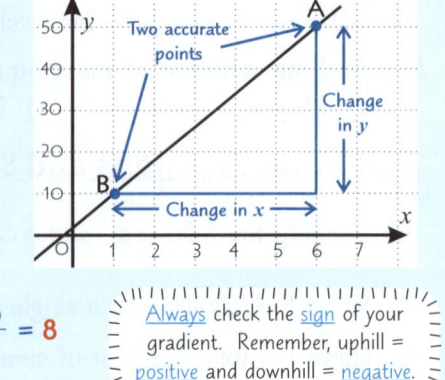

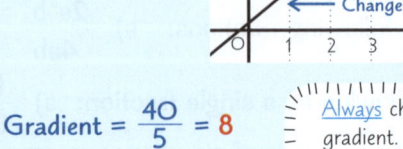

Always check the sign of your gradient. Remember, uphill = positive and downhill = negative.

Finding gradients is often an uphill battle...

Learn the three steps for finding the gradient then have a bash at this practice question. Take care — you might not be able to pick two points with nice, positive coordinates. Fun times ahoy.

Q1 Find the gradient of the line shown on the right. [2 marks]

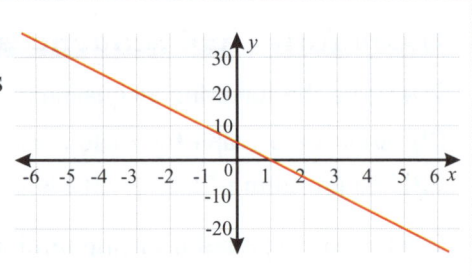

Line Segments

Put down your pen. Take a deep breath. It's time for the most exciting topic in this book — line segments...

The Midpoint of a Line

The 'MIDPOINT OF A LINE SEGMENT' is the POINT THAT'S BANG IN THE MIDDLE of it.

Finding the coordinates of a midpoint is pretty easy. **LEARN THESE THREE STEPS**...

1) Find the average of the x-coordinates.
2) Find the average of the y-coordinates.
3) Plonk them in brackets.

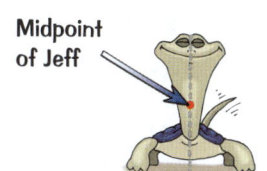

EXAMPLE: P and Q have coordinates (1, 2) and (6, 6). Find the midpoint of the line PQ.

Average of x-coordinates = $\frac{1+6}{2}$ = 3.5

Average of y-coordinates = $\frac{2+6}{2}$ = 4

Coordinates of midpoint = **(3.5, 4)**

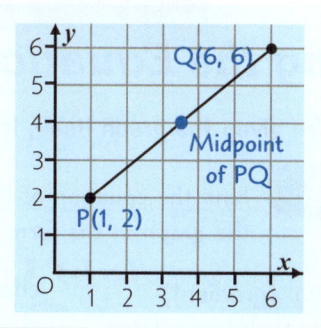

Use Pythagoras to find the Distance Between Points

You need to know how to find the straight-line distance between two points on a graph. You can do this by turning the straight line into a right-angled triangle and then using Pythagoras' theorem.

Pythagoras' Theorem

Pythagoras' theorem is $a^2 + b^2 = c^2$. This allows you to find the longest length of a right-angled triangle (c), as long as you know the lengths of the two smaller sides (a and b). Learn more about it on p.75.

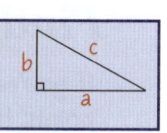

This is how you use the theorem to find the distance between any two points...

1) Sketch a straight line to join up the two points. Then turn the sketch into a right-angled triangle.
2) Find the lengths of the shorter sides of the triangle by subtracting the coordinates.
3) Use Pythagoras to find the length of the longest side. (That's your answer.)

EXAMPLE: Point P has coordinates (10, 3) and point Q has coordinates (2, 9). Find the length of the line PQ.

① Draw lines to make the line PQ the longest side of a right-angled triangle.

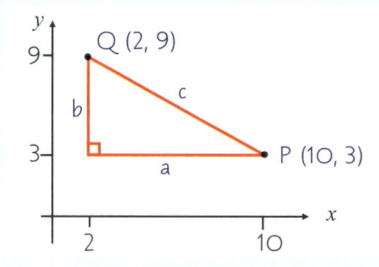

② Find the lengths of the shorter sides:
Length of side a = 10 − 2 = 8
Length of side b = 9 − 3 = 6

③ Use Pythagoras to find side c:
$c^2 = a^2 + b^2 = 8^2 + 6^2 = 64 + 36 = 100$
So: c = $\sqrt{100}$ = **10**

If you only do half the work, you'll only reach your midpoint-ential...

If you wanna make tricky line segment questions a bit less tricky then draw a diagram. It'll help loads.

Q1 Point A has coordinates (5, 2) and point B has coordinates (9, 8). Find:

a) The coordinates of the midpoint of AB. [2 marks]

b) The length from point A to point B. [5 marks]

Section Four — Graphs

y = mx + c

Using '$y = mx + c$' is the most straightforward way of dealing with straight-line equations, and it's very useful in exams. The first thing you have to do though is rearrange the equation into the standard format like this:

Straight line:	Rearranged into '$y = mx + c$'		where:
$y = 2 + 3x$	→ $y = 3x + 2$	($m = 3$, $c = 2$)	'm' = gradient of the line.
$x - y = 0$	→ $y = x + 0$	($m = 1$, $c = 0$)	'c' = 'y-intercept' (where it hits the y-axis)
$4x - 3 = 5y$	→ $y = \frac{4}{5}x - \frac{3}{5}$	($m = \frac{4}{5}$, $c = -\frac{3}{5}$)	

WATCH OUT: people mix up 'm' and 'c' when they get something like $y = 5 + 2x$. Remember, 'm' is the number in front of the 'x' and 'c' is the number on its own.

Finding the Equation of a Straight-Line Graph

When you're given the graph itself, it's quick and easy to find the equation of the straight line.

EXAMPLE: Find the equation of the line on the graph in the form $y = mx + c$.

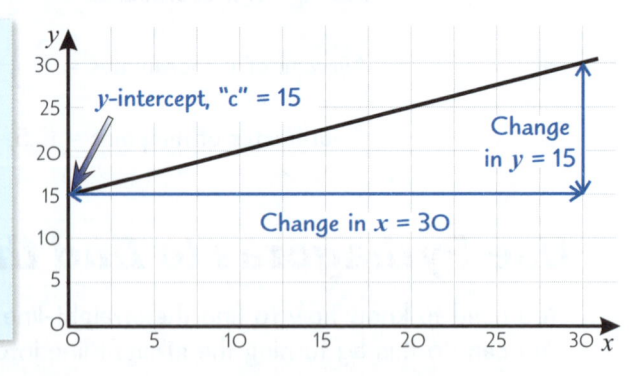

1) Find 'm' (gradient) and 'c' (y-intercept).

$$'m' = \frac{\text{change in } y}{\text{change in } x} = \frac{15}{30} = \frac{1}{2}$$

'c' = 15

2) Use these to write the equation in the form $y = mx + c$.

$$y = \frac{1}{2}x + 15$$

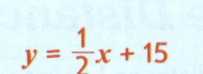

Finding the Equation of a Line Through Two Points

If you're given two points on a line you can find the gradient, then you can use the gradient and one of the points to find the equation of the line. This is super handy, so practise it until you can do it in your sleep.

EXAMPLE: Find the equation of the straight line that passes through $(-2, 9)$ and $(3, -1)$. Give your answer in the form $y = mx + c$.

1) Use the two points to find 'm' (gradient).

$$m = \frac{\text{change in } y}{\text{change in } x} = \frac{-1 - 9}{3 - (-2)} = \frac{-10}{5} = -2$$

So $y = -2x + c$

2) Substitute one of the points into the equation you've just found.

Substitute $(-2, 9)$ into equation: $9 = -2(-2) + c$
$9 = 4 + c$

3) Rearrange the equation to find 'c'.

$c = 9 - 4$
$c = 5$

4) Substitute back into $y = mx + c$:

$y = -2x + 5$

You might be asked to give your equation in other forms such as $ax + by + c = 0$. Just rearrange your $y = mx + c$ equation to get it in this form. It's no biggie.

Remember $y = mx + c$ — it'll keep you on the straight and narrow...

Remember the steps for finding equations and try out your new-found graph skills.

Q1 Find the equation of the line on the graph to the right. [2 marks]

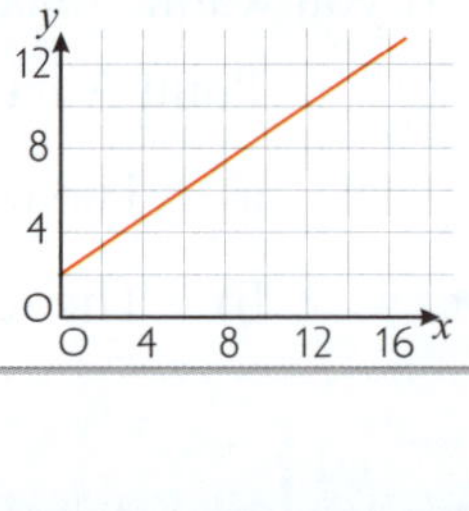

Q2 Line Q goes through $(0, 5)$ and $(4, 7)$.
Find the equation of Line Q in the form $y = mx + c$. [3 marks]

Section Four — Graphs

Parallel and Perpendicular Lines

On p.56 you saw how to write the equation of a straight line. Once you know the equation of a line you can work out the equation of a straight line that's parallel or perpendicular to it.

Parallel Lines Have the Same Gradient

Parallel lines all have the same gradient, which means their $y = mx + c$ equations all have the same value of m.
So the lines: $y = 2x + 3$, $y = 2x$ and $y = 2x - 4$ are all parallel.

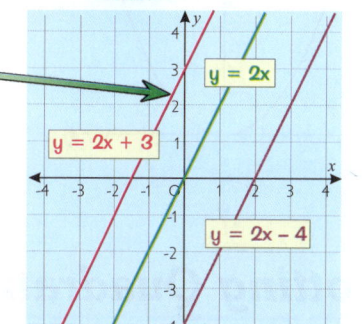

EXAMPLE: Line J has a gradient of –0.25. Find the equation of Line K, which is parallel to Line J and passes through point (2, 3).

Lines J and K are parallel so their gradients are the same $\Rightarrow m = -0.25$

$y = -0.25x + c$

when $x = 2$, $y = 3$:
$3 = (-0.25 \times 2) + c \Rightarrow 3 = -0.5 + c$
$c = 3.5$

$y = -0.25x + 3.5$

1) First find the 'm' value for Line K.
2) Substitute the value for 'm' into $y = mx + c$ to give you the 'equation so far'.
3) Substitute the x and y values for the given point on Line K and solve for 'c'.
4) Write out the full equation.

Perpendicular Line Gradients

Perpendicular lines cross at a right angle, and if you multiply their gradients together you'll get –1. Pretty nifty that.

If the gradient of the first line is m, the gradient of the other line will be $-\frac{1}{m}$, because $m \times -\frac{1}{m} = -1$.

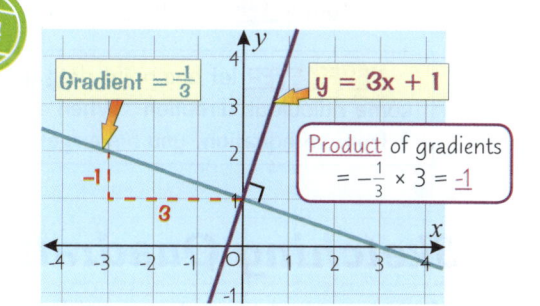

Gradient $= \frac{-1}{3}$
$y = 3x + 1$
Product of gradients $= -\frac{1}{3} \times 3 = -1$

EXAMPLE: Lines A and B are perpendicular and intersect at (3, 3). If Line A has the equation $3y - x = 6$, what is the equation of Line B?

Find 'm' (the gradient) for Line A.	$3y - x = 6 \Rightarrow 3y = x + 6$ $\Rightarrow y = \frac{1}{3}x + 2$, so $m_A = \frac{1}{3}$
Find the 'm' value for the perpendicular line (Line B).	$m_B = -\frac{1}{m_A} = -1 \div \frac{1}{3} = -3$
Put this into $y = mx + c$ to give the 'equation so far'.	$y = -3x + c$
Put in the x and y values of the point and solve for 'c'.	$x = 3$, $y = 3$ gives: $3 = (-3 \times 3) + c$ $\Rightarrow 3 = -9 + c \Rightarrow c = 12$
Write out the full equation.	$y = -3x + 12$

Learn how to calculate gradients and you'll get the top grade-ients...

So basically, use one gradient to find the other, then use the known x and y values to work out c.

Q1 Find the equation of the line parallel to $2x + 2y = 3$ which passes through the point (1, 4). Give your answer in the form $y = mx + c$. [3 marks]

Q2 Show that the lines $y + 5x = 2$ and $5y = x + 3$ are perpendicular. [3 marks]

Section Four — Graphs

Quadratic Graphs

Quadratic functions take the form y = anything with x^2 (but no higher powers of x).
x^2 graphs all have the same symmetrical bucket shape.

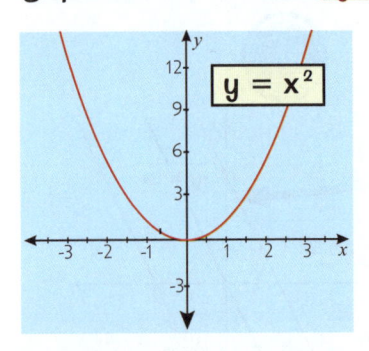

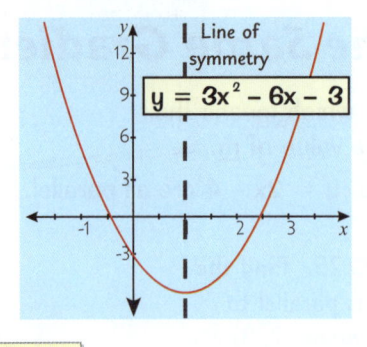

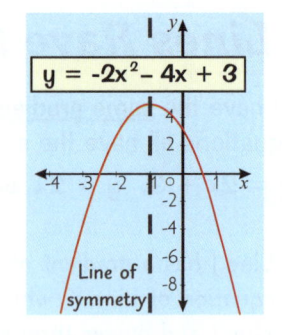

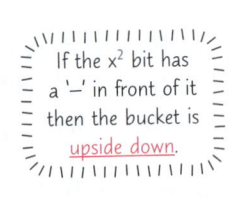

$y = x^2$

$y = 3x^2 - 6x - 3$ — Line of symmetry

$y = -2x^2 - 4x + 3$ — Line of symmetry

If the x^2 bit has a '–' in front of it then the bucket is upside down.

Plotting Quadratics

EXAMPLE: Complete the table of values for the equation $y = x^2 + 2x - 3$ and then plot the graph.

x	-4	-3	-2	-1	0	1	2
y	5	0	-3	-4	-3	0	5

1) Substitute each x-value into the equation to get each y-value.

   E.g. $y = (-4)^2 + (2 \times -4) - 3 = 5$

2) Plot the points and join them with a completely smooth curve.

This point is obviously wrong

NEVER EVER let one point drag your graph off in some ridiculous direction. When a graph is generated from an equation, you never get spikes or lumps.

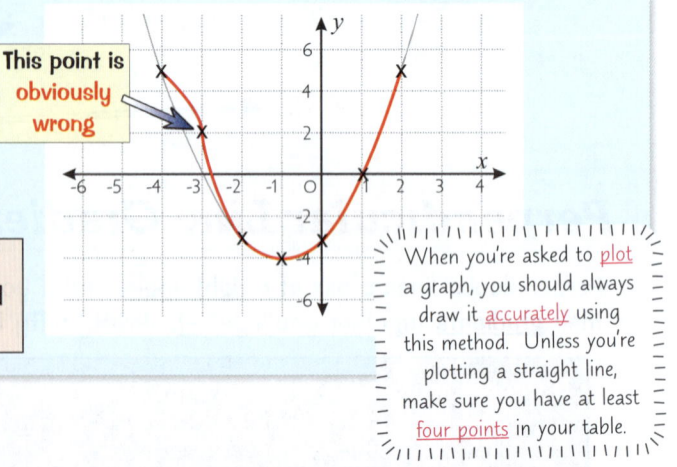

When you're asked to plot a graph, you should always draw it accurately using this method. Unless you're plotting a straight line, make sure you have at least four points in your table.

Sketching Quadratics

If you're asked to sketch a graph, you won't have to use graph paper or be dead accurate — just find and label the important points and make sure the graph is roughly in the correct position on the axes.

EXAMPLE: Sketch the graph of $y = -x^2 - 2x + 8$, labelling the turning point and x-intercepts with their coordinates.

For more on solving quadratic equations, see p.42-44.

1 Find all the information you're asked for.

Solve $-x^2 - 2x + 8 = 0$ to find the x-intercepts.
$-x^2 - 2x + 8 = -(x + 4)(x - 2) = 0$ so $x = -4, x = 2$

Use symmetry to find the turning point of the curve:
The x-coordinate of the turning point is halfway between -4 and 2.

$x = \frac{-4 + 2}{2} = -1$

$y = -(-1)^2 - 2(-1) + 8 = 9$

So the turning point is $(-1, 9)$.

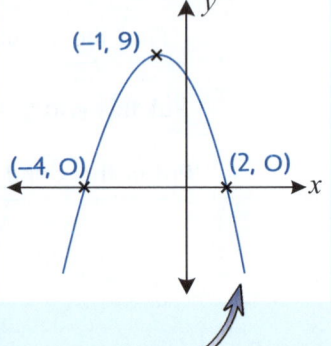

2 Use the information you know to sketch the curve and label the important points. The x^2 is negative, so the curve is n-shaped.

(−1, 9) (−4, 0) (2, 0)

How refreshing — a page on graphs. Not seen one of those in a while...

Fun fact* — the gradient at a turning point on a quadratic will always equal zero.

Q1 Plot the graph of $y = x^2 - 4x - 1$ for values of x between –2 and 6. [4 marks]

*fun not guaranteed.

Section Four — Graphs

Harder Graphs

Graphs come in all sorts of shapes, sizes and wiggles — here are the first of 4 more types you need to know:

x^3 Graphs: $y = ax^3 + bx^2 + cx + d$ (b, c and d can be zero)

All x^3 graphs (also known as cubic graphs) have a wiggle in the middle — sometimes it's a flat wiggle, sometimes it's more pronounced. $-x^3$ graphs always go down from top left, $+x^3$ ones go up from bottom left.

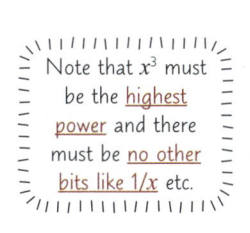

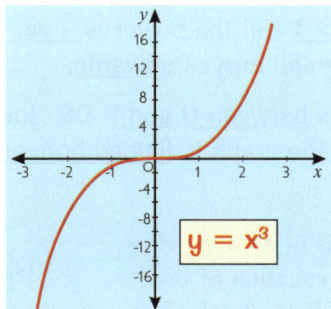

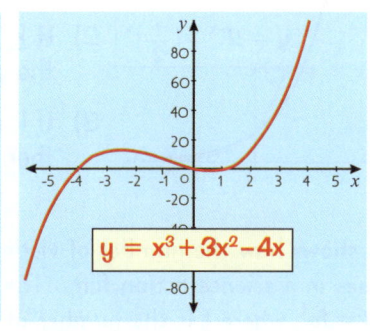

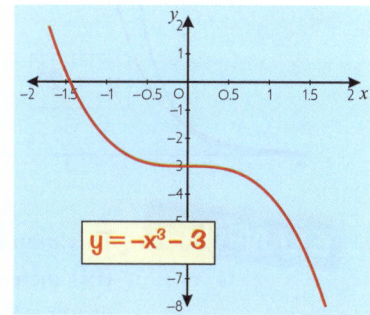

Note that x^3 must be the highest power and there must be no other bits like $1/x$ etc.

$y = x^3$

$y = x^3 + 3x^2 - 4x$

$y = -x^3 - 3$

EXAMPLE:

Draw the graph of $y = x^3 + 4x^2$ for values of x between -4 and $+2$.

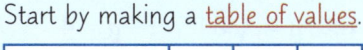

Start by making a table of values.

x	-4	-3	-2	-1	0	1	2
$y = x^3 + 4x^2$	0	9	8	3	0	5	24

Plot the points and join them with a lovely smooth curve. DON'T use your ruler — that would be a bit daft.

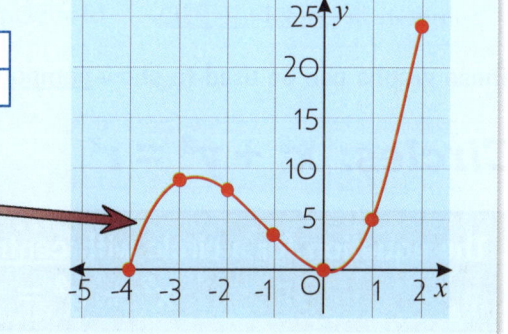

$1/x$ (Reciprocal) Graphs: $y = A/x$ or $xy = A$

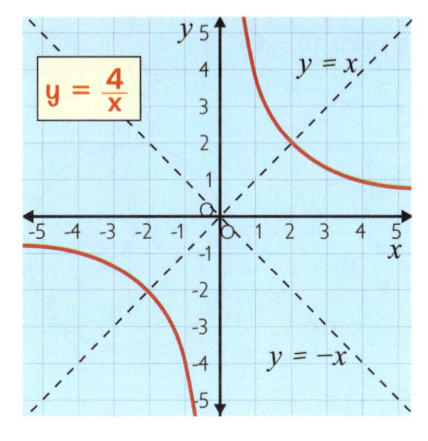

$y = \dfrac{4}{x}$

$y = -\dfrac{4}{x}$

These are all the same basic shape, except the negative ones are in opposite quadrants to the positive ones (as shown). The two halves of the graph don't touch. The graphs don't exist for $x = 0$.

They're all symmetrical about the lines $y = x$ and $y = -x$.

(You get this type of graph with inverse proportion — see p.22.)

If you need to draw a reciprocal graph, use the same method as drawing x^3 graphs.

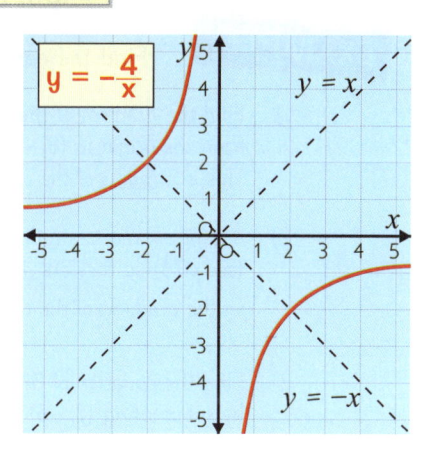

Funny... Those cubic graphs don't look anything like a cube...

Make sure you can recognise and describe the shapes of cubic and reciprocal graphs — you might need to sketch some simple examples too, so better get practising...

Q1   Draw the graph of $x^3 - 4x^2 + 2$ for values of x between -1 and 4.   [4 marks]

Harder Graphs

Here are two more graph types you need to be able to sketch. Knowing what you're aiming for really helps.

k^x Graphs: $y = k^x$ or $y = k^{-x}$ (k is some positive number)

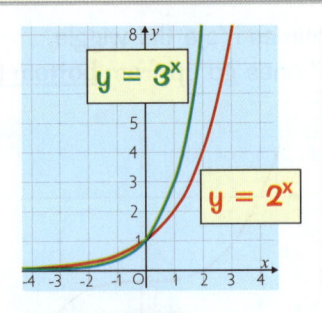

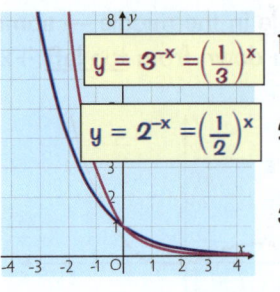

1) These 'exponential' graphs ($y = k^x$) are always above the x-axis, and always go through the point (0, 1).

2) If $k > 1$ and the power is +ve, the graph curves upwards.

   If k = 1, the graph is the same as y = 1.

3) If k is between 0 and 1 OR the power is negative, then the graph is flipped horizontally.

EXAMPLE:
This graph shows how the number of victims of an alien virus (N) increases in a science fiction film. The equation of the graph is $N = fg^t$, where t is the number of days into the film. f and g are positive constants. Find the values of f and g.

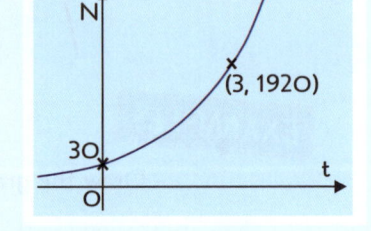

When $t = 0$, $N = 30$ so substitute these values into the equation: *$g^0 = 1$, so you can find f.*

$30 = fg^0 \Rightarrow 30 = f \times 1 \Rightarrow f = 30$

Substitute in $t = 3$, $N = 1920$: $N = 30g^t \Rightarrow 1920 = 30g^3 \Rightarrow g = \sqrt[3]{64} \Rightarrow g = 4$

These graphs can be used to show compound growth ($y = k^x$) or compound decay ($y = k^{-x}$) — see p.27.

Circles: $x^2 + y^2 = r^2$

The equation for a circle with centre (0, 0) and radius r is:
$$x^2 + y^2 = r^2$$

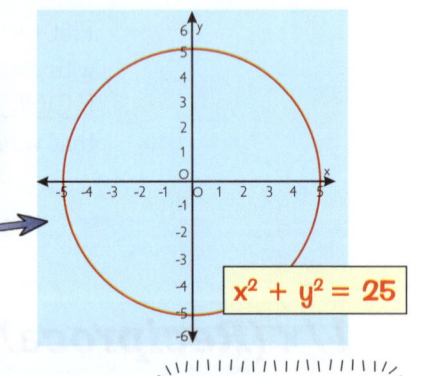

$x^2 + y^2 = 25$ is a circle with centre (0, 0).
$r^2 = 25$, so the radius, r, is 5.

$x^2 + y^2 = 100$ is a circle with centre (0, 0).
$r^2 = 100$, so the radius, r, is 10.

EXAMPLE:
Find the equation of the tangent to $x^2 + y^2 = 100$ at the point (8, −6).

A tangent is a straight line that touches a single point on a circle.

1) Find the gradient of the line from the origin to (8, −6). This is a radius of the circle.

   Gradient = $\dfrac{\text{Change in } y}{\text{Change in } x} = \dfrac{-6 - 0}{8 - 0} = \dfrac{-3}{4}$

2) A tangent meets a radius at 90°, (see p.73) so they are perpendicular so the gradient of the tangent is $-\dfrac{1}{m}$.

   Gradient of tangent $= -\dfrac{1}{m} = -\dfrac{1}{\frac{-3}{4}} = \dfrac{4}{3}$

3) Find the equation of the tangent by substituting (8, −6) into $y = mx + c$.

   $y = mx + c \Rightarrow (-6) = \dfrac{4}{3}(8) + c$

   $-6 = \dfrac{32}{3} + c$

   $c = -\dfrac{50}{3}$

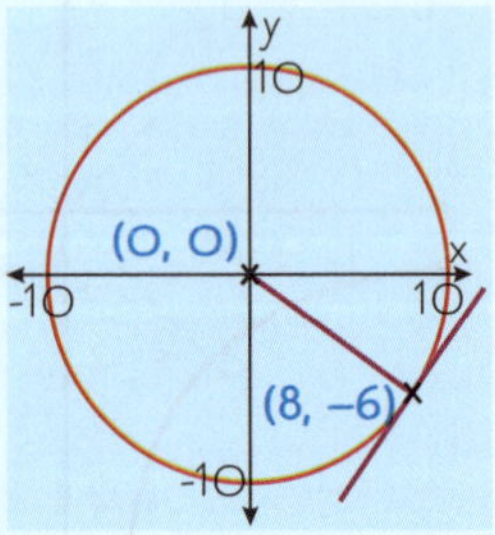

The equation of the tangent is $y = \dfrac{4}{3}x - \dfrac{50}{3}$

Graphs — the only place where squares make a circle...

Learn what type of graph you get from each sort of equation. Then try this Exam Practice Question.

Q1   The point (5, 12) lies on a circle with centre (0, 0).
     Find the radius and equation of the circle.   [4 marks]

Section Four — Graphs

Solving Equations Using Graphs

You can plot graphs to find <u>approximate solutions</u> to simultaneous equations or other awkward equations. Plot the equations you want to solve and the solution lies where the lines <u>intersect</u>.

Plot Both Graphs and See Where They Cross

EXAMPLES:

1. Draw and use a graph to solve the simultaneous equations $y = \frac{1}{2}x$ and $y = -2x + 5$.

1) Use the 'table of values' method to draw the two lines (see p.54).
2) Read off the <u>x and y values</u> where the two lines <u>cross</u>.
   The solution is $x = 2, y = 1$.

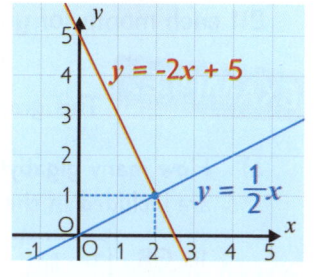

2. Use the graph of $y = 2x^2 - 3x$ (on the right) to estimate both solutions to the equation $2x^2 - 3x = 5$.

$2x^2 - 3x = 5$ is what you get when you put $y = 5$ into the graph's equation, so:
1) <u>Draw</u> a line at $y = 5$.
2) Read the <u>x-values</u> where the curve <u>crosses</u> this line.
   The solutions are about $x = -1$ and $x = 2.5$.

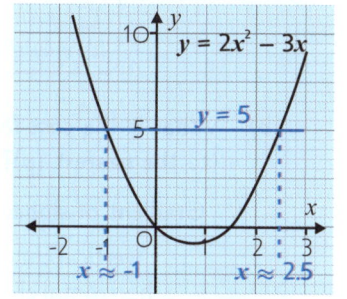

3. By plotting the equations, estimate the points of intersection of the graphs $y = x^2 + 2x - 4$ and $y = 2x + 1$.

1) Make a <u>table of values</u> for each equation and <u>draw both graphs</u>.
2) Read the <u>x and y values</u> where the lines cross.
   The values are about $x = 2.2, y = 5.5$ and $x = -2.2, y = -3.5$.

If you're sitting an M8 exam you might be asked to estimate the solutions to simultaneous equations involving a quadratic and linear equation by plotting the graphs. This example shows how to do it.

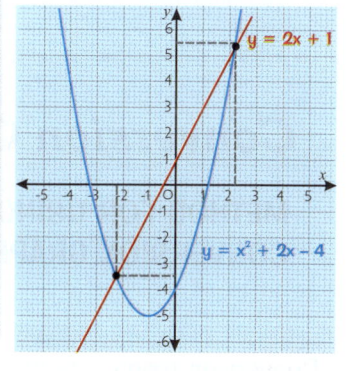

Using Graphs to Solve Tricky Quadratic Equations

Some quadratic equations need <u>rearranging</u> so that you can use graphs to solve them.

EXAMPLE: The graph of $y = 2x^2 - 3x$ is shown on the right. Find the equation of the line you would need to draw on the graph to solve $2x^2 - 5x + 1 = 0$

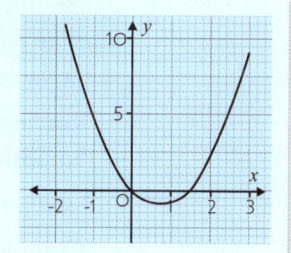

This is a bit nasty — the trick is to rearrange the given equation $2x^2 - 5x + 1 = 0$ so that you have $2x^2 - 3x$ (the graph) on one side.

$$2x^2 - 5x + 1 = 0$$

Adding $2x - 1$ to both sides: $2x^2 - 3x = 2x - 1$ So the line needed is $y = 2x - 1$.

The sides of this equation represent the two graphs $y = 2x^2 - 3x$ and $y = 2x - 1$. Plotting $y = 2x - 1$ on the graph and finding where it crossed the quadratic would give solutions for $2x^2 - 5x + 1 = 0$.

What do you call a giraffe with no eyes? A graph...

Get your graph-plotting pencils ready and have a go at this Practice Question:

Q1 Plot the graph of $y = x^2 + 2x - 8$ and use it to estimate the solutions to $-2 = x^2 + 2x - 8$ (to 1 d.p).   [6 marks]

Section Four — Graphs

Real-Life Graphs

Now and then, graphs mean something more interesting than just y = x³ + 4x² – 6x + 4...

Graphs Can Show Billing Structures

Many bills are made up of two charges — a <u>fixed charge</u> and a <u>cost per unit</u>. E.g. You might pay £11 each month for your phone line, and then be charged 3p for each minute of calls you make.

EXAMPLE: This graph shows how a broadband bill is calculated.

a) How many gigabytes (GB) of Internet usage are included in the <u>basic monthly cost</u>?

18 GB — The first section of the graph is <u>horizontal</u>. You're charged <u>£24</u> even if you <u>don't</u> use the Internet during the month. It's only after you've used <u>18 GB</u> that the bill starts rising.

b) What is the cost for each <u>additional gigabyte</u> (to the nearest 1p)?

Gradient of sloped section = cost per GB

$$\frac{\text{vertical change}}{\text{horizontal change}} = \frac{11}{19} = £0.5789... \text{ per GB}$$

To the nearest 1p this is **£0.58**

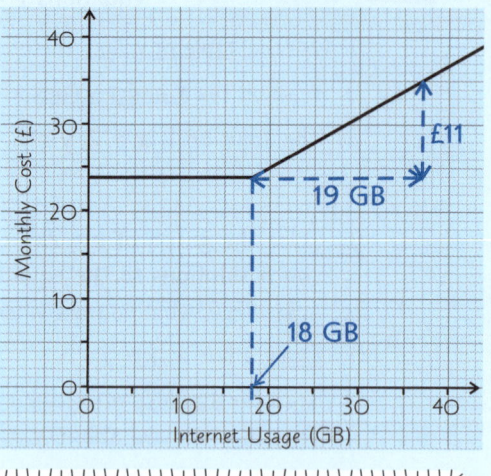

No matter what the graph, the <u>gradient</u> is always the <u>y-axis unit PER the x-axis unit</u> (see p.64).

Conversion Graphs are Easy to Use

METHOD FOR USING CONVERSION GRAPHS:
1. <u>Draw a line</u> from a value on <u>one axis</u>.
2. When you hit the <u>LINE</u>, <u>change direction</u> and go straight to <u>the other axis</u>.
3. <u>Read off the value</u> from this axis. The two values are <u>equivalent</u>.

Conversion graphs are so <u>simple</u> to use that the examiners often wrap them up in tricky questions.

EXAMPLE: Sam went on holiday to Florida and paid $360 for a camera. The same camera in Coleraine costs £250. Where was the camera cheaper? Show your working.

$360 is way off the graph, so find a point which will make calculating easy. The easiest way is to read off the value for $36 and multiply by 10.

Reading off the graph, $36 = £22
So $360 = £22 × 10 = £220

Now compare the values and add your conclusion.

£220 is less than £250, so the camera was cheaper in Florida.

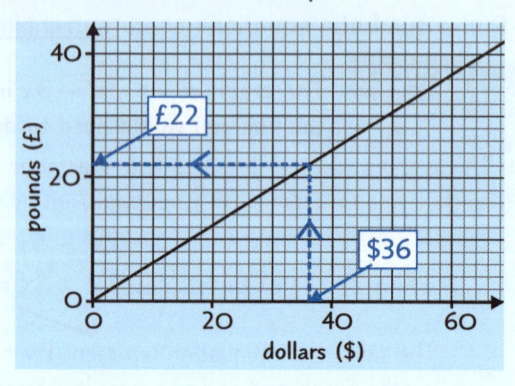

Exam marks per unit of brainpower...

Distance-time graphs are real-life graphs too — see p.63.

Q1   A taxi charges a minimum fare of £4.50, which includes the first three miles.
     It then charges 80p for each additional mile.
     Draw a graph to show the cost of journeys of up to 10 miles.   [4 marks]

Section Four — Graphs

Distance-Time Graphs

M7

Ah, what could be better than some nice D/T graphs? OK, so a slap-up meal with Hugh Jackman might be better. Unfortunately this section isn't called 'Tea With The Stars' so a D/T graph will have to do...

Distance-Time Graphs

Distance-time graphs can look a bit awkward at first, but they're not too bad once you get your head around them.

Just remember these 4 important points:

1) At any point, GRADIENT = SPEED.
2) The STEEPER the graph, the FASTER it's going.
3) FLAT SECTIONS are where it is STOPPED.
4) If the gradient's negative, it's COMING BACK.

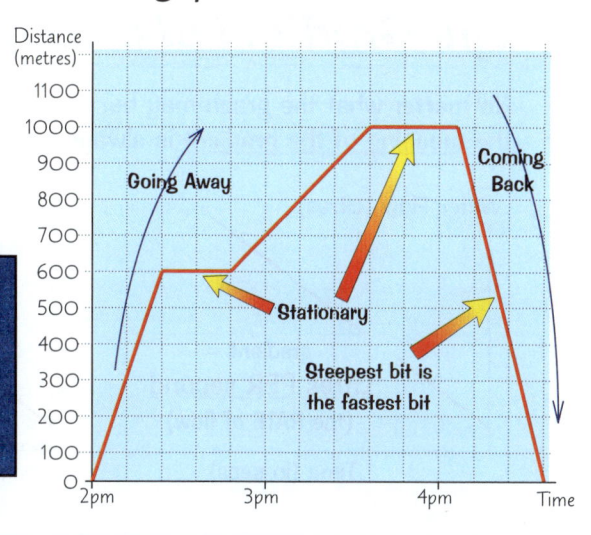

EXAMPLE:

Henry went out for a ride on his bike. After a while he got a puncture and stopped to fix it. This graph shows the first part of Henry's journey.

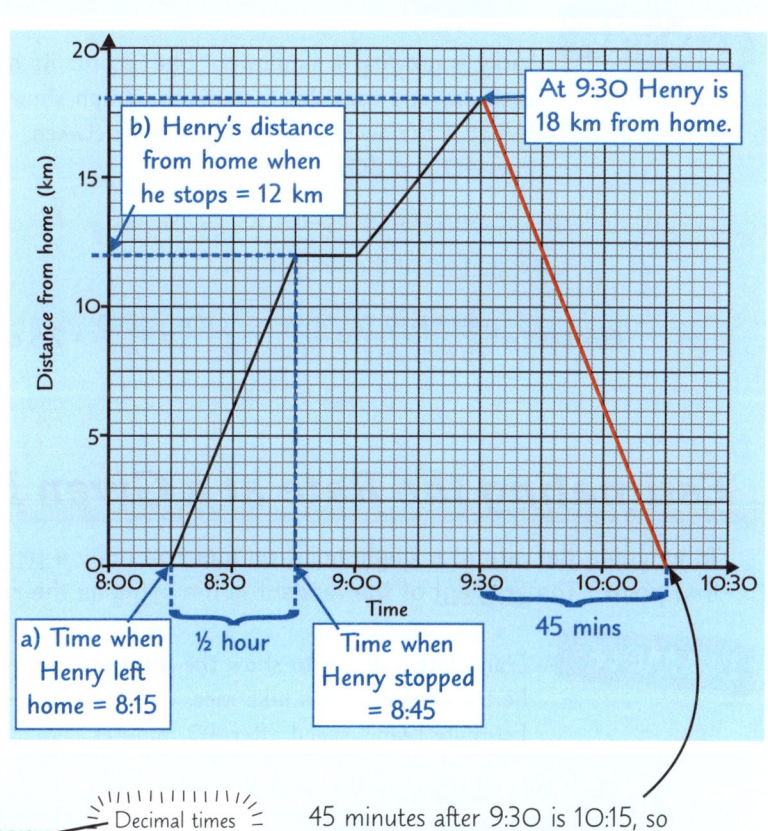

a) What time did Henry leave home?

He left home at the point where the line starts. **At 8:15**

b) How far did Henry cycle before getting a puncture?

The horizontal part of the graph is where Henry stopped. **12 km**

c) What was Henry's speed before getting a puncture?

Using the speed formula (p.67) is the same as finding the gradient.

speed = $\frac{\text{distance}}{\text{time}}$ = $\frac{12 \text{ km}}{0.5 \text{ hours}}$
= **24 km/h**

d) At 9:30 Henry turns round and cycles home at 24 km/h. Complete the graph to show this.

You have to work out how long it will take Henry to cycle the 18 km home:

time = $\frac{\text{distance}}{\text{speed}}$ = $\frac{18 \text{ km}}{24 \text{ km/h}}$ = **0.75 hours**

0.75 × 60 mins = **45 mins**

Decimal times are yuck, so convert it to minutes.

45 minutes after 9:30 is 10:15, so that's the time Henry gets home. Now you can complete the graph.

At 9:30 Henry is 18 km from home.

a) Time when Henry left home = 8:15
½ hour
Time when Henry stopped = 8:45
45 mins

b) Henry's distance from home when he stops = 12 km

D-T Graphs — filled with highs and lows...

... like my bungee jumping career. The way to get good at distance-time graphs is to practise using them.

Q1 a) Using the graph above, how long did Henry stop for? [1 mark]

b) What was Henry's speed after he had repaired the puncture, before he turned back home? [2 marks]

Section Four — Graphs

Gradients of Real-Life Graphs

Gradients are great — they tell you all sorts of stuff, like 'you're accelerating', or 'you need a spirit level'.

The Gradient of a Graph Represents the Rate

No matter what the graph may be, the meaning of the gradient is always simply: **(y-axis UNITS) PER (x-axis UNITS)**

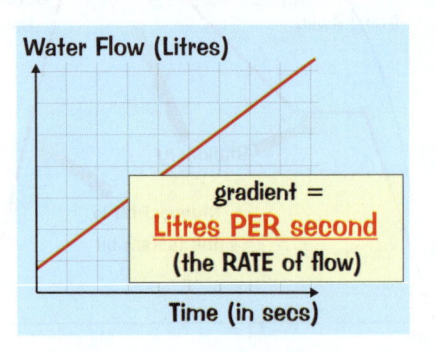

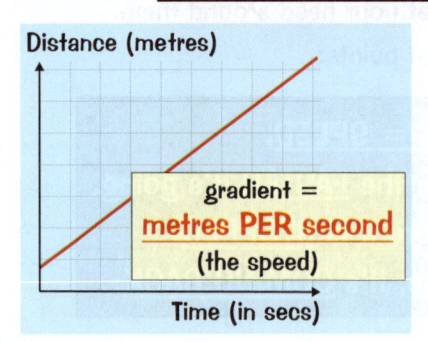

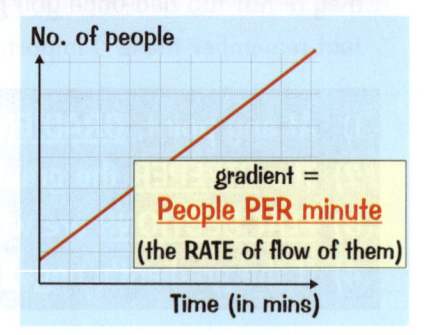

- Water Flow (Litres) vs Time (in secs): gradient = Litres PER second (the RATE of flow)
- Distance (metres) vs Time (in secs): gradient = metres PER second (the speed)
- No. of people vs Time (in mins): gradient = People PER minute (the RATE of flow of them)

Finding the Average Gradient

EXAMPLE: Vicky is growing a sunflower. She records its height each day and uses this to draw the graph shown. What is the average growth per day between days 40 and 80?

1) Draw a straight line connecting the points.
2) Find the gradient of the straight line.

$$\text{Gradient} = \frac{\text{change in } y}{\text{change in } x} = \frac{200 - 100}{80 - 40} = \frac{100}{40} = 2.5 \text{ cm per day}$$

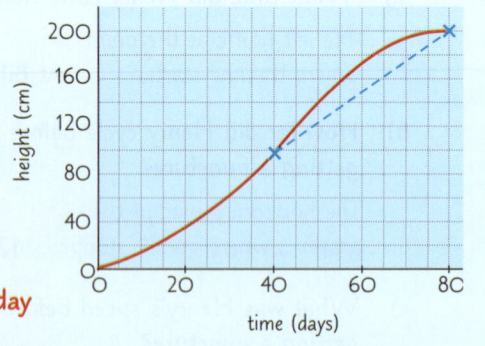

Estimating the Rate at a Given Point

To estimate the rate at a single point on a curve, draw a tangent that touches the curve at that point. The gradient of the tangent is the same as the rate at the chosen point.

EXAMPLE: Dan plots a graph to show the distance he travelled during a bike race. Estimate Dan's speed after 40 minutes.

1) Draw a tangent to the curve at 40 minutes.
2) Find the gradient of the straight line.

$$\text{Gradient} = \frac{\text{change in } y}{\text{change in } x} = \frac{14 - 10}{55 - 40} = \frac{4}{15} \text{ miles per minute}$$
$$= 16 \text{ miles per hour}$$

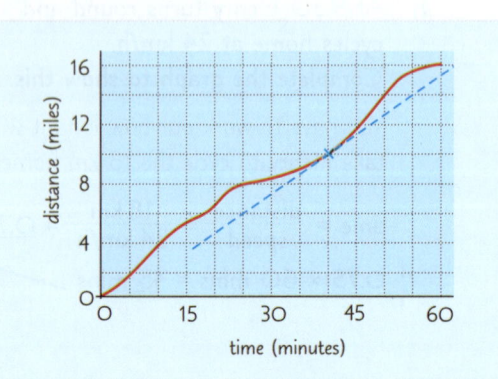

I think I'll have bacon and eggs for tea... wait, no, fish cakes...

Sorry, I was going off on a tangent. Just remember to look at the units and keep a ruler to hand and you'll have no problem with this. Also practise finding the gradient, just to make sure you've got it nailed.

Q1   On the sunflower height graph, estimate the rate of growth on day 20.   [2 marks]

Section Four — Graphs

Revision Questions for Section Four

Well, that wraps up Section Four — time to put yourself to the test and find out how much you really know.
- Try these questions and tick off each one when you get it right.
- When you've done all the questions for a topic and are completely happy with it, tick off the topic.

Straight Lines, Gradients and Line Segments (p54-57)

1) Sketch the lines a) $y = -x$, b) $y = -4$, c) $x = 2$
2) Draw the graph of $y = \frac{1}{2}x + 1$ for values of x from −2 to 2.
3) A and B have coordinates (−1, 5) and (4, −2), respectively.
   a) Find the midpoint of the line AB.
   b) Find the length of the line AB.
4) Find the equation of the graph on the right. 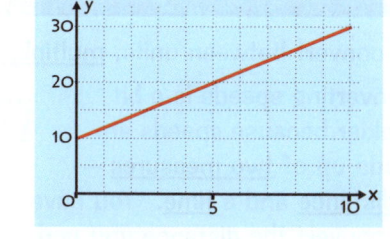
5) Find the equation of the line passing through (3, −6) and (6, −3).
6) Decide whether these lines are parallel, perpendicular or neither to $y = 3x + 5$
   a) $y = -\frac{1}{3}x + 2$ b) $y = 7 + 3x$ c) $y = \frac{1}{3}(x + 15)$
7) Find the equation of the line passing through (4, 2) which is perpendicular to $y = 2x - 1$.

Quadratic Graphs and Harder Graphs (p58-60)

8) a) Create and complete a table of values for $-3 \leq x \leq 1$ for the equation $y = x^2 + 3x - 7$.
   b) Plot the graph of $y = x^2 + 3x - 7$, labelling the turning point with its exact coordinates.
9) Describe in words and with a sketch the forms of these graphs:
   a) $y = ax^3$ b) $xy = a$;   c) $y = k^x$ $(k > 1)$ d) $x^2 + y^2 = r^2$
10) The increasing population of rats over time (shown on the graph on the right) is modelled by the equation $P = ab^t$, where P = population, t = number of months and a and b are positive constants. Find a and b. 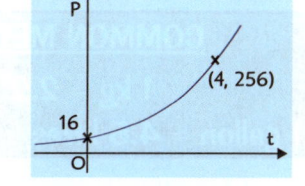
11) The point (−2, 6) lies on a circle with centre (0, 0). Find the radius and equation of the circle.

Solving Equations (p61)

12) By plotting their graphs, solve the simultaneous equations $4y - 2x = 32$ and $3y - 12 = 3x$
13) By plotting the graphs, find approximate solutions to the simultaneous equations: $y = x^2 + 2x - 4$ and $y = 6 - x$.
14) Find the equation of the line you would need to draw on the graph shown on the right to solve $x^2 + 4x = 0$

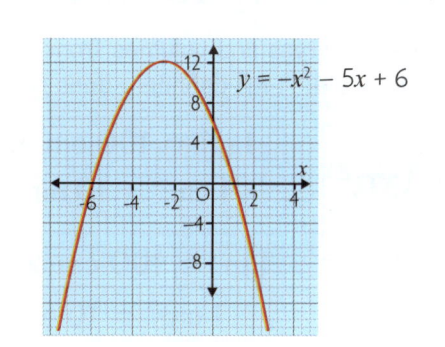

Real-Life Graphs and Gradients (p62-64)

15) Sweets'R'Yum sell chocolate drops. They charge 90p per 100 g for the first kg, then 60p per 100 g after that. Plot a graph to show the cost of buying up to 3 kg of chocolate drops.
16) What does a horizontal line mean on a distance-time graph?
17) The graph to the right shows the distance travelled by a sledge on a slope. Find:
    a) the time taken for the sledge to travel 300 m,
    b) the speed of the sledge at 6 seconds.

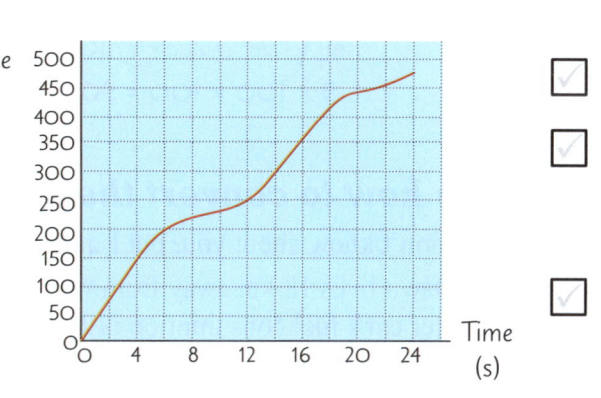

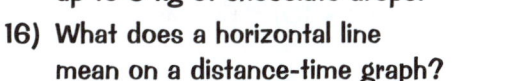

Unit Conversions

Ah, units. Metric units are most commonly used nowadays, but imperial units still crop up quite a bit too.

Metric Units

COMMON METRIC CONVERSIONS
1 cm = 10 mm   1 tonne = 1000 kg   1 m = 100 cm   1 litre = 1000 ml
1 km = 1000 m   1 litre = 1000 cm³   1 kg = 1000 g   1 cm³ = 1 ml

To convert between units, multiply or divide by the conversion factor.

Converting speeds is a bit trickier because speeds are made up of two measures — a distance and a time. You have to convert the distance unit and the time unit separately.

EXAMPLE: A rabbit's top speed is 56 km/h. How fast is this in m/s?
1) First convert from km/h to m/h:
   56 km/h = (56 × 1000) m/h = 56 000 m/h
2) Now convert from m/h to m/s:
   56 000 m/h = (56 000 ÷ 60 ÷ 60) m/s = 15.6 m/s (1 d.p.)

Always check your answer looks sensible — if it's not then chances are you divided instead of multiplying or vice versa.

Imperial Units

COMMON IMPERIAL CONVERSIONS
1 Yard = 3 Feet   1 Foot = 12 Inches   1 Gallon = 8 Pints
1 Stone = 14 Pounds   1 Pound = 16 Ounces

COMMON METRIC-IMPERIAL CONVERSIONS
1 kg ≈ 2.2 pounds   1 foot ≈ 30 cm
1 gallon ≈ 4.5 litres   1 mile ≈ 1.6 km (or 5 miles ≈ 8 km)

EXAMPLE: Convert 10 pounds into kg.
2.2 pounds ≈ 1 kg
So 10 pounds ≈ 10 ÷ 2.2
≈ 4.5 kg

Converting Area and Volume Measurements

Converting areas and volumes from one unit to another is an exam disaster that you have to know how to avoid. 1 m² definitely does NOT equal 100 cm². Remember this and read on for why.

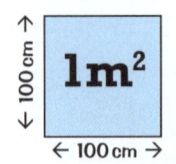

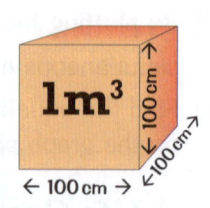

1 m² = 100 cm × 100 cm = 10 000 cm²
1 cm² = 10 mm × 10 mm = 100 mm²

1 m³ = 100 cm × 100 cm × 100 cm = 1 000 000 cm³
1 cm³ = 10 mm × 10 mm × 10 mm = 1000 mm³

EXAMPLES:

1. Convert 9 m² to cm².
To change area measurements from m² to cm² multiply by 100 twice.
9 × 100 × 100 = 90 000 cm²

2. Convert 60 000 mm³ to cm³.
To change volume measurements from mm³ to cm³ divide by 10 three times.
60 000 ÷ (10 × 10 × 10) = 60 cm³

Learn how to convert these questions into marks...

Hmm, I don't know about you, but I quite fancy a conversion-based question after all that.

Q1 Dawn lives 18 km away from work. She drives to work and back 5 days a week. Her car's fuel consumption is 28 mpg (miles per gallon). 1 gallon ≈ 4.5 litres. How many litres of petrol does she use each week travelling to and from work?   [4 marks]

Speed, Density and Pressure

Speed, density and pressure. Just a matter of learning the formulas, bunging in numbers and watching the units.

Speed = Distance ÷ Time

Speed is the distance travelled per unit time, e.g. the number of km per hour or metres per second.

$$\text{SPEED} = \frac{\text{DISTANCE}}{\text{TIME}} \qquad \text{TIME} = \frac{\text{DISTANCE}}{\text{SPEED}} \qquad \text{DISTANCE} = \text{SPEED} \times \text{TIME}$$

Formula triangles are a handy tool for remembering formulas like these. The speed one is shown below.

HOW DO YOU USE FORMULA TRIANGLES?
1) COVER UP the thing you want to find and WRITE DOWN what's left showing.
2) Now PUT IN THE VALUES and CALCULATE — check the UNITS in your answer.

EXAMPLE: A car travels 9 miles at 36 miles per hour. How many minutes does it take?

Write down the formula, put in the values and calculate:

$$\text{time} = \frac{\text{distance}}{\text{speed}} = \frac{9 \text{ miles}}{36 \text{ mph}} = 0.25 \text{ hours} = 15 \text{ minutes}$$

Density = Mass ÷ Volume

Density is the mass per unit volume of a substance. It's usually measured in kg/m^3 or g/cm^3.

$$\text{DENSITY} = \frac{\text{MASS}}{\text{VOLUME}} \qquad \text{VOLUME} = \frac{\text{MASS}}{\text{DENSITY}} \qquad \text{MASS} = \text{DENSITY} \times \text{VOLUME}$$

EXAMPLE: A giant 'Wunda-Choc' bar has a density of 1.3 g/cm^3. If the bar's volume is 1800 cm^3, what is the mass of the bar in kg?

Write down the formula, put in the values and calculate:

mass = density × volume
= $1.3 \text{ g/cm}^3 \times 1800 \text{ cm}^3 = 2340 \text{ g}$
= 2.34 kg

CHECK YOUR UNITS MATCH
If the density is in g/cm^3, the volume must be in cm^3 and you'll get a mass in g.

Pressure = Force ÷ Area

'N' stands for 'Newtons'.

Pressure is the amount of force acting per unit area. It's usually measured in N/m^2, or pascals (Pa).

$$\text{PRESSURE} = \frac{\text{FORCE}}{\text{AREA}} \qquad \text{AREA} = \frac{\text{FORCE}}{\text{PRESSURE}} \qquad \text{FORCE} = \text{PRESSURE} \times \text{AREA}$$

EXAMPLE: A cylindrical barrel with a weight of 200 N rests on horizontal ground. The radius of the circular face resting on the ground is 0.4 m. Calculate the pressure exerted by the barrel on the ground to 1 d.p.

Work out the area of the circular face: $\pi \times 0.4^2 = 0.5026... \text{ m}^2$

Write down the pressure formula, put in the values and calculate:

$$\text{pressure} = \frac{\text{force}}{\text{area}} = \frac{200 \text{ N}}{0.5026... \text{ m}^2} = 397.8873... \text{ N/m}^2$$
$$= 397.9 \text{ N/m}^2 \text{ (1 d.p.)}$$

Formula triangles — it's all a big cover-up...

Write down the formula triangles from memory, then use them to generate the formulas.

Q1 A solid lead cone has a vertical height of 60 cm and a base radius of 20 cm. If the density of lead is 11.34 g/cm^3, find the mass of the cone in kg to 3 s.f. [3 marks]

Hint: you'll need to find the volume of the cone to answer this question — see p.90.

Section Five — Measures and Angles

Five Angle Rules

M3

If you know <u>all</u> these rules <u>thoroughly</u>, you'll at least have a fighting chance of working out problems with lines and angles. If you don't — you've no chance. Sorry to break it to you like that.

5 Simple Rules — that's all

1) <u>Angles in a triangle</u> add up to <u>180°</u>.

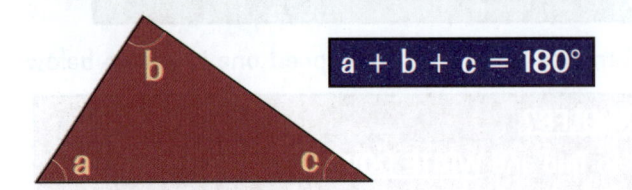

$a + b + c = 180°$

2) <u>Angles on a straight line</u> add up to <u>180°</u>.

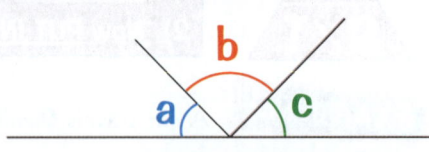

$a + b + c = 180°$

3) <u>Angles in a quadrilateral</u> add up to <u>360°</u>.

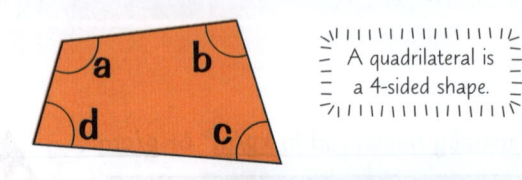

A quadrilateral is a 4-sided shape.

$a + b + c + d = 360°$

You can <u>see why</u> this is if you split the quadrilateral into <u>two triangles</u> along a <u>diagonal</u>. Each triangle has angles adding up to 180°, so the two together have angles adding up to 180° + 180° = 360°.

4) <u>Angles round a point</u> add up to <u>360°</u>.

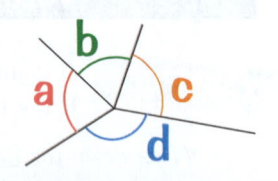

$a + b + c + d = 360°$

5) <u>Isosceles triangles</u> have 2 sides the same and 2 angles the same.

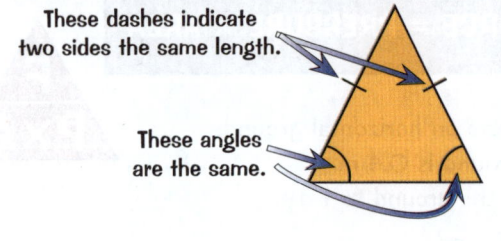

In an isosceles triangle, you only need to know <u>one angle</u> to be able to find the other two.

These dashes indicate two sides the same length.

These angles are the same.

EXAMPLE: Find the size of angle x.

$180° - 40° = 140°$

<u>The two angles on the right are the same</u> (they're both x) and they must add up to 140°, so $2x = 140°$, which means $x = 70°$.

The first rule of angle club is "you don't talk about angle club"...

All the basic facts are pretty easy really, but examiners love to combine them in questions to confuse you. There are some examples of these on p.70, but have a go at this one as a warm-up.

Q1   Find the size of the angle marked x.

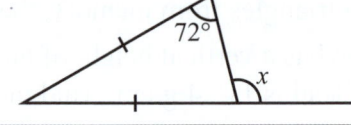

72°

[2 marks]

Section Five — Measures and Angles

Parallel Lines

Parallel lines are quite straightforward really. (They're also quite straight. And parallel.)
There are a few rules you need to learn — make sure you don't get them mixed up.

Angles Around Parallel Lines

When a line crosses two parallel lines, it forms special sets of angles.

1) The two bunches of angles formed at the points of intersection are the same.
2) There are only actually two different angles involved (labelled a and b here), and they add up to 180° (from rule 2 on the previous page).
3) Vertically opposite angles (ones opposite each other) are equal (in the diagram, a and a are vertically opposite, as are b and b).

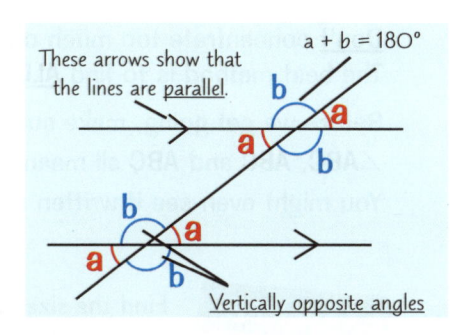

These arrows show that the lines are parallel.
$a + b = 180°$
Vertically opposite angles

Alternate, Allied and Corresponding Angles

The diagram above has some characteristic shapes to look out for — and each shape contains a specific pair of angles. The angle pairs are known as alternate, allied, corresponding and adjacent angles.

You need to spot the characteristic Z, C, U and F shapes:

ALTERNATE ANGLES

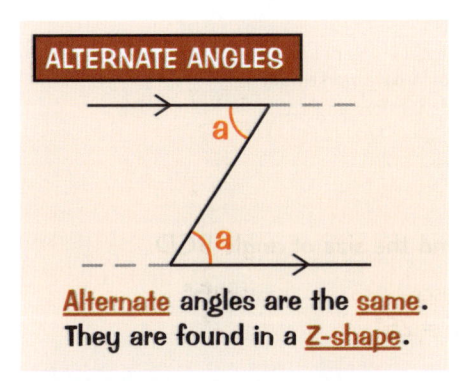

Alternate angles are the same.
They are found in a Z-shape.

ALLIED ANGLES

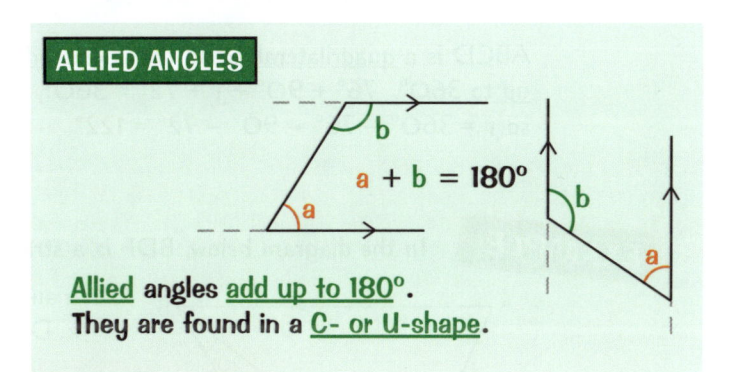

$a + b = 180°$

Allied angles add up to 180°.
They are found in a C- or U-shape.

CORRESPONDING ANGLES

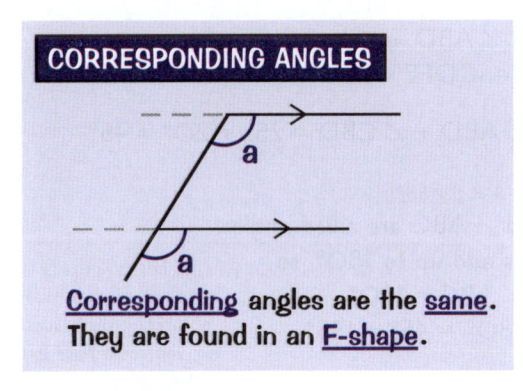

Corresponding angles are the same.
They are found in an F-shape.

ADJACENT ANGLES

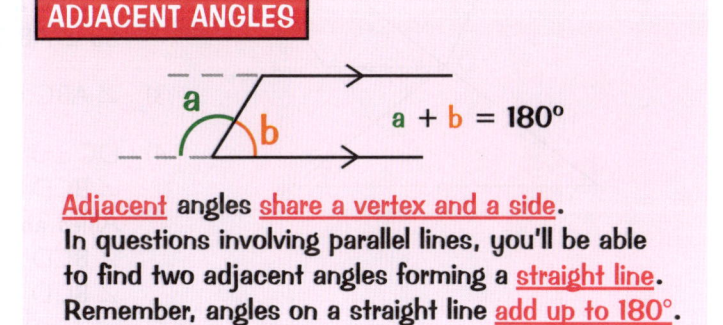

$a + b = 180°$

Adjacent angles share a vertex and a side.
In questions involving parallel lines, you'll be able to find two adjacent angles forming a straight line.
Remember, angles on a straight line add up to 180°.

It's OK to use the letters Z, C, U and F to help you identify the rule — but you must use the proper names (alternate, allied, etc.) in the exam.

Aim for a gold medal in the parallel lines...

Watch out for hidden parallel lines in other geometry questions — the little arrows are a dead giveaway.

Q1 Find the value of x.

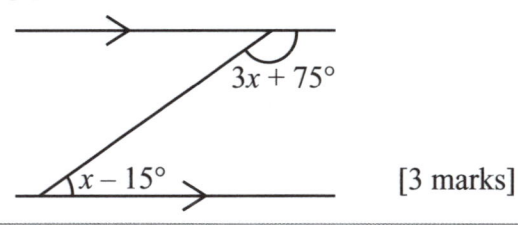

$3x + 75°$
$x - 15°$

[3 marks]

Section Five — Measures and Angles

Geometry Problems

My biggest geometry problem is that I have to do geometry problems in the first place. *Sigh*
Ah well, best get practising — these problems aren't going to solve themselves.

Try Out All The Rules One By One

Don't concentrate too much on the angle you have been asked to find.
The best method is to find ALL the angles in whatever order they become obvious.

Before we get going, make sure you're familiar with three-letter angle notation, e.g. ∠ABC.
∠ABC, ABC and ABĈ all mean 'the angle formed at B' (it's always the middle letter).
You might even see it written as just B̂.

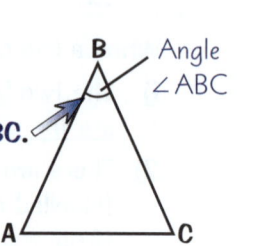

EXAMPLE: Find the size of angles x and y.

Write down everything you know (or can work out) about the shape:

Triangle ABD is isosceles,
so ∠ BAD = ∠ ABD = 76°.
That means ∠ ADB = 180° − 76° − 76° = 28°.
∠ ADC is a right angle (= 90°),
so angle x = 90° − 28° = 62°

ABCD is a quadrilateral, so all the angles add up to 360°. 76° + 90° + y + 72° = 360°,
so y = 360° − 76° − 90° − 72° = **122°**

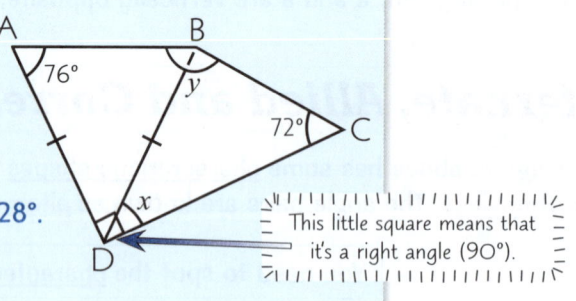

This little square means that it's a right angle (90°).

You could have worked out angle y before angle x.

EXAMPLE: In the diagram below, BDF is a straight line. Find the size of angle BCD.

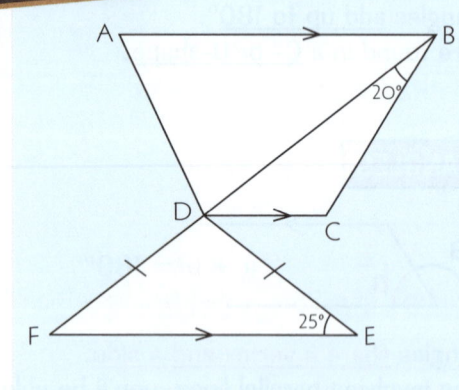

1) Triangle DEF is isosceles, so...
   ∠ DFE = ∠ DEF = 25°

2) FE and AB are parallel, so...
   ∠ DFE and ∠ ABD are alternate angles.
   So ∠ ABD = ∠ DFE = 25°.

3) ∠ ABC = ∠ ABD + ∠ CBD = 25° + 20° = 45°

4) DC and AB are parallel, so...
   ∠ BCD and ∠ ABC are allied angles.
   Allied angles add up to 180°, so
   ∠ BCD + ∠ ABC = 180°
   ∠ BCD = 180° − 45° = **135°**.

There's often more than one way of tackling these questions — e.g. you could have found angle BDC using the properties of parallel lines, then used angles in a triangle to find BCD.

Missing: angle x. If found, please return to Amy...

Geometry problems often look a lot worse than they are — don't panic, just write down everything you can work out. Watch out for hidden parallel lines and isosceles triangles — they can help you work out angles.

Q1 Find the size of angle x.
[3 marks]

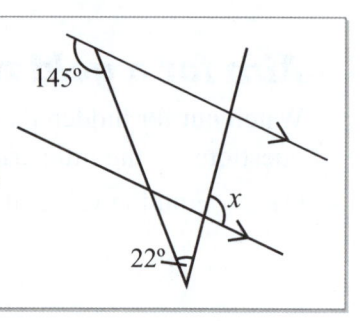

Section Five — Measures and Angles

Angles in Shapes

A polygon is a <u>many-sided shape</u>, and can be <u>regular</u> or <u>irregular</u>. A regular polygon (p.83) is one where all the <u>sides</u> are the <u>same length</u> and all the <u>angles</u> are the <u>same size</u>. This page is all about angles — yippee...

Exterior and Interior Angles

You need to know <u>what</u> exterior and interior angles are and <u>how to find them</u>.

For ANY POLYGON (regular or irregular):

SUM OF EXTERIOR ANGLES = 360°

INTERIOR ANGLE = 180° − EXTERIOR ANGLE

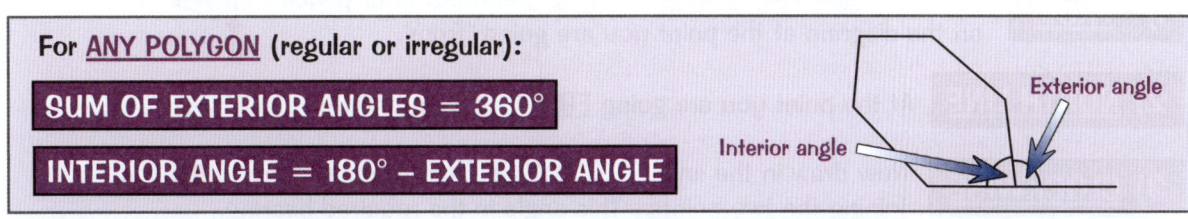

For REGULAR POLYGONS only:

EXTERIOR ANGLE = $\frac{360°}{n}$

(n is the number of sides)

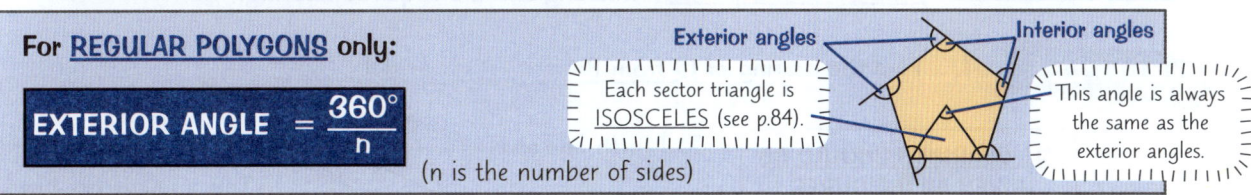

Each sector triangle is <u>ISOSCELES</u> (see p.84).

This angle is always the same as the exterior angles.

EXAMPLE: Find the exterior and interior angles of a regular octagon.

Octagons have 8 sides: exterior angle = $\frac{360°}{n} = \frac{360°}{8}$ = **45°**

Use the exterior angle to find the interior angle: interior angle = 180° − exterior angle
= 180° − 45° = **135°**

The Tricky One — Sum of Interior Angles

This formula for the <u>sum of the interior angles</u> works for <u>ALL</u> polygons, even irregular ones:

SUM OF INTERIOR ANGLES = (n − 2) × 180°

This is because a polygon can be divided up into (n − 2) triangles, and the sum of angles in a triangle is 180°. Try it for yourself on the polygons above.

EXAMPLE: Find the <u>sum of the interior angles</u> of the polygon on the right.

The polygon is a hexagon, so n = 6: Sum of interior angles = (n − 2) × 180°
= (6 − 2) × 180° = **720°**

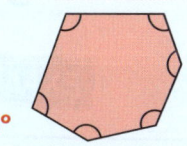

Don't panic if those pesky examiners put algebra in an interior angle question. It looks worse than it is.

EXAMPLE: Find the value of x in the diagram on the right.

First, find the <u>sum of the interior angles</u> of the 5-sided shape:

Sum of interior angles = (n − 2) × 180°
= (5 − 2) × 180° = 540°

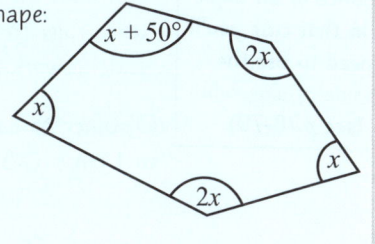

Now write an equation and solve it to find x:

$2x + x + 2x + x + (x + 50°)$ = 540°

$7x + 50°$ = 540° → $7x$ = 490° → x = **70°**

EXCLUSIVE: Heptagon lottery winner — "I'm just a regular guy"...

Learn all the formulas above, and remember whether they go with regular or irregular polygons.

Q1 Find the size of the interior angle of a regular 10-sided shape. [2 marks]

Q2 A regular polygon has exterior angles of 72°. What is the name of the polygon? [2 marks]

Bearings

Bearings. They'll be useful next time you're off sailing. Or in your Maths exam.

Bearings

To find or plot a bearing you must remember <u>the three key words</u>:

1) **'FROM'** — <u>Find the word 'FROM' in the question</u>, and put your pencil on the diagram at the point you are going '<u>from</u>'.

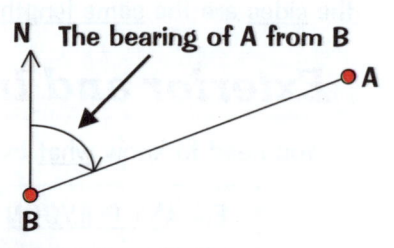

2) **NORTH LINE** — At the point you are going <u>FROM</u>, <u>draw in a NORTH LINE</u>.

3) **CLOCKWISE** — Now draw in the angle CLOCKWISE <u>from the north line to the line joining the two points</u>. This angle is the required bearing.

EXAMPLES:

1. Find the bearing of Q <u>from</u> P.

   1) 'From P'
   2) North line at P
   3) Clockwise, from the N-line. This angle is the bearing of Q from P. Measure it with your protractor — 245°.

   ALL BEARINGS SHOULD BE GIVEN AS 3 FIGURES
   e.g. 176°, 034° (not 34°), 005° (not 5°), 018° etc.

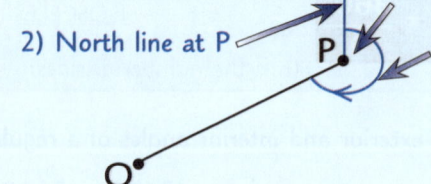

2. The bearing of Z from Y is 110°. Find the bearing of Y from Z.

   See page 69 for allied angles.

   First sketch a diagram so you can see what's going on.
   Angles a and b are <u>allied</u>, so they add up to <u>180°</u>.
   Angle b = 180° − 110° = 70°
   So bearing of Y from Z = 360° − 70° = 290°.

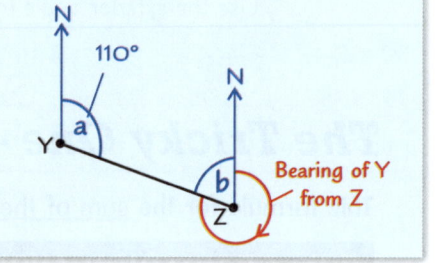

Bearings Questions and Scale Drawings

EXAMPLE: A hiker walks 2 km from point A, on a bearing of 036°. If the scale of the map below is 2 cm to 1 km, how far is the hiker now from his car?

If you're doing an M8 exam, you might get asked to CALCULATE a distance or an angle — in that case you'll need to use the cosine or sine rule (see p.78-79).

First, draw a line at a <u>bearing of 036°</u> from point A. <u>1 km</u> is <u>2 cm</u> on the map and the hiker walks <u>2 km</u>, so make the line from A <u>4 cm</u> long.

You want the distance of the hiker from the car, so use a ruler to measure it on the map, then use the scale to work out the <u>real distance</u> it represents.

Distance to car on map = 3 cm. 2 cm = 1 km, so 1 cm = 0.5 km, therefore 3 cm = 1.5 km.

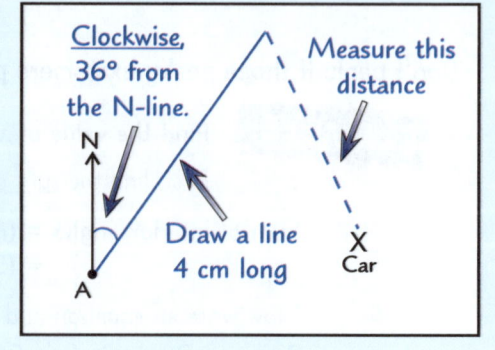

Please bear with me while I figure out where we are...

Learn the three key words above and scribble them out from memory.
Now try these practice questions.

Q1 A cinema is on a bearing of 035° from Ellie's house and is 5 miles away. Mark the cinema on this map. [3 marks]

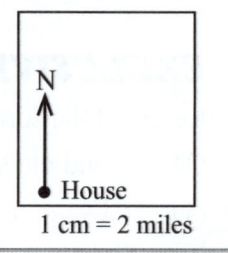

1 cm = 2 miles

Section Five — Measures and Angles

Circle Geometry

I'm afraid that was only a brief interlude on bearings before returning to some more geometry rules — it's now time to plunge you into the depths of mathematical peril with a 2-page extravaganza on circle theorems.

8 ~~Simple~~ Rules to Learn

The 8th rule is on the next page.

1) A TANGENT and a RADIUS meet at 90°.

A TANGENT is a line that just touches a single point on the circumference of a circle. A tangent always makes an angle of exactly 90° with the radius it meets at this point.

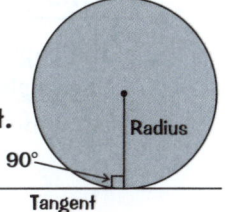

2) TWO RADII form an ISOSCELES TRIANGLE.

Radii is the plural of radius.

Unlike other isosceles triangles they don't have the little tick marks on the sides to remind you that they are the same — the fact that they are both radii is enough to make it an isosceles triangle.

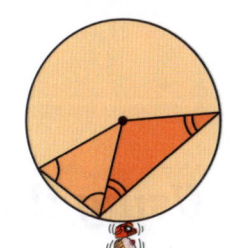

3) The angle at the CENTRE of a circle is TWICE the angle at the CIRCUMFERENCE.

The angle subtended at the centre of a circle is EXACTLY DOUBLE the angle subtended at the circumference of the circle from the same two points (two ends of the same chord).

'Angle subtended at' is just a posh way of saying 'angle made at'.

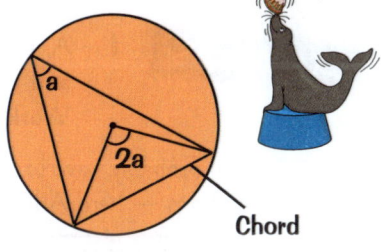

4) The ANGLE in a SEMICIRCLE is 90°.

A triangle drawn from the two ends of a diameter will ALWAYS make an angle of 90° where it hits the circumference of the circle, no matter where it hits.

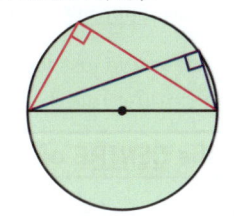

5) Angles in the SAME SEGMENT are EQUAL.

All triangles drawn from a chord will have the same angle where they touch the circumference. Also, the two angles on opposite sides of the chord add up to 180°.

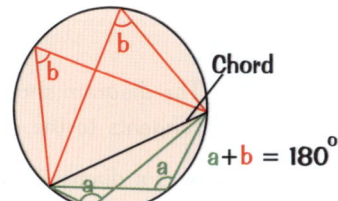

$a + b = 180°$

6) OPPOSITE ANGLES in a CYCLIC QUADRILATERAL add up to 180°.

A cyclic quadrilateral is a 4-sided shape with every corner touching the circle. Both pairs of opposite angles add up to 180°.

$a + c = 180°$
$b + d = 180°$

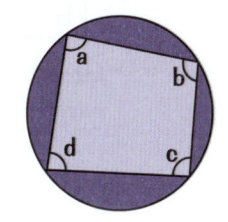

7) TANGENTS from the SAME POINT are the SAME LENGTH.

Two tangents drawn from an outside point are always equal in length, creating two congruent right-angled triangles as shown.

There's more about congruence on p.85.

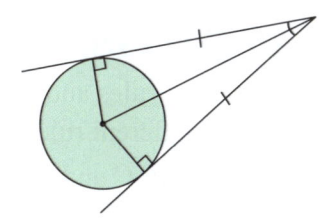

What? No Exam Practice Questions? I feel cheated.

Section Five — Measures and Angles

Circle Geometry

More circle theorems? But I've had enough. Can't I go home now?

The Final Rule

8) The ALTERNATE SEGMENT THEOREM.

The angle between a tangent and a chord is always equal to 'the angle in the opposite segment' (i.e. the angle made at the circumference by two lines drawn from ends of the chord).

This is probably the hardest rule — make sure you're able to recognise when you have two angles that fit the criteria. In particular, look out for a chord and a tangent that meet.

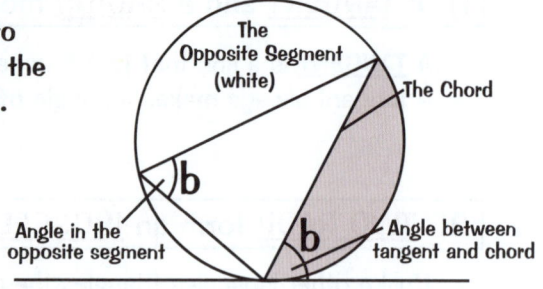

Using the Circle Theorems

EXAMPLES:

1. A, B, C and D are points on the circumference of the circle, and O is the centre of the circle. Angle ADC = 109°. Work out the size of angles ABC and AOC.

You'll probably have to use more than one rule to solve circle theorem questions — here, ABCD is a cyclic quadrilateral so use rule 6:

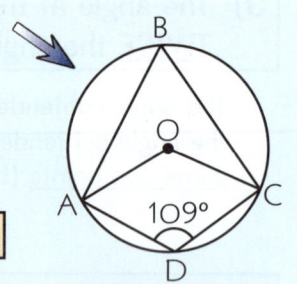

6) OPPOSITE ANGLES in a CYCLIC QUADRILATERAL add up to 180°.

Angles ADC and ABC are opposite, so **angle ABC = 180° − 109° = 71°**.

Now, angles ABC (which you've just found) and AOC both come from chord AC, so you can use rule 3:

3) The angle at the CENTRE of a circle is TWICE the angle at the CIRCUMFERENCE.

So angle AOC is double angle ABC, which means **angle AOC = 71° × 2 = 142°**.

2. The diagram shows the triangle ABC, where lines BA and BC are tangents to the circle. Show that line AC is NOT a diameter.

If AC was a diameter passing through the centre, O, then OA and OC would be radii, and angle CAB = angle ACB = 90° by rule 1:

1) A TANGENT and a RADIUS meet at 90°.

However, this would mean that ABC isn't a triangle as you can't have a triangle with two 90° angles, so **AC cannot be a diameter**.

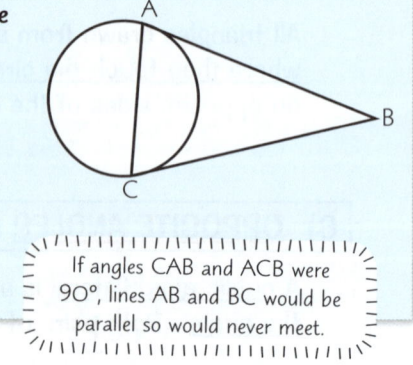

If angles CAB and ACB were 90°, lines AB and BC would be parallel so would never meet.

All this talk of segments and tangerines is making me hungry...

Learn all 8 rules and practise using them — sometimes the best approach is to try different rules until you find one that works.

Q1   A, B, C and D are points on the circumference of the circle with centre O. The line EF is a tangent to the circle, and touches the circle at D. Angle ADE is 63°. Find the size of angles ABD and ACD.   [2 marks]

Section Five — Measures and Angles

Pythagoras' Theorem

Once upon a time there lived a clever chap called Pythagoras. He made famous a clever theorem...

Pythagoras' Theorem *is Used on Right-Angled Triangles*

Pythagoras' theorem only works for RIGHT-ANGLED TRIANGLES.
It uses two sides to find the third side.

The formula for Pythagoras' theorem is: $a^2 + b^2 = c^2$

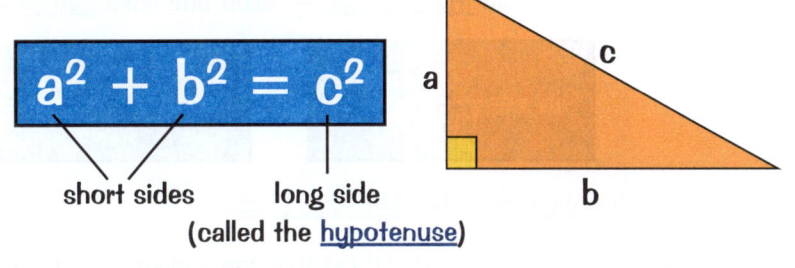

short sides — long side (called the hypotenuse)

The formula can be quite tricky to use, so below it's been broken down into three simple steps. Follow these steps, and you won't go far wrong.

1) SQUARE THEM	SQUARE THE TWO NUMBERS that you are given, (use the x^2 button if you've got your calculator).	
2) ADD or SUBTRACT	To find the longest side, ADD the two squared numbers. To find a shorter side, SUBTRACT the smaller from the larger.	$a^2 + b^2 = c^2$ $c^2 - b^2 = a^2$
3) SQUARE ROOT	Once you've got your answer, take the SQUARE ROOT (use the $\sqrt{}$ button on your calculator).	$c = \sqrt{a^2 + b^2}$ $a = \sqrt{c^2 - b^2}$

EXAMPLES:

1. Find the length of side PQ in this triangle.

1) Square them: $a^2 = 5^2 = 25$, $b^2 = 12^2 = 144$
2) You want to find the longest side, so ADD: $a^2 + b^2 = c^2$
   $25 + 144 = 169$
3) Square root: $c = \sqrt{169} = 13$, so PQ = **13 cm**

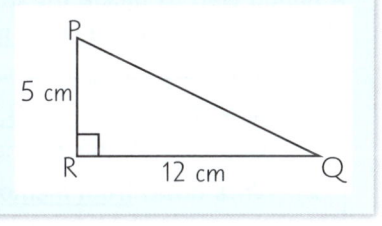

Always check the answer's sensible — 13 cm is longer than the other two sides, but not too much longer, so it seems OK.

2. Find the length of SU to 1 decimal place.

1) Square them: $b^2 = 3^2 = 9$, $c^2 = 6^2 = 36$
2) You want to find a shorter side, so SUBTRACT: $c^2 - b^2 = a^2$
   $36 - 9 = 27$
3) Square root: $a = \sqrt{27} = 5.196...$,
   so SU = **5.2 m (to 1 d.p.)**

Check the answer is sensible — yes, it's a bit shorter than the longest side.

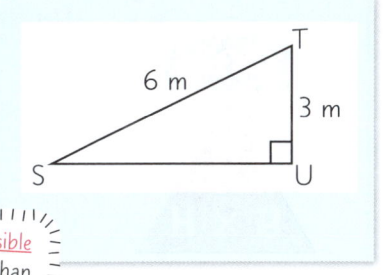

Remember, if it's not a right angle, it's a wrong angle...

Once you've learned all the Pythagoras facts, try these Exam Practice Questions.

Q1 Find the length of AC correct to 1 decimal place. [3 marks]

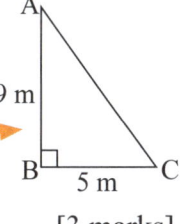

Q2 A 4 m long ladder leans against a wall. Its base is 1.2 m from the wall. How far up the wall does the ladder reach? Give your answer in metres to 1 decimal place. [3 marks]

Section Five — Measures and Angles

Trigonometry

Trigonometry — it's a big scary word. But it's not a big scary topic. An *important* topic, yes. An *always cropping up* topic, definitely. But scary? Pur-lease. Takes more than a triangle to scare me. Read on...

The 3 Trigonometry Formulas

There are three basic trig formulas — each one links two sides and an angle of a right-angled triangle.

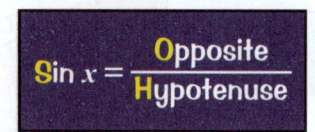

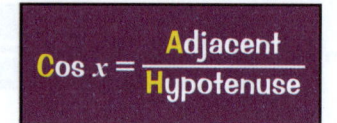

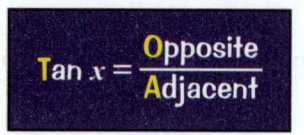

$$\sin x = \frac{\text{Opposite}}{\text{Hypotenuse}} \qquad \cos x = \frac{\text{Adjacent}}{\text{Hypotenuse}} \qquad \tan x = \frac{\text{Opposite}}{\text{Adjacent}}$$

- The Hypotenuse is the LONGEST SIDE.
- The Opposite is the side OPPOSITE the angle being used (x).
- The Adjacent is the (other) side NEXT TO the angle being used.

1) Whenever you come across a trig question, work out which two sides of the triangle are involved in that question — then pick the formula that involves those sides.
2) To find the angle — use the inverse, i.e. press SHIFT or 2ndF, followed by sin, cos or tan (and make sure your calculator is in DEG mode) — your calculator will display $\sin^{-1}$, $\cos^{-1}$ or $\tan^{-1}$.
3) Remember, you can only use the sin, cos and tan formulas above on right-angled triangles — you may have to add lines to the diagram to create one.

Formula Triangles Make Things Simple

There's more about formula triangles on p.67 if you need to jog your memory.

A handy way to tackle trig questions is to convert the formulas into formula triangles. Then you can use the same method every time, no matter which side or angle is being asked for.

1) Label the three sides O, A and H (Opposite, Adjacent and Hypotenuse).
2) Write down from memory 'SOH CAH TOA'.
3) Decide which two sides are involved: O,H A,H or O,A and select SOH, CAH or TOA accordingly.
4) Turn the one you choose into a FORMULA TRIANGLE:

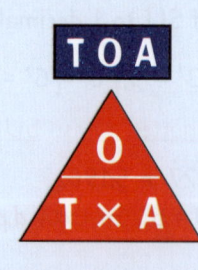

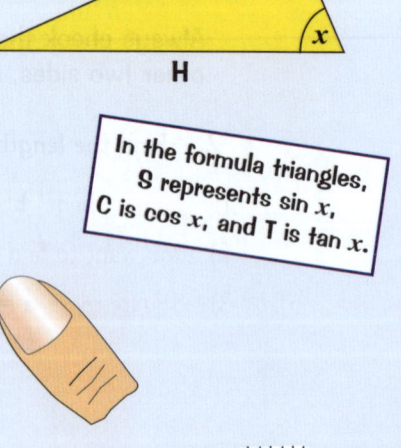

SOH $\dfrac{O}{S \times H}$ **CAH** $\dfrac{A}{C \times H}$ **TOA** $\dfrac{O}{T \times A}$

In the formula triangles, S represents sin x, C is cos x, and T is tan x.

5) Cover up the thing you want to find (with your finger), and write down whatever is left showing.
6) Translate into numbers and work it out.
7) Finally, check that your answer is sensible.

If you can't make SOH CAH TOA stick, try using a mnemonic like 'Strange Orange Hamsters Creep Around Houses Tripping Over Ants'.

SOH CAH TOA — the not-so-secret formula for success...

You need to know this stuff off by heart — so go over this page a few times until you've got those formulas firmly lodged and all ready to reel off in the exam. All set? Trigtastic...

Section Five — Measures and Angles

Trigonometry

Here are some lovely examples using the method from p.76 to help you through the trials of trigonometry...

Examples:

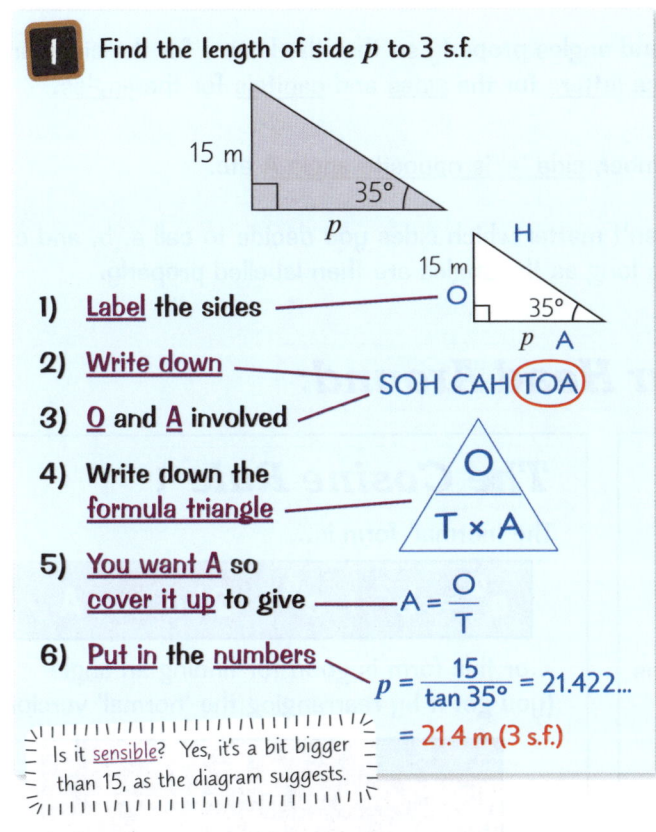

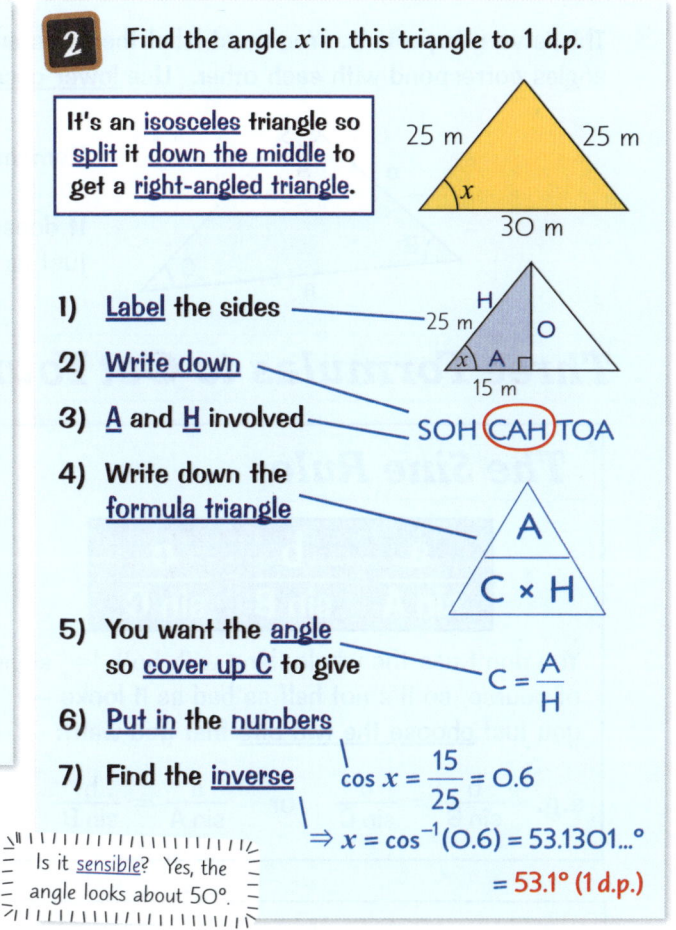

1 Find the length of side p to 3 s.f.

(Triangle: 15 m side, 35° angle, side p)

1) **Label** the sides
2) **Write down** SOH CAH **TOA**
3) **O** and **A** involved
4) Write down the **formula triangle** — O / (T × A)
5) **You want A** so **cover it up** to give — $A = \frac{O}{T}$
6) **Put in** the numbers — $p = \frac{15}{\tan 35°} = 21.422...$
   = **21.4 m (3 s.f.)**

Is it sensible? Yes, it's a bit bigger than 15, as the diagram suggests.

2 Find the angle x in this triangle to 1 d.p.

It's an **isosceles** triangle so **split** it **down the middle** to get a **right-angled triangle**.

(Triangle: 25 m, 25 m, 30 m; split gives 25 m hypotenuse, 15 m adjacent, angle x)

1) **Label** the sides
2) **Write down** SOH **CAH** TOA
3) **A** and **H** involved
4) Write down the **formula triangle** — A / (C × H)
5) You want the **angle** so **cover up C** to give — $C = \frac{A}{H}$
6) **Put in** the numbers — $\cos x = \frac{15}{25} = 0.6$
7) Find the **inverse** — $\Rightarrow x = \cos^{-1}(0.6) = 53.1301...°$
   = **53.1° (1 d.p.)**

Is it sensible? Yes, the angle looks about 50°.

Angles of Elevation and Depression

Trigonometry can also be used to solve problems with <u>real-life context</u> — sometimes this involves the terms <u>angle of elevation</u> or <u>angle of depression</u>. The diagram below shows what these angles look like in a made-up boat-and-cliff scenario.

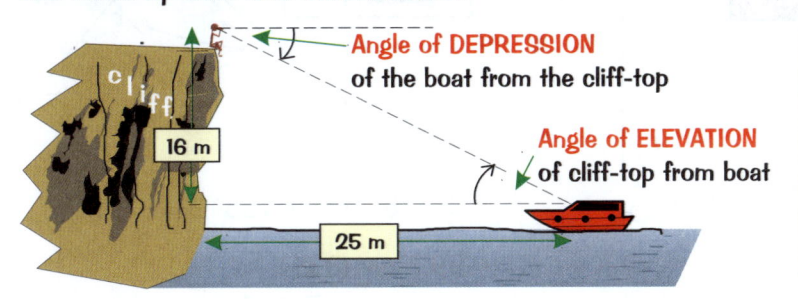

(Diagram: cliff 16 m tall, 25 m from boat, showing Angle of DEPRESSION of the boat from the cliff-top, and Angle of ELEVATION of cliff-top from boat)

1) The **Angle of Depression** is the angle **downwards** from the horizontal.
2) The **Angle of Elevation** is the angle **upwards** from the horizontal.
3) The angles of elevation and depression are **equal**.

I do trigonometry outdoors cos I always get a great sin tan...

Make sure you can follow what's going on in the examples above then have a go at these...

Q1 Find the value of x and give your answer to 1 decimal place.

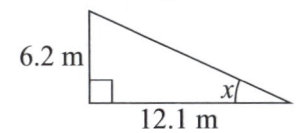

(Right-angled triangle: 6.2 m vertical, 12.1 m horizontal, angle x)

[3 marks]

Q2 A 3.2 m ladder is leaning against a vertical wall. It is at an angle of 68° to the horizontal ground. How far does the ladder reach up the wall? Give your answer to 3 s.f.

[3 marks]

Section Five — Measures and Angles

The Sine and Cosine Rules

Normal trigonometry using SOH CAH TOA etc. can only be applied to right-angled triangles. Which leaves us with the question of what to do with other-angled triangles. Step forward the Sine and Cosine Rules...

Labelling the Triangle

This is very important. You must label the sides and angles properly so that the letters for the sides and angles correspond with each other. Use lower case letters for the sides and capitals for the angles.

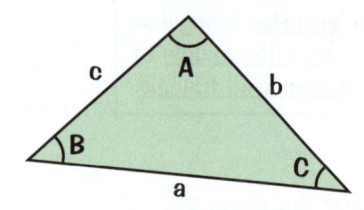

Remember, side 'a' is opposite angle A etc.

It doesn't matter which sides you decide to call a, b, and c, just as long as the angles are then labelled properly.

Three Formulas to Get Your Head Around:

The Sine Rule

$$\frac{a}{\sin A} = \frac{b}{\sin B} = \frac{c}{\sin C}$$

You don't use the whole thing with both '=' signs of course, so it's not half as bad as it looks — you just choose the two bits that you want:

e.g. $\frac{b}{\sin B} = \frac{c}{\sin C}$ or $\frac{a}{\sin A} = \frac{b}{\sin B}$

The Cosine Rule

The 'normal' form is...

$$a^2 = b^2 + c^2 - 2bc \cos A$$

...or this form is good for finding an angle (you get it by rearranging the 'normal' version):

$$\text{or } \cos A = \frac{b^2 + c^2 - a^2}{2bc}$$

Area of the Triangle

This formula comes in handy when you know two sides and the angle between them:

$$\text{Area of triangle} = \tfrac{1}{2} ab \sin C$$

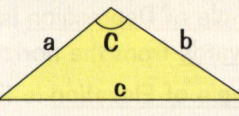

Of course, there's a simple formula for calculating the area using the base length and height (see p.86). The formula here is for when you don't know those values.

EXAMPLE: Triangle XYZ has XZ = 18 cm, YZ = 13 cm and angle XZY = 58°. Find the area of the triangle, giving your answer correct to 3 significant figures.

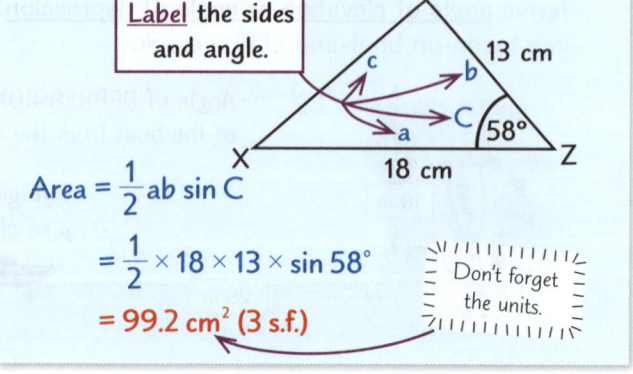

Label the sides and angle.

Area = $\tfrac{1}{2}$ ab sin C

= $\tfrac{1}{2} \times 18 \times 13 \times \sin 58°$

= 99.2 cm² (3 s.f.)

Don't forget the units.

...and step back again. Hope you enjoyed a moment in the spotlight...

Make sure you know how to use the three formulas on this page. Now have a go at this area question (and fear not — you can have a go at some sine and cosine rule problems on the next page)...

Q1 Triangle FGH has FG = 9 cm, FH = 12 cm and angle GFH = 37°. Find its area, giving your answer correct to 3 significant figures. [2 marks]

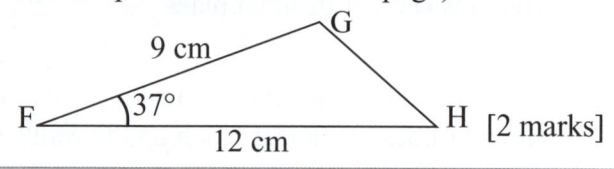

Section Five — Measures and Angles

The Sine and Cosine Rules

There are four main question types where the sine and cosine rules would be applied. So learn the exact details of these four examples and you'll be laughing. WARNING: if you laugh too much your socks might fall off.

The Four Examples

1 TWO ANGLES given plus ANY SIDE — SINE RULE needed.

Find the length of AB for the triangle below.

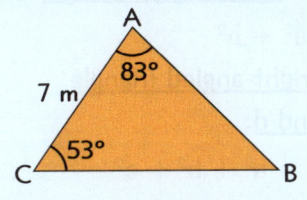

1) Don't forget the obvious... $B = 180° - 83° - 53° = 44°$

2) Put the numbers into the sine rule. $\dfrac{b}{\sin B} = \dfrac{c}{\sin C}$ $\Rightarrow \dfrac{7}{\sin 44°} = \dfrac{c}{\sin 53°}$

3) Rearrange to find c. $\Rightarrow c = \dfrac{7 \times \sin 53°}{\sin 44°} = 8.05$ m (3 s.f.)

2 TWO SIDES given plus an ANGLE NOT ENCLOSED by them — SINE RULE needed.

Find angle ABC for the triangle shown below.

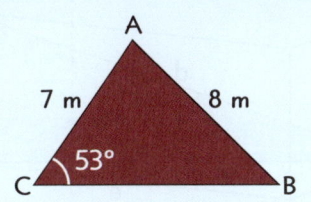

1) Put the numbers into the sine rule. $\dfrac{b}{\sin B} = \dfrac{c}{\sin C}$ $\Rightarrow \dfrac{7}{\sin B} = \dfrac{8}{\sin 53°}$

2) Rearrange to find sin B. $\Rightarrow \sin B = \dfrac{7 \times \sin 53°}{8} = 0.6988...$

3) Find the inverse. $\Rightarrow B = \sin^{-1}(0.6988...) = 44.3°$ (1 d.p.)

3 TWO SIDES given plus the ANGLE ENCLOSED by them — COSINE RULE needed.

Find the length CB for the triangle shown below.

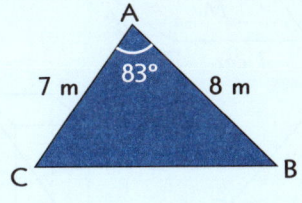

1) Put the numbers into the cosine rule. $a^2 = b^2 + c^2 - 2bc \cos A$ $= 7^2 + 8^2 - 2 \times 7 \times 8 \times \cos 83°$ $= 99.3506...$

2) Take square roots to find a. $a = \sqrt{99.3506...} = 9.97$ m (3 s.f.)

4 ALL THREE SIDES given but NO ANGLES — COSINE RULE needed.

Find angle CAB for the triangle shown.

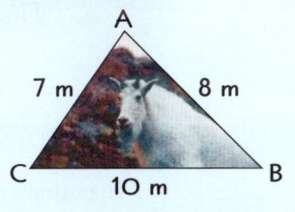

1) Use this version of the cosine rule. $\cos A = \dfrac{b^2 + c^2 - a^2}{2bc}$

2) Put in the numbers. $= \dfrac{49 + 64 - 100}{2 \times 7 \times 8}$

3) Take the inverse to find A. $= \dfrac{13}{112} = 0.11607...$

$\Rightarrow A = \cos^{-1}(0.11607...) = 83.3°$ (1 d.p.)

You might come across a triangle that isn't labelled ABC — just relabel it yourself to match the sine and cosine rules.

---

4 examples + 3 formulas + 2 rules = 1 trigonometric genius...

You need to get really good at spotting which of the four methods to use, so try these practice questions.

Q1 Find the length of side AB for triangle ABC. [3 marks]

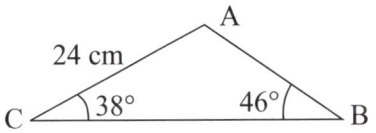

Q2 Find the size of angle RPQ for triangle PQR. [3 marks]

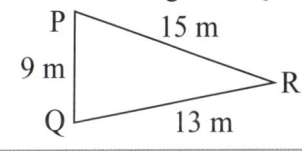

Section Five — Measures and Angles

3D Pythagoras

This is a 3D version of the 2D Pythagoras theorem you saw on page 75. There's just one simple formula — learn it and the world's your oyster...

3D Pythagoras for Cuboids — $a^2 + b^2 + c^2 = d^2$

Cuboids have their own formula for calculating the length of their longest diagonal:

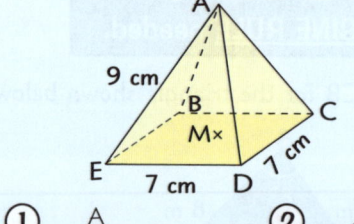

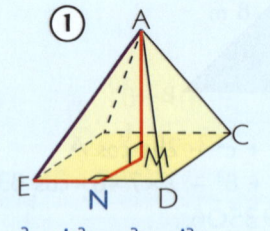

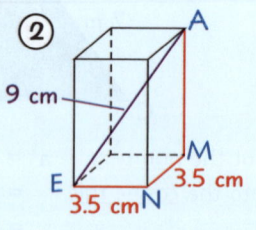

$$a^2 + b^2 + c^2 = d^2$$

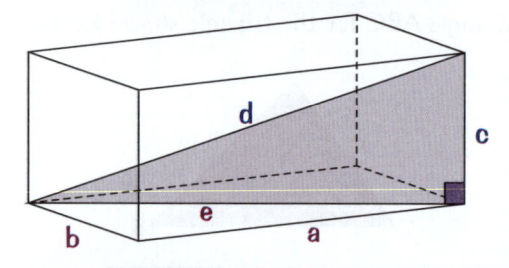

In reality it's nothing you haven't seen before — it's just 2D Pythagoras' theorem being used twice:

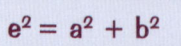

1) a, b and e make a right-angled triangle so
$$e^2 = a^2 + b^2$$

2) Now look at the right-angled triangle formed by e, c and d:
$$d^2 = e^2 + c^2 = a^2 + b^2 + c^2$$

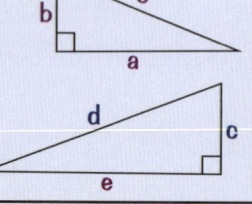

EXAMPLE: Find the exact length of the diagonal BH for the cube in the diagram.

1) Write down the formula. $a^2 + b^2 + c^2 = d^2$
2) Put in the numbers. $4^2 + 4^2 + 4^2 = BH^2$
3) Take the square root to find BH. $\Rightarrow BH = \sqrt{48} = 4\sqrt{3}$ cm

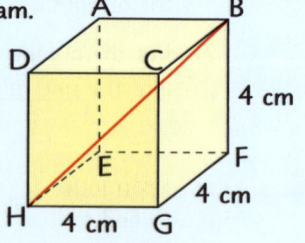

The Cuboid Formula can be used in Other 3D Shapes

EXAMPLE: In the square-based pyramid shown, M is the midpoint of the base. Find the vertical height AM.

1) Label N as the midpoint of ED.

   Then think of EN, NM and AM as three sides of a cuboid, and AE as the longest diagonal in the cuboid (like d in the section above).

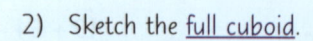

2) Sketch the full cuboid.

3) Write down the 3D Pythagoras formula. $a^2 + b^2 + c^2 = d^2$

4) Rewrite it using side labels. $EN^2 + NM^2 + AM^2 = AE^2$

5) Put in the numbers and solve for AM. $\Rightarrow 3.5^2 + 3.5^2 + AM^2 = 9^2$

   $\Rightarrow AM = \sqrt{81 - 2 \times 12.25} = 7.52$ cm (3 s.f.)

Wow — just what can't right-angled triangles do...

You need to be ready to tackle 3D questions in the exam, so have a go at this Exam Practice Question.

Q1 Find the length AH in the cuboid shown to 3 s.f.

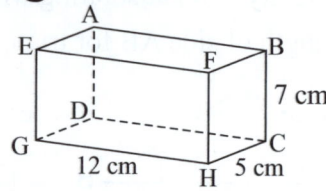

[3 marks]

Section Five — Measures and Angles

3D Trigonometry

3D trig may sound tricky, and I suppose it is a bit... but it's actually just using the same old rules.

Angle Between Line and Plane — Use a Diagram

If you've got a 3D problem involving angles, chances are you're going to have to use 3D trigonometry to solve it. The key trick here is to draw out 2D diagrams to get the side or angle you want. Normally this means you end up finding the angle between a line and a plane — there's a three-step method to help you with this:

A plane is just a flat surface.

1) Make a right-angled triangle between the line and the plane.

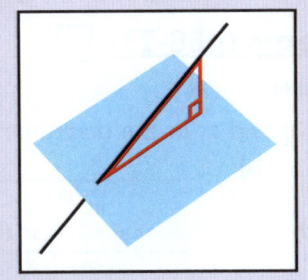

2) Draw a simple 2D sketch of this triangle and mark on the lengths of two sides (you might have to use Pythagoras to find one).

3) Use trigonometry to find the angle.

Have a look at p.75-77 to jog your memory about Pythagoras and trig.

EXAMPLE: ABCDE is a square-based pyramid with M as the midpoint of its base. Find the angle the edge AE makes with the base.

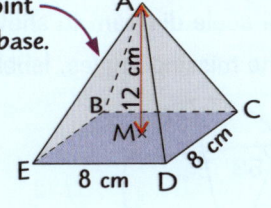

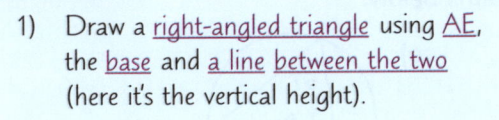

1) Draw a right-angled triangle using AE, the base and a line between the two (here it's the vertical height).

   Label the angle you need to find.

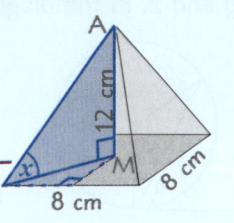

2) Now sketch this triangle in 2D and label it.

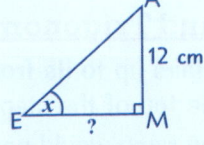

   You have to use Pythagoras (on the base triangle with the dashed outline) to find EM.

   $EM^2 = 4^2 + 4^2 = 32$
   $\Rightarrow EM = \sqrt{32}$ cm

3) Finally, use trigonometry to find x.
   (EM is adjacent to x, AM is opposite to x — use SOH CAH TOA)

   T = O/A
   $\tan x$ = opposite ÷ adjacent
   $= 12 \div \sqrt{32}$
   $= 2.1213...$
   $x = \tan^{-1}(2.1213...)$
   $= 64.8°$ (1 d.p.)

SOHCAHTOA Returns — out now in 3D...

If you need to find an angle in a 3D question, don't panic — just put those standard trig formulas to work.

Q1 Find the size of the angle between the line PV and the plane PQRS in the cuboid shown.

[4 marks]

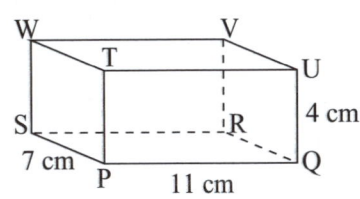

Section Five — Measures and Angles

Revision Questions for Section Five

This section had a lot of new methods and rules — check you can use them by working through this page.
- Try these questions and tick off each one when you get it right.
- When you've done all the questions for a topic and are completely happy with it, tick off the topic.

Conversions and Speed, Density and Pressure (p66-67)

1) Convert: a) 5.6 litres to cm³   b) 3 m/s to km/h   c) 8 feet to cm
   d) 12 m³ to cm³   e) 1280 mm² to cm²   f) 2.75 cm³ to mm³
2) Find the volume of a snowman if its density is 0.4 g/cm³ and its mass is 5 kg.
3) Find the area of an object in contact with horizontal ground, if the pressure it exerts on the ground is 120 N/m² and the force acting on the object is 1320 N.

Angles and Geometry Problems (p68-71)

4) Write down the five simple angle rules.
5) Find the missing angles, labelled x, y and z, in the diagrams below.
   a) [triangle with angles 83°, 71°, x]   b) [parallel lines with 112°, y]   c) [isoceles triangle with 58°, z]
6) Find the exterior angle of a regular heptagon to 1 d.p. What is the sum of its interior angles?

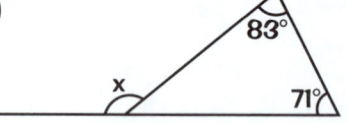

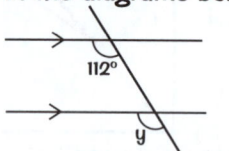

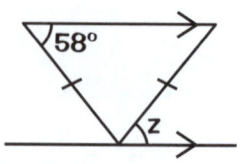

Bearings and Circle Geometry (p72-74)

7) Describe how to find a bearing from point A to point B.
8) A helicopter flies 25 km on a bearing of 210°, then 20 km on a bearing of 040°. Draw a scale diagram to show this. Use a scale of 1 cm = 5 km.
9) Find the missing angles, labelled x, y and z, in the diagrams below.
   a) [circle with 53°, x]   b) [circle with 21°, y]   c) [circle with 57°, z]

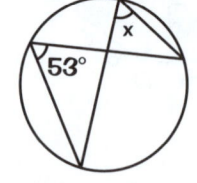

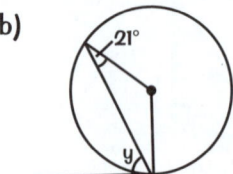

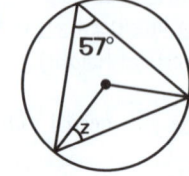

Pythagoras' Theorem and Trigonometry (p75-77)

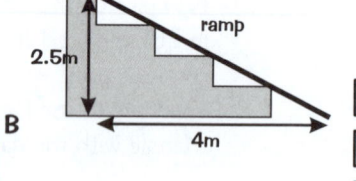

10) A museum has a flight of stairs up to its front door (see diagram). A ramp is to be put over the top of the steps for wheelchair users. Calculate the length that the ramp would need to be to 3 s.f.
11) Write down the three trigonometry formula triangles.
12) Find the size of angle x in triangle ABC to 1 d.p. 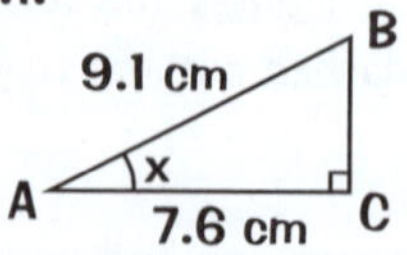
13) A seagull is sitting on top of a 2.8 m high lamp-post. It sees a bag of chips on the ground, 7.1 m away from the base of the lamp-post. Calculate the angle of depression of the chips from the top of the lamp-post, correct to 1 d.p.

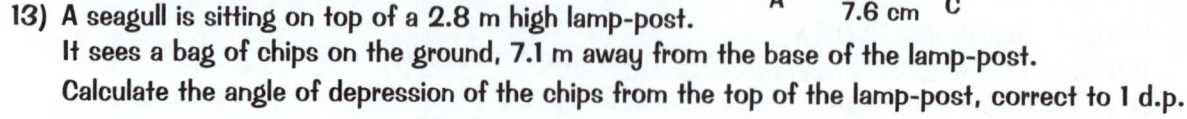

The Sine and Cosine Rules (p78-79)

14) Write down the sine and cosine rules and the formula (involving sin) for the area of any triangle.
15) List the 4 different types of sine/cosine rule questions and which rule you need for each.
16) Triangle PQR has side PQ = 12 cm, side QR = 9 cm and angle PQR = 63°. Find its area.
17) Triangle JKL has side JK = 7 cm, side JL = 11 cm and angle JLK = 32°. Find angle JKL.
18) In triangle FGH side FH = 8 cm, side GH = 9 cm and angle FHG = 47°. Find the length of side FG.

3D Pythagoras and Trigonometry (p80-81)

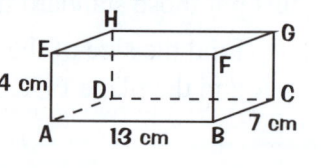

19) Find the length of the longest diagonal in a 5 m × 6 m × 9 m cuboid.
20) Find the angle between the line BH and the plane ABCD in this cuboid.

Section Five — Measures and Angles

Section Six — Shapes and Area

Properties of 2D Shapes

Here's a nice easy page to get you started on 2D shapes.

Line Symmetry

This is where you draw one or more MIRROR LINES across a shape and both sides fold exactly together.

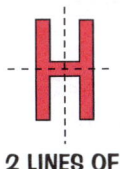

H	E	⬇	✦	N	M
2 LINES OF SYMMETRY	1 LINE OF SYMMETRY	1 LINE OF SYMMETRY	3 LINES OF SYMMETRY	NO LINES OF SYMMETRY	1 LINE OF SYMMETRY

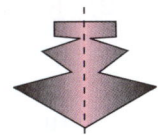

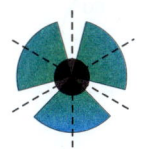

Rotational Symmetry

This is where you can rotate the shape into different positions that look exactly the same.

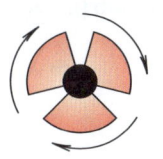

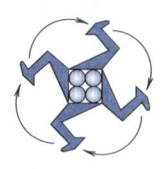

T	Z	S	(fan)	(triskelion)
Order 1	Order 2	Order 2	Order 3	Order 4

The ORDER OF ROTATIONAL SYMMETRY is the posh way of saying: 'how many different positions look the same'. You should say the Z-shape above has 'rotational symmetry of order 2'.

When a shape has only 1 position you can either say that it has 'rotational symmetry of order 1' or that it has 'NO rotational symmetry'.

Regular Polygons

In a regular polygon, all sides are the same length and all angles are the same size. Learn the names of these regular polygons and how many sides they have. (An equilateral triangle and a square are both regular polygons — see the next page for their properties.)

In an irregular polygon, the sides and angles aren't all equal.

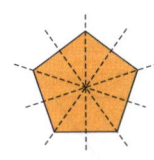

REGULAR PENTAGON
5 sides
5 lines of symmetry
Rotational symmetry of order 5

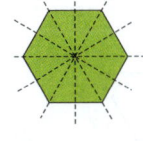

REGULAR HEXAGON
6 sides
6 lines of symmetry
Rotational symmetry of order 6

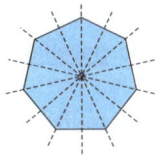

REGULAR HEPTAGON
7 sides
7 lines of symmetry
Rotational symmetry of order 7

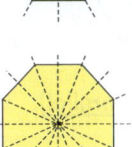

REGULAR OCTAGON
8 sides
8 lines of symmetry
Rotational symmetry of order 8

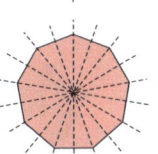

REGULAR NONAGON
9 sides
9 lines of symmetry
Rotational symmetry of order 9

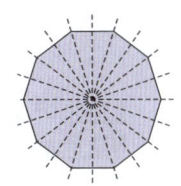

REGULAR DECAGON
10 sides
10 lines of symmetry
Rotational symmetry of order 10

Mirror line, mirror line on the wall...

Make sure you learn the two different types of symmetry, and dazzle your friends by spotting them in everyday shapes like road signs, warning signs and letters.

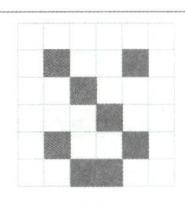

Q1 Make two copies of the pattern to the right.
    a) Shade two squares to make a pattern with one line of symmetry.   [1 mark]
    b) Shade two squares to make a pattern with rotational symmetry of order 2.   [1 mark]

Properties of 2D Shapes

This page is jam-packed with details about triangles and quadrilaterals — and you need to learn them all.

Triangles

1) **EQUILATERAL TRIANGLES**
   3 equal sides and
   3 equal angles of 60°.
   3 lines of symmetry,
   rotational symmetry order 3.

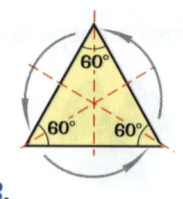

2) **RIGHT-ANGLED TRIANGLES**
   1 right angle (90°).
   No lines of symmetry
   (unless it's also isosceles).
   No rotational symmetry.

   The little square means it's a right angle.

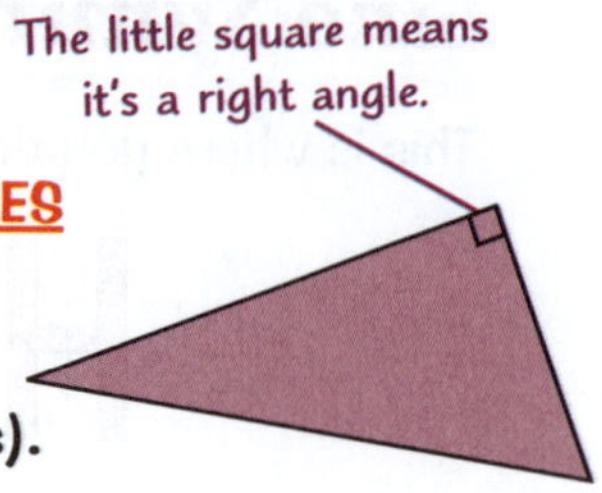

3) **ISOSCELES TRIANGLES**
   2 sides the same.
   2 angles the same.
   1 line of symmetry.
   No rotational symmetry.

   These dashes mean that the two sides are the same length.

4) **SCALENE TRIANGLES**
   All three sides different.
   All three angles different.
   No symmetry (pretty obviously).

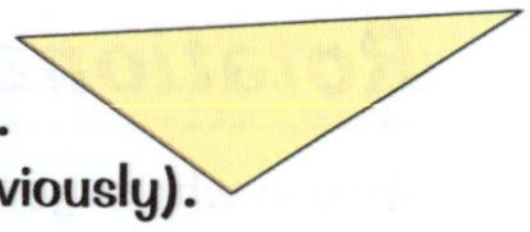

An acute-angled triangle has 3 acute angles (angles less than 90°), and an obtuse-angled triangle has one obtuse angle (an angle between 90° and 180°).

Quadrilaterals

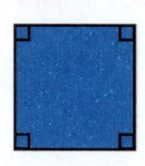

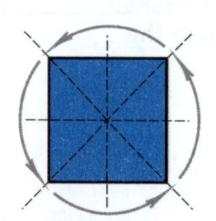

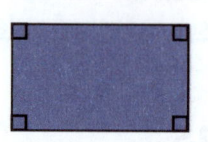

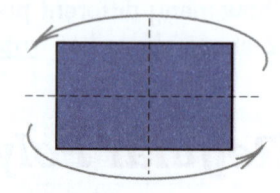

1) **SQUARE**
   4 equal angles of 90° (right angles).
   4 lines of symmetry, rotational symmetry order 4.

2) **RECTANGLE**
   4 equal angles of 90° (right angles).
   2 lines of symmetry, rotational symmetry order 2.

3) **RHOMBUS** (A square pushed over) 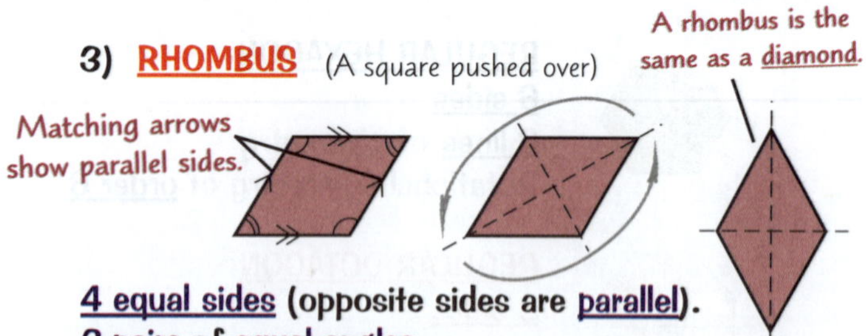
   Matching arrows show parallel sides.
   A rhombus is the same as a diamond.
   4 equal sides (opposite sides are parallel).
   2 pairs of equal angles.
   2 lines of symmetry, rotational symmetry order 2.

4) **PARALLELOGRAM** (A rectangle pushed over) 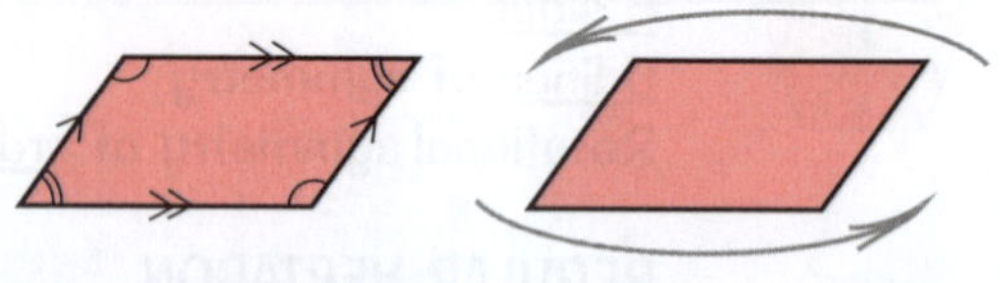
   2 pairs of equal sides (each pair are parallel).
   2 pairs of equal angles.
   NO lines of symmetry, rotational symmetry order 2.

5) **TRAPEZIUM** 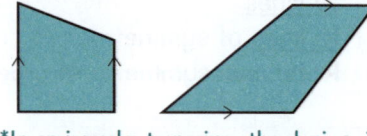
   1 pair of parallel sides.
   NO lines of symmetry*.
   No rotational symmetry.

   *In an isosceles trapezium, the sloping sides are the same length. An isosceles trapezium has 1 line of symmetry.

6) **KITE**
   2 pairs of equal sides.
   1 pair of equal angles.
   1 line of symmetry.
   No rotational symmetry.

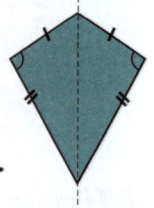

Kite facts — 2 pairs of equal sides, 1 line of symmetry, Gemini...

Learn the names (and spellings) and properties of all the shapes on this page, then try this question:

Q1   A quadrilateral has all 4 sides the same length and two pairs of equal angles.
     Identify the quadrilateral, and write down its order of rotational symmetry.   [2 marks]

Section Six — Shapes and Area

Similar Shapes

Similar shapes are <u>exactly the same shape</u>, but can be <u>different sizes</u> (they can also be <u>rotated</u> or <u>reflected</u>).

SIMILAR — same shape, <u>different size</u>.

Don't confuse similar shapes with <u>congruent</u> shapes. <u>Congruent</u> shapes are the <u>same shape</u> AND the <u>same size</u> (they too can be <u>reflected</u> or <u>rotated</u>).

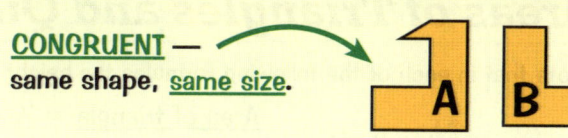

CONGRUENT — same shape, <u>same size</u>.

Similar Triangles

Generally, for two shapes to be <u>similar</u>, all the <u>angles</u> must match and the <u>sides</u> must be <u>proportional</u>. But for <u>triangles</u>, there are <u>three special conditions</u> — if any one of these is true, you know they're similar.

Two triangles are similar if:

1) All the <u>angles</u> match up
   i.e. the angles in one triangle are the same as the other.

2) All three <u>sides</u> are <u>proportional</u>
   i.e. if <u>one</u> side is twice as long as the corresponding side in the other triangle, <u>all</u> the sides are twice as long as the corresponding sides.

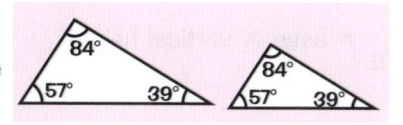

3) Any <u>two sides</u> are <u>proportional</u> and the <u>angle between them</u> is the <u>same</u>.

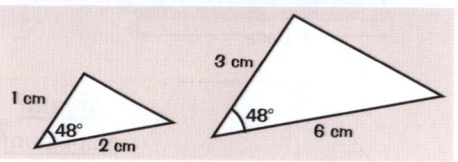

Watch out — if one of the triangles has been rotated or flipped over, it might look as if they're not similar, but don't be fooled.

EXAMPLE: Show that triangles ABC and ADE are similar.

∠BAC = ∠EAD (vertically opposite angles)
∠ABC = ∠ADE (alternate angles)
∠BCA = ∠AED (alternate angles)

See p.69 for more on angles around parallel lines.

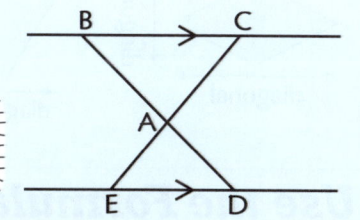

The angles in triangle ABC are the same as the angles in triangle ADE, so the triangles are similar.

Use Similarity to Find Missing Lengths

You might have to use the <u>properties</u> of similar shapes to find missing distances, lengths etc. — you'll need to use <u>scale factors</u> (see p.97) to find the lengths of missing sides.

EXAMPLE: Suzanna is swimming in the sea. When she is at point B, she is 20 m from a rock that is 8 m tall at its highest point. There is a lighthouse 50 m away from Suzanna that is directly behind the rock. From her perspective, the top of the lighthouse is in line with the top of the rock. How tall is the lighthouse?

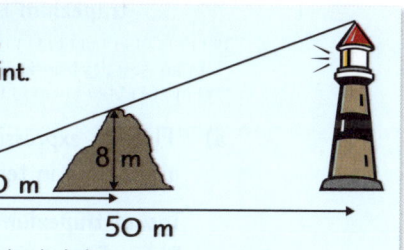

The triangles formed between Suzanna and the rock and Suzanna and the lighthouse are <u>similar</u>, so work out the <u>scale factor</u>: scale factor = $\frac{50}{20}$ = 2.5

Now <u>use</u> the scale factor to work out the height of the lighthouse: height = 8 × 2.5 = **20 m**

Butter and margarine — similar products...

To help remember the difference between similarity and congruence, think '<u>similar siblings, congruent clones</u>' — siblings are alike but not the same, clones are identical.

Q1 Find the length of DB.   [2 marks]

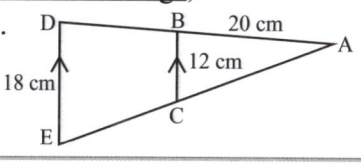

Section Six — Shapes and Area

Area — Triangles and Quadrilaterals

There are lots of area formulas coming up on the next two pages for you to learn. I'm assuming you already know the formulas for the area of a rectangle (A = l × w) and the area of a square (A = l²).

l = length, w = width

Areas of Triangles and Quadrilaterals

Note that in each of the following formulas the height must be the vertical height, not the sloping height.

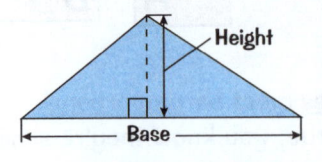

Area of triangle = ½ × base × vertical height

$$A = ½ × b × h_v$$

If you're studying for M8 exams, you'll know the alternative formula is:
Area of triangle = ½ ab sin C
This is covered on p.78.

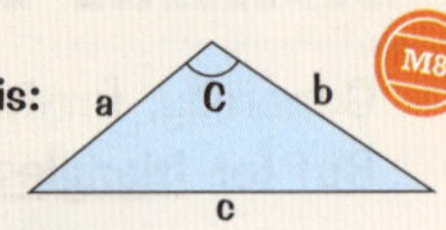

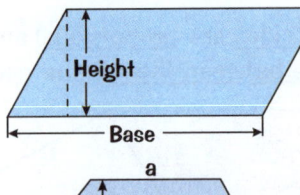

Area of parallelogram = base × vertical height

$$A = b × h_v$$

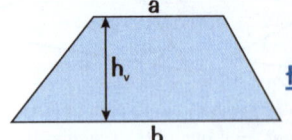

Area of trapezium = average of parallel sides × distance between them (vertical height)

$$A = ½(a + b) × h_v$$

The formula for the area of a rhombus or a kite is the same:

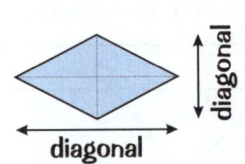

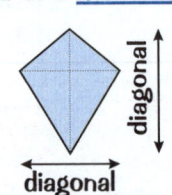

Area of rhombus or kite = ½ × diagonal × diagonal

$$A = ½ × d × d$$

Use the Formulas to Solve Problems

Examiners like to sneak bits of algebra into area and perimeter questions — you'll often have to set up and then solve an equation to find a missing side length or area of a shape. Meanies.

EXAMPLE: The shape on the right shows a square with sides of length x cm drawn inside an isosceles trapezium. The base of the trapezium is three times as long as one side of the square.

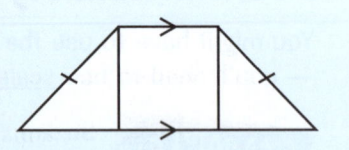

In an isosceles trapezium, the sloping sides are the same length.

a) Find an expression for the area of the trapezium in terms of x.

Top of trapezium = side of square = x cm
Base of trapezium = 3 × side of square = $3x$ cm
Height of trapezium = side of square = x cm
Area of trapezium = ½($x + 3x$) × x = $2x^2$ cm²

b) The area of the trapezium is 60.5 cm². Find the side length of the square.

Set your equation from part a) equal to 60.5 and solve to find x:

$2x^2 = 60.5$
$x^2 = 30.25$
$x = 5.5$ cm

No jokes about my vertical height please...

If you have a composite shape (a shape made up of different shapes stuck together), split it into triangles and quadrilaterals, work out the area of each bit and add them together.

Q1 The triangle and rectangle shown on the right have the same area. Find the value of x. [2 marks]

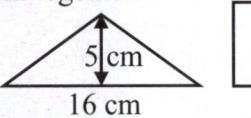

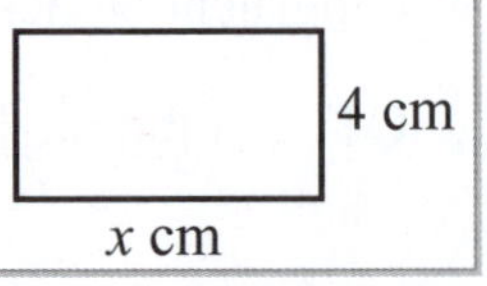

5 cm, 16 cm, 4 cm, x cm

Section Six — Shapes and Area

Area — Circles

Yes, I thought I could detect some groaning when you realised that this is another page of formulas. Just imagine all these circles are biscuits that you're going to eat once you've finished this page.

Area and Circumference of Circles

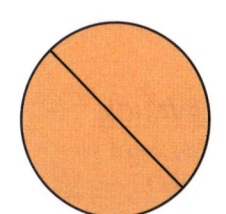

Area of circle = π × (radius)²
Remember that the radius is half the diameter.

$$A = \pi r^2$$

Circumference = π × diameter
= 2 × π × radius

$$C = \pi D = 2\pi r$$

For these formulas, use the π button on your calculator. For non-calculator questions, use π ≈ 3.142.

Areas of Sectors and Lengths of Arcs

These next ones are a bit more tricky — before you try and learn the formulas, make sure you know what a sector and an arc are (I've helpfully labelled the diagrams below — I'm nice like that).

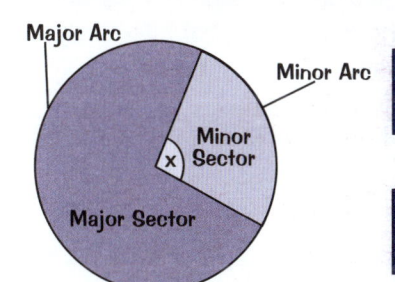

Area of Sector = $\frac{x}{360}$ × Area of full Circle   (Pretty obvious really, isn't it?)

Length of Arc = $\frac{x}{360}$ × Circumference of full Circle   (Obvious again, no?)

EXAMPLE: In the diagram on the right, a sector with angle 60° has been cut out of a circle with radius 3 cm. Find the exact area of the shaded shape.

First find the angle of the shaded sector (this is the major sector):
360° − 60° = 300°

Then use the formula to find the area of the shaded sector:

area of sector = $\frac{x}{360} \times \pi r^2 = \frac{300}{360} \times \pi \times 3^2$
$= \frac{5}{6} \times \pi \times 9 = \frac{15}{2} \pi$ cm²

'Exact area' means leave your answer in terms of π.

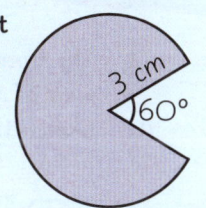

Make sure you know these circle-y terms too:

Chord — a straight line that joins two points on a circle's circumference.

Segment — the region between a chord and its arc.

Tangent — a straight line that just touches a single point on a circle's circumference.

Pi r not square — pi are round. Pi are tasty...

Oo, one more thing — if you're asked to find the perimeter of a semicircle or quarter circle, don't forget to add on the straight edges too. It's an easy mistake to make, and it'll cost you marks.

Q1 For the shape on the right, find to 2 decimal places:
a) the area of the sector,   [2 marks]   b) the arc length.   [2 marks]

150°
8 cm

Section Six — Shapes and Area

Plans and Elevations

Plans and elevations are just different views of a 3D solid shape — looking at it from the front, side and top.

The Three Different Views

There are three different types of view — front elevations, side elevations and plans (these three types can also be called projections).

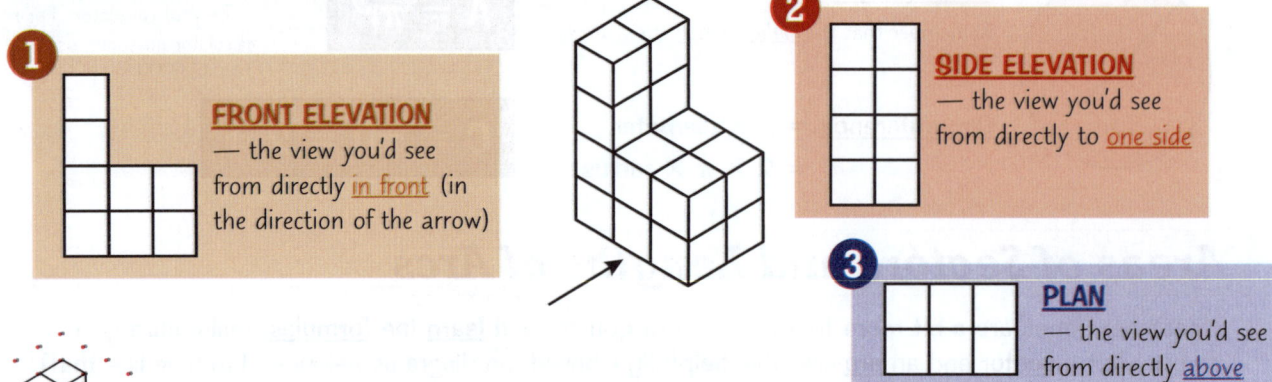

① FRONT ELEVATION — the view you'd see from directly in front (in the direction of the arrow)

② SIDE ELEVATION — the view you'd see from directly to one side

③ PLAN — the view you'd see from directly above

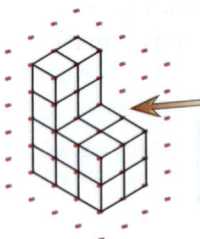

Don't be thrown if you're given a diagram on isometric (dotty) paper like this — it works in just the same way. If you have to draw shapes on isometric paper, just join the dots. You should only draw vertical and diagonal lines (no horizontal lines).

Drawing Elevations

EXAMPLES:

1. The front elevation and plan view of a shape are shown below. Sketch the solid shape.

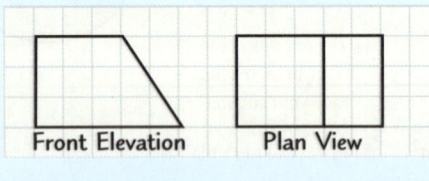

   Front Elevation   Plan View

   Just piece together the original shape from the information given — here you get a prism (see p.90) in the shape of the front elevation.

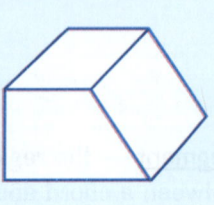

2. a) On the cm square grid, draw the front elevation of the prism from the direction of the arrow.
   b) Draw a plan of the prism on the grid.

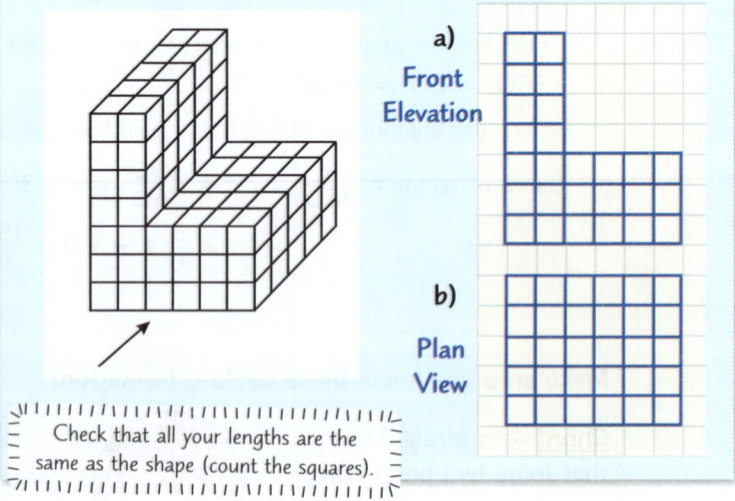

   a) Front Elevation
   b) Plan View

   Check that all your lengths are the same as the shape (count the squares).

Elevations — enough to send you dotty...

This type of question's not too bad — just take your time and sketch the diagrams carefully. Watch out for questions on isometric paper — they might look confusing, but they can actually be easier than other questions.

Q1 For the shape on the right, draw:
   a) The front elevation (from the direction of the arrow), [1 mark]
   b) The side elevation, [1 mark]
   c) The plan view. [1 mark]

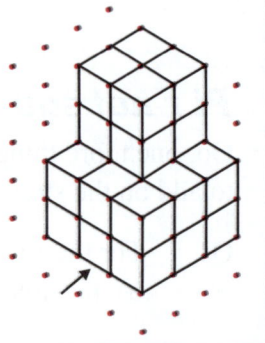

Section Six — Shapes and Area

3D Shapes — Surface Area

It's time now to move on to the next dimension — yep, that's right, 3D shapes. I can hardly contain my excitement. If you do really well on these next few pages, we might even get on to time travel. Oooooo.

Vertices, Faces and Edges

There are different parts of 3D shapes you need to be able to spot. These are vertices (corners), faces and edges. You might be asked for the number of vertices, faces and edges in the exam — just count them up, and don't forget the hidden ones.

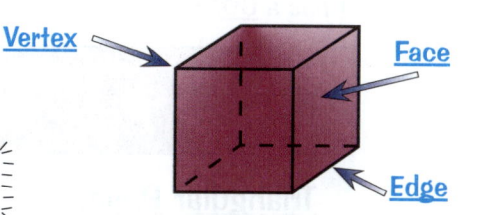

Curved faces are sometimes called surfaces.

Surface Area

1) SURFACE AREA only applies to 3D objects — it's just the total area of all the faces added together.
2) SURFACE AREA OF SOLID = AREA OF NET (remember that a net is just a 3D shape folded out flat). So if it helps, imagine the net and add up the area of each bit.
3) SPHERES, CONES AND CYLINDERS have surface area formulas:

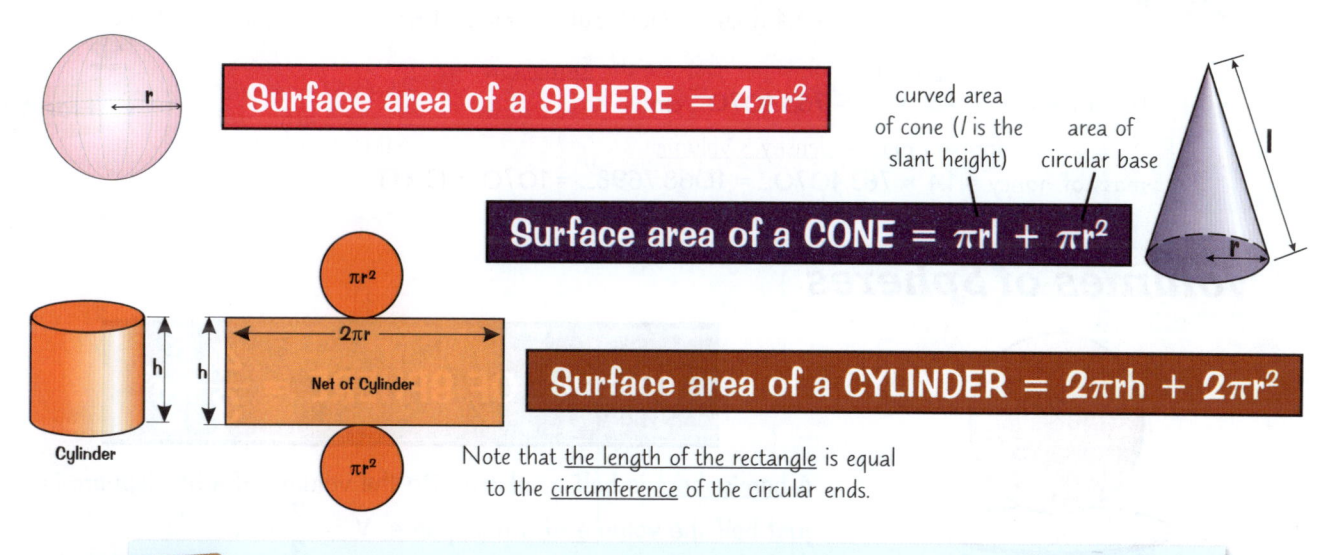

Surface area of a SPHERE = $4\pi r^2$

Surface area of a CONE = $\pi r l + \pi r^2$

curved area of cone (l is the slant height)   area of circular base

Surface area of a CYLINDER = $2\pi r h + 2\pi r^2$

Note that the length of the rectangle is equal to the circumference of the circular ends.

EXAMPLE: Find the exact surface area of a hemisphere with radius 4 cm.

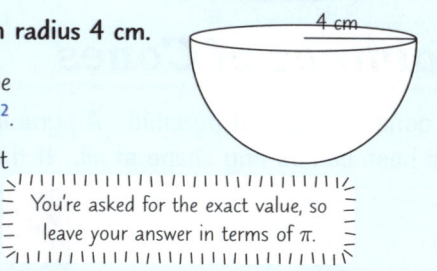

A hemisphere is half a sphere — so the surface area of the curved face is $4\pi r^2 \div 2 = 2\pi r^2 = 2 \times \pi \times 4^2 = 32\pi$ cm^2.
Don't forget the area of the flat face though — this is just the area of a circle with radius 4 cm: $\pi r^2 = 16\pi$ cm^2.
So the total surface area is $32\pi + 16\pi = 48\pi$ cm^2.

You're asked for the exact value, so leave your answer in terms of π.

Beware of the space-time vertex...

Don't get confused if you're sketching a net — most shapes have more than one net (for example, a cube has about a million. I'm not exaggerating. Well, maybe a little). Anyway, make sure you know how to use all the formulas on this page, then try this lovely practice question:

Q1 The surface area of a cone with radius 5 cm is 125π cm^2.
Find the slant height, l, of the cone. [3 marks]

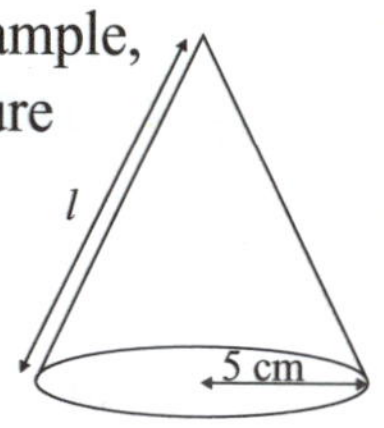

Section Six — Shapes and Area

3D Shapes — Volume

I'm fairly certain that you already know that the volume of a cuboid is length × width × height (and a cube is length³) — if not, you do now. Luckily for you, there's still more to learn about volumes of 3D shapes.

Volumes of Prisms

A PRISM is a solid (3D) object which is the same shape all the way through — i.e. it has a CONSTANT AREA OF CROSS-SECTION.

VOLUME OF PRISM = CROSS-SECTIONAL AREA × LENGTH

$V = A \times L$

Triangular Prism

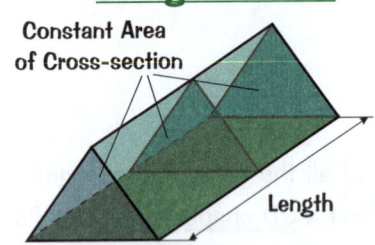

Constant Area of Cross-section

Length

Cylinder

Here, the cross-sectional area is a circle, so the formula for the volume of a cylinder is:

$V = \pi r^2 h$

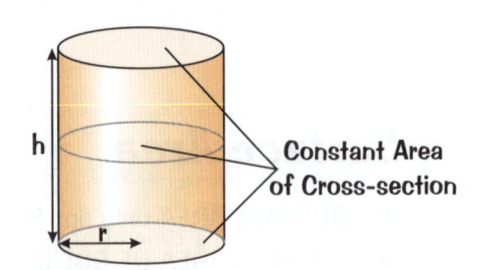

Constant Area of Cross-section

EXAMPLE: Honey comes in cylindrical jars with radius 4.5 cm and height 12 cm. The density of honey is 1.4 g/cm³. Work out the mass of honey in this jar to 3 s.f.

First, work out the volume of the jar — just use the formula above:
$V = \pi r^2 h = \pi \times 4.5^2 \times 12 = 763.4070...$ cm³

See p.67 for more on density.

Now use the formula mass = density × volume:
mass of honey = 1.4 × 763.4070... = 1068.7698... = **1070 g (3 s.f.)**

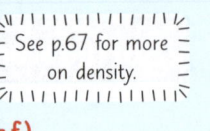

Volumes of Spheres

VOLUME OF SPHERE = $\frac{4}{3}\pi r^3$

A hemisphere is half a sphere. So the volume of a hemisphere is just half the volume of a full sphere, $V = \frac{2}{3}\pi r^3$.

Volumes of Cones

A cone is a type of pyramid. A pyramid is a shape that goes from a flat base up to a point at the top. Its base can be any shape at all. If the base is a circle then it's called a cone.

VOLUME OF CONE = $\frac{1}{3} \times \pi r^2 \times h_v$

Make sure you use the vertical (perpendicular) height in the formula — don't get confused with the slant height, which you used to find the surface area of a cone.

No, a cone isn't 'just as good' — all the other Pharaohs will laugh...

There are lots of formulas for 3D shapes — check you know which measurement each letter stands for.

Q1 A cone and a sphere both have radius 9 cm. Their volumes are the same. Find the vertical height, *h*, of the cone. [4 marks]

Section Six — Shapes and Area

3D Shapes — Volume

Another page on volumes now, but this is a bit of a weird one. It's all about volumes of frustums (cones with their top bits chopped off). As long as you can calculate the volume of a cone I reckon you'll be ok...

Volumes of Frustums

A frustum of a cone is what's left when the top part of a cone is cut off parallel to its circular base.

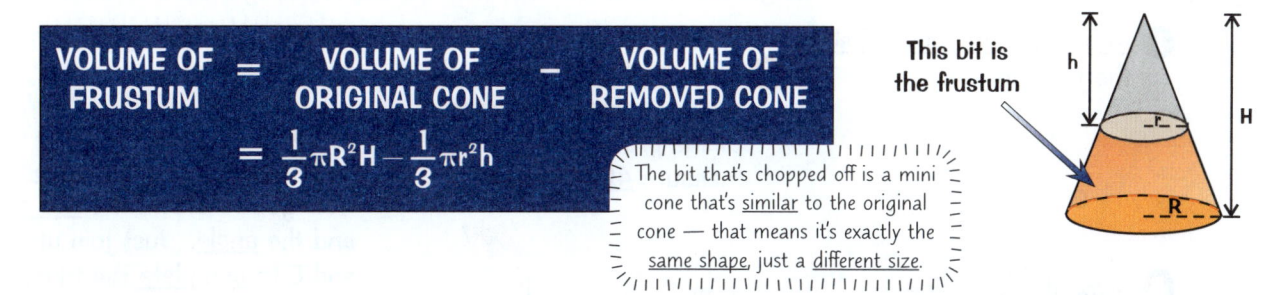

VOLUME OF FRUSTUM = VOLUME OF ORIGINAL CONE − VOLUME OF REMOVED CONE

$$= \frac{1}{3}\pi R^2 H - \frac{1}{3}\pi r^2 h$$

The bit that's chopped off is a mini cone that's similar to the original cone — that means it's exactly the same shape, just a different size.

This bit is the frustum

EXAMPLE: A waste paper basket is the shape of a frustum formed by removing a cone of height 10 cm and radius 7 cm from a cone of height 50 cm and radius 35 cm. Find the volume of the waste paper basket to 3 significant figures.

Volume of original cone = $\frac{1}{3}\pi R^2 H = \frac{1}{3} \times \pi \times 35^2 \times 50 = 64140.850...$ cm^3

Volume of removed cone = $\frac{1}{3}\pi r^2 h = \frac{1}{3} \times \pi \times 7^2 \times 10 = 513.126...$ cm^3

Volume of frustum = 64140.850... − 513.126... = 63627.723... = **63600 cm^3 (3 s.f.)**

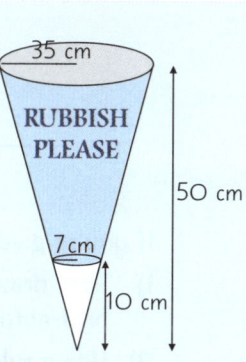

EXAMPLE: A funnel is formed by removing a cone of height 2.4 cm from a cone of height 12 cm and radius 10 cm, and then attaching a cylinder of height 8 cm and radius 2 cm. Find the exact volume of the funnel.

Volume of original cone = $\frac{1}{3}\pi R^2 H = \frac{1}{3} \times \pi \times 10^2 \times 12 = 400\pi$ cm^3

Radius of removed cone = 2 cm (the radius of the removed cone is the same as the radius of the cylinder)

Volume of removed cone = $\frac{1}{3}\pi r^2 h = \frac{1}{3} \times \pi \times 2^2 \times 2.4 = 3.2\pi$ cm^3

Volume of frustum = $400\pi - 3.2\pi = 396.8\pi$ cm^3

Volume of cylinder = V = $\pi r^2 h = \pi \times 2^2 \times 8 = 32\pi$ cm^3

Volume of funnel = $396.8\pi + 32\pi = $ **428.8π cm^3**

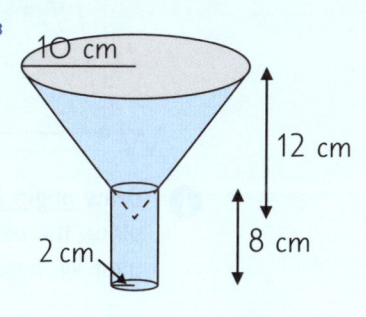

Hands up if you're finding this topic a bit frust-rating...

A common misconception is that a frustum is actually called a frustRum. (I thought this until about a year ago. It blew my mind.)

Q1 The diagram on the right shows an hourglass made from two identical frustums. Calculate the volume of the hourglass.   [4 marks]

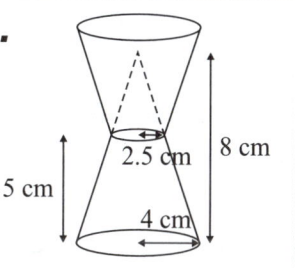

Section Six — Shapes and Area

Construction

How you construct triangles and quadrilaterals depends on what info you're given. If you've got enough sides and angles you can use a ruler and a protractor. Otherwise you might need to use compasses (see p.93).

Constructing using a Ruler and a Protractor

EXAMPLES:

1. Construct triangle DEF. DE = 5 cm, DF = 3 cm, and angle EDF = 40°.

① Roughly sketch and label the triangle.

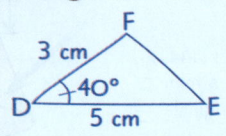

② Draw the base line.

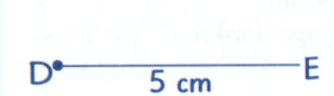

③ Draw angle EDF (the angle at D) — place the centre of the protractor over D, measure 40° and put a dot.

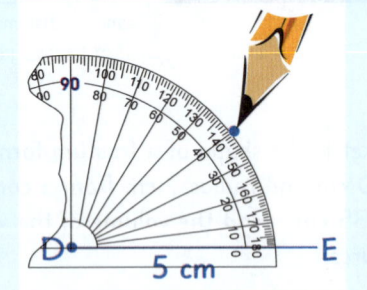

Remember — angle ABC means the angle between lines AB and BC.

④ Measure 3 cm towards the dot and label it F. Join up D and F. Now you've drawn the two sides and the angle. Just join up F and E to complete the triangle.

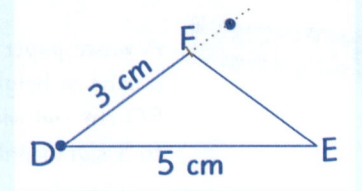

If you're given two angles and one side the method for constructing a triangle is similar:

1) First draw the side you have, make it the base and make it the right length. Then use your protractor to measure the two angles at each end of the line (marking them out with dots).
2) Use a ruler to draw from each end towards the dots you've marked out.
3) The point where these lines meet is the third corner of the triangle.

2. Finish constructing quadrilateral WXYZ on the right, so that angle ZWX = 30° and XYZ = 160°.

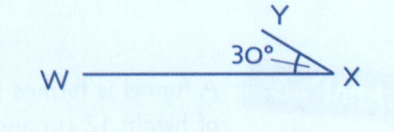

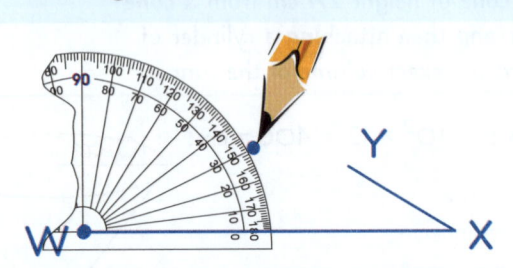

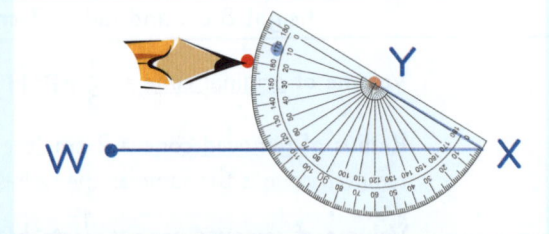

① Draw angle ZWX (the angle at W) — place the centre of the protractor over W, measure 30° and put a dot.

② Draw angle XYZ (the angle at Y) — place the centre of the protractor over Y, measure 160° and put a dot.

③ Draw from W towards the blue dot and from Y towards the red dot. The point at which both lines meet completes the quadrilateral.

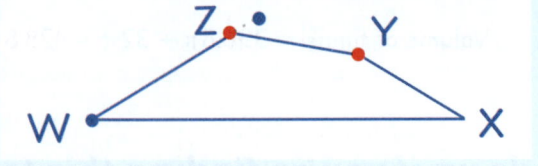

Pencils at the ready — three, two, one... Construct...

Constructions are always better when drawn with a nice sharp pencil. So remember to get that sharpener out and make sure your pencils, like your brain, are sharp before the exam.

Q1   Construct triangle PQR where PQ = 6 cm, angle RPQ = 70° and angle PQR = 30°.   [2 marks]

Section Six — Shapes and Area

Construction

Don't just read the page through once and hope you'll remember it — get your ruler, compasses and pencil out and have a go. It's the only way of testing whether you really know this stuff.

Constructing Triangles Using Compasses

EXAMPLE: Construct the triangle ABC where AB = 6 cm, BC = 4 cm, AC = 5 cm.

1) First, sketch and label a triangle so you know roughly what's needed. It doesn't matter which line you make the base line.

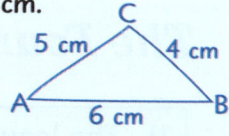

2) Draw the base line. Label the ends A and B.

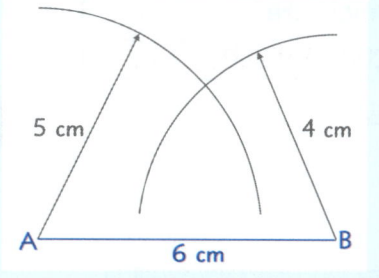

3) For AC, set the compasses to 5 cm, put the point at A and draw an arc. For BC, set the compasses to 4 cm, put the point at B and draw an arc.

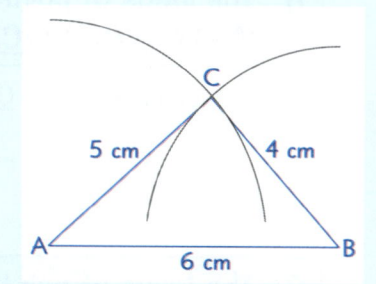

4) Where the arcs cross is point C. Now you can finish your triangle.

Constructing Equilateral Triangles

1) You might be asked to draw an accurate equilateral triangle without a protractor.

2) Follow the method shown in this diagram (make sure you leave the compass settings the same for each step).

3) If you just want a 60° angle, you can ignore Step 3 where you join up the triangle.

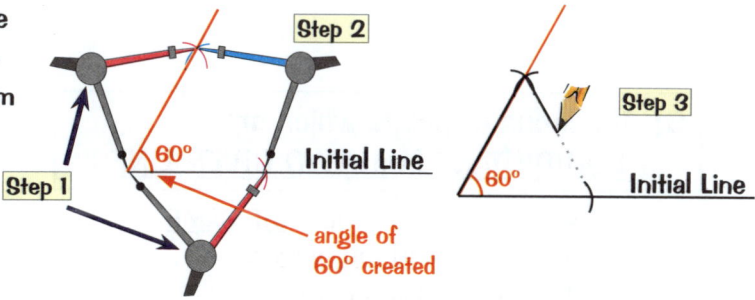

Construct Right Angles to Draw the Perpendicular

1) If you're asked to draw a perpendicular from a point to a line, you'll be given a line and a point, like this: A ——— B   •

2) Follow the method in the diagram to draw the perpendicular. This is the shortest distance between the point and the line.

3) You can use this method if you just want an accurate 90° angle — simply put the initial point on the line itself, where you want the angle to be.

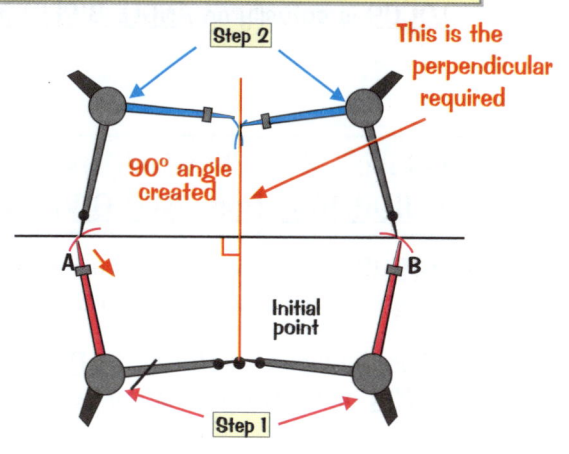

My compasses don't construct anything — they just point north...

You can't do these constructions 'by eye' or with a protractor. You've got to do them with compasses — so don't rub out your compass marks, or the examiner won't know you used the proper method.

Q1   Construct an equilateral triangle with sides of 5 cm. Leave visible construction marks. [2 marks]

Loci and Construction

A LOCUS (another ridiculous maths word) is simply:

A LINE or REGION that shows all the points which fit a given rule.

Make sure you learn how to draw these PROPERLY using a ruler and compasses as shown below.

The Four Different Types of Loci

Loci is just the plural of locus.

1) The locus of points which are 'A FIXED DISTANCE from a given POINT'.

This locus is simply a CIRCLE.

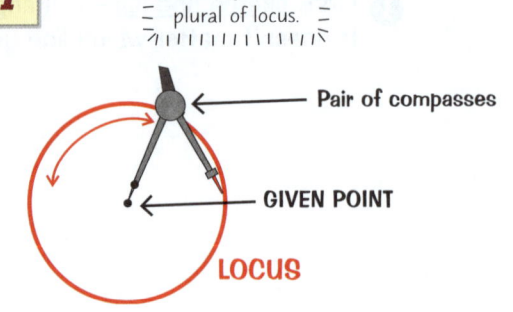

2) The locus of points which are 'A FIXED DISTANCE from a given LINE'.

This locus is a SAUSAGE SHAPE.

It has straight sides (drawn with a ruler) and ends which are perfect semicircles (drawn with compasses).

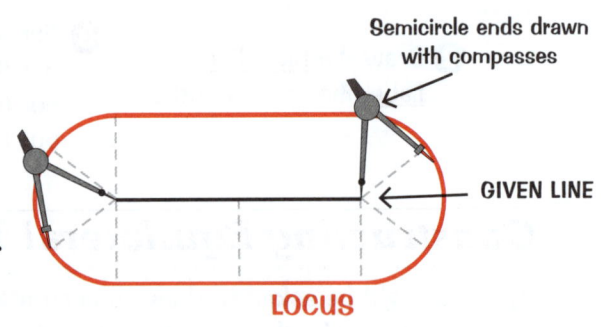

3) The locus of points which are 'EQUIDISTANT from TWO GIVEN LINES'.

1) Keep the compass setting THE SAME while you make all four marks.
2) Make sure you leave your compass marks showing.
3) You get two equal angles — i.e. this LOCUS is actually an ANGLE BISECTOR.

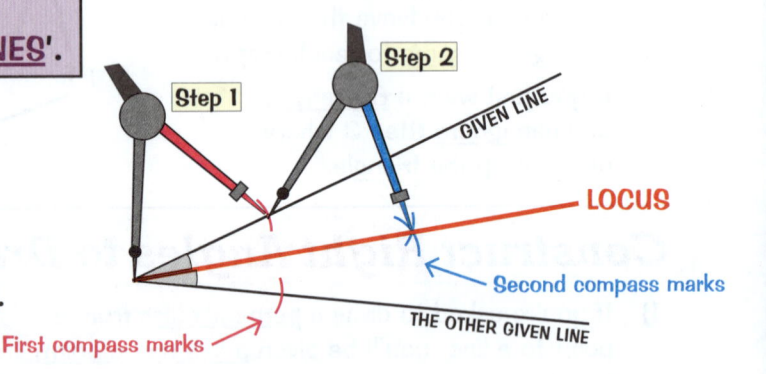

4) The locus of points which are 'EQUIDISTANT from TWO GIVEN POINTS'.

(In the diagram below, A and B are the two given points.)

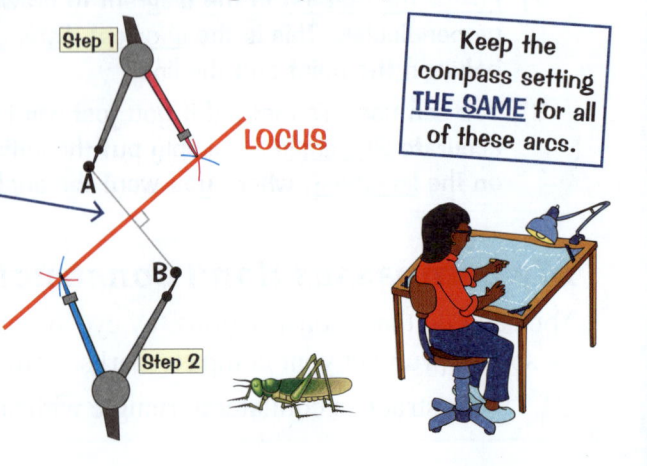

This LOCUS is all points which are the same distance from A as they are from B.

This time the locus is actually the PERPENDICULAR BISECTOR of the line joining the two points.

The perpendicular bisector of line segment AB is a line at right angles to AB, passing through the midpoint of AB. This is the method to use if you're asked to draw it.

Keep the compass setting THE SAME for all of these arcs.

Section Six — Shapes and Area

Loci and Construction — Examples

Now you know what loci are, and how to do all the constructions you need, it's time to put them all together.

Finding a Locus that Satisfies Lots of Rules

In the exam, you might be given a situation with lots of different conditions, and asked to find the region that satisfies all the conditions. To do this, just draw each locus, then see which bit you want.

EXAMPLE: On the square below, shade the region that is within 3 cm of vertex A and closer to vertex B than vertex D.

The shaded area is the region you want.

It's a square, so this diagonal is equidistant from B and D. The bit above the line is closer to B than D.

If it wasn't a square you'd have to CONSTRUCT the equidistant line with compasses using the method on p.94.

Construct a quarter circle 3 cm from A using compasses — you want the region within it.

You might be given the information as a wordy problem — work out what you're being asked for and draw it.

EXAMPLE: Tessa is organising a village fete. The fete will take place on a rectangular field, shown in the diagram below. Tessa is deciding where an ice cream van can go. It has to be at least 1 m away from each edge of the field, and closer to side AB than side CD. There is a maypole at M, and the ice cream van must be at least 2 m away from the maypole. The diagram is drawn to a scale of 1 cm = 1 m. Show on it where the ice cream van can go.

Start by drawing lines 1 cm away from each side (to represent 1 m) — use a ruler to measure along each edge. The ice cream van must go within these lines.

Draw a line equidistant from AB and CD (measure the length of side BC and divide it by two). The ice cream van has to go above this line.

Use compasses to draw a circle 2 cm away from M. The ice cream van has to go outside the circle.

The shaded area shows where the ice cream van can go.

Always leave your construction lines showing.
They show the examiner that you used the proper method.

Stay at least 3 m away from point C — or I'll release the hounds...

I can't stress this enough — make sure you draw your diagrams ACCURATELY (using a ruler and compasses) — like in this Exam Practice Question:

Q1 The gardens of a stately home are shown on the diagram. The public can visit the gardens, but must stay at least 2 m away from the rectangular pond and at least 2 m away from each of the statues (labelled A and B). Make a copy of this diagram using a scale of 1 cm = 2 m and indicate on it the areas where the public can go. [4 marks]

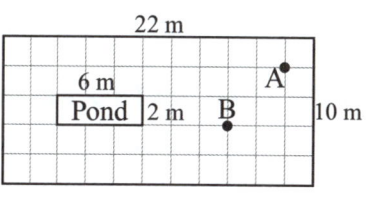

Section Six — Shapes and Area

M7 Translation, Rotation and Reflection

There are four <u>transformations</u> you need to know — the first three are <u>translation</u>, <u>rotation</u> and <u>reflection</u>.

Translations

In a <u>translation</u>, the <u>amount</u> the shape moves by is given as a <u>vector</u> written $\binom{x}{y}$ — where x is the <u>horizontal movement</u> (i.e. to the <u>right</u>) and y is the <u>vertical movement</u> (i.e. <u>up</u>). If the shape moves <u>left and down</u>, x and y will be <u>negative</u>. Shapes are <u>congruent</u> under translation, meaning the angles and side lengths are preserved (p.85).

In the exam, you might be asked to do more than one transformation on a shape. Don't panic — just do them one at a time.

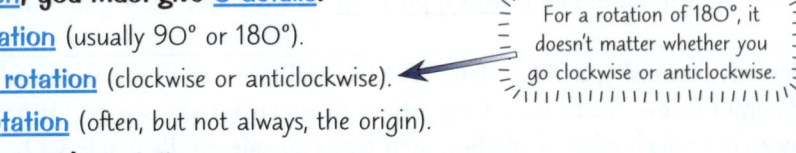

EXAMPLE:
a) Describe the transformation that maps triangle ABC onto A'B'C'.
b) Describe the transformation that maps triangle ABC onto A"B"C".

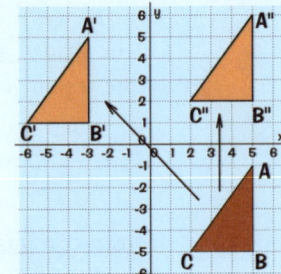

a) To get from A to A', you need to move <u>8 units left</u> and <u>6 units up</u>, so...
The transformation from ABC to A'B'C' is a translation by the vector $\binom{-8}{6}$.

b) The transformation from ABC to A"B"C" is a translation by the vector $\binom{0}{7}$.

Rotations

To describe a <u>rotation</u>, you must give <u>3 details</u>:
1) The <u>angle of rotation</u> (usually 90° or 180°).
2) The <u>direction of rotation</u> (clockwise or anticlockwise).
3) The <u>centre of rotation</u> (often, but not always, the origin).

Shapes are <u>congruent</u> under rotation.

For a rotation of 180°, it doesn't matter whether you go clockwise or anticlockwise.

EXAMPLE:
a) Describe the transformation that maps triangle ABC onto A'B'C'.
b) Describe the transformation that maps triangle ABC onto A"B"C".

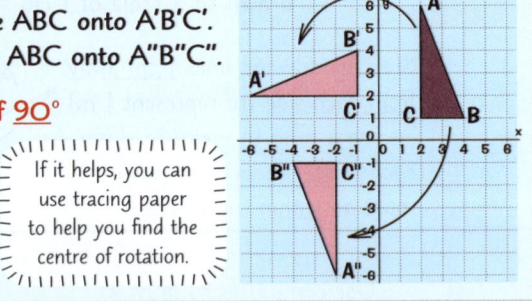

a) The transformation from ABC to A'B'C' is a rotation of <u>90°</u> anticlockwise about the <u>origin</u>.

b) The transformation from ABC to A"B"C" is a rotation of <u>180°</u> clockwise (or anticlockwise) about the <u>origin</u>.

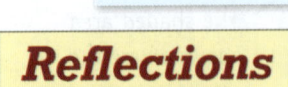

If it helps, you can use tracing paper to help you find the centre of rotation.

Reflections

For a <u>reflection</u>, you must give the <u>equation</u> of the <u>mirror line</u>. Shapes are <u>congruent</u> under reflection as well.

EXAMPLE:
a) Describe the transformation that maps shape A onto shape B.
b) Describe the transformation that maps shape A onto shape C.

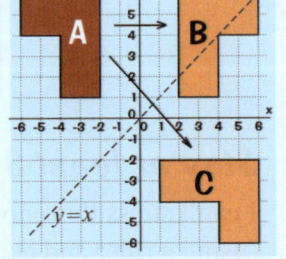

a) The transformation from A to B is a reflection in the y-axis (the line $x = 0$).
b) The transformation from A to C is a reflection in the line $y = x$.

Moving eet to ze left — a perfect translation...

The reason that shapes are <u>congruent</u> under translation, reflection and rotation is because their <u>size</u> and <u>shape</u> don't change, just their position and orientation. Now have a go at this question:

Q1 On a grid, copy shape A above and rotate it 90° clockwise about the point (−1, −1). [2 marks]

Section Six — Shapes and Area

Enlargement

One more transformation coming up — enlargements. They're the trickiest, but also the most fun (honest).

Enlargements M7

1) For an enlargement, you must specify:
   - The scale factor.
   - The centre of enlargement.

   $$\text{scale factor} = \frac{\text{new length}}{\text{old length}}$$

   Shapes are similar under enlargement — the position and the size change, but the angles and ratios of the sides don't (see p.85).

2) If a scale factor is bigger than 1, the shape gets bigger.
   If a scale factor is smaller than 1 (e.g. $\frac{1}{2}$), it gets smaller.

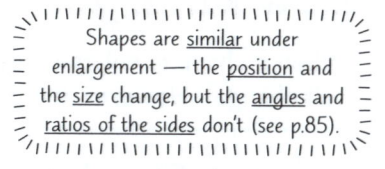

EXAMPLE: Describe the transformation that maps triangle B onto triangle A.

Use the formula above to find the scale factor (just choose one side):

$$\text{scale factor} = \frac{3}{6} = \frac{1}{2}$$

For the centre of enlargement, draw lines that go through corresponding vertices of both shapes and see where they cross.

So the transformation from B to A is an enlargement of scale factor $\frac{1}{2}$, centre (2, 6)

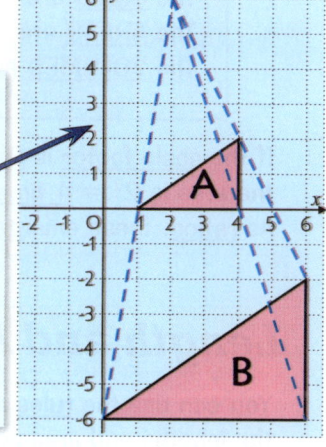

3) The scale factor also tells you the relative distance of old points and new points from the centre of enlargement — this is very useful for drawing an enlargement, because you can use it to trace out the positions of the new points.

EXAMPLE: Enlarge the shaded shape by a scale factor of $\frac{1}{2}$, about centre O.

1) Draw lines going from the centre to each corner of the original shape. The corners of the new shape will be on these lines.
2) The scale factor is $\frac{1}{2}$, so make each corner of the new shape half as far from O as it is in the original shape.

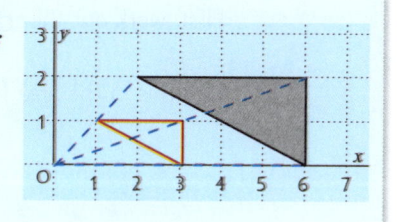

Negative Scale Factors M8

1) If the scale factor is negative then the shape pops out the other side of the enlargement centre.
2) If the scale factor is −1, it's exactly the same as a rotation of 180°.

EXAMPLE: Enlarge shape A below by a scale factor of −3, centre (1, 1). Label the transformed shape B.

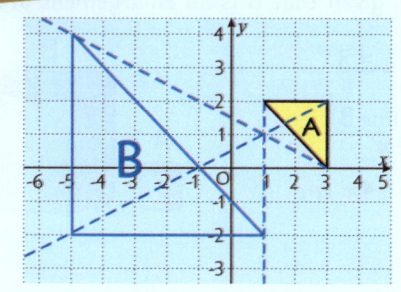

1) First, draw lines going through (1, 1) from each vertex of shape A.
2) Then, multiply the distance from each vertex to the centre of enlargement by 3, and measure this distance coming out the other side of the centre of enlargement. So on shape A, vertex (3, 2) is 2 right and 1 up from (1, 1) — so the corresponding point on shape B will be 6 left and 3 down from (1, 1). Do this for every point.
3) Join the points you've drawn to form shape B.

Scale factors — they're enough to put the fear of cod into you...

Here's some practice of doing more than one transformation in a single question. Jeez, I spoil you.

Q1 On a grid, draw triangle A with vertices (2, 1), (4, 1) and (4, 2). Enlarge it by a scale factor of 2 from centre of enlargement (3, 8), then reflect it in the line $y = 0$. [4 marks] M7

Section Six — Shapes and Area

Enlargement — Area and Volume

You've learnt the basics of enlargement. Now it's time to work in some whole new dimensions.

How Enlargement Affects Length, Area and Volume

When a shape is enlarged, its perimeter and area, or surface area and volume (if it's a 3D shape), will change. However, they don't all change by the same value as the scale factor:

> **For a SCALE FACTOR n:**
> The SIDES are n times bigger
> The AREAS are n^2 times bigger
> The VOLUMES are n^3 times bigger
>
> **And:**
> $n = \dfrac{\text{new length}}{\text{old length}}$ $n^2 = \dfrac{\text{new area}}{\text{old area}}$
>
> $n^3 = \dfrac{\text{new volume}}{\text{old volume}}$

If the scale factor is 2, the lengths are twice as long (meaning the perimeter will be twice as big), the area is $2^2 = 4$ times as big and the volume is $2^3 = 8$ times as big.
As ratios, these enlargements are 1 : 2 (length), 1 : 4 (area) and 1 : 8 (volume).

Length and Area for 2D Shapes

You can use the rules above to solve problems involving the lengths and areas of enlarged shapes.

Remember, if one shape is an enlargement of another, then the two shapes are similar.

EXAMPLE: Star A has sides of length 7.5 cm and star B has sides of length 30 cm. The area of star A is 120 cm². Find the area of star B, given that B is an enlargement of A.

First, work out the scale factor, n: $n = \dfrac{\text{Length B}}{\text{Length A}} = \dfrac{30}{7.5} = 4$

Use this in the area formula: $n^2 = \dfrac{\text{Area B}}{\text{Area A}} \Rightarrow 4^2 = \dfrac{\text{Area B}}{120}$

$\Rightarrow$ Area of B = 120 × 16 = **1920 cm²**

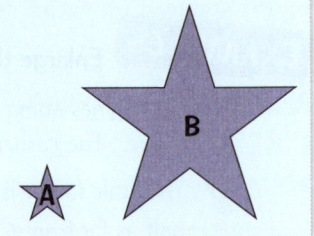

Surface Area and Volume for 3D Shapes

You can do the same with 3D shapes that have been enlarged, to work out the new volume.

EXAMPLE: Cylinder A has surface area 6π cm², and cylinder B has surface area 54π cm². The volume of cylinder A is 2π cm³. Find the volume of cylinder B, given that B is an enlargement of A.

First, work out the scale factor, n: $n^2 = \dfrac{\text{Area B}}{\text{Area A}} = \dfrac{54\pi}{6\pi} = 9$, so n = 3

Use this in the volume formula: $n^3 = \dfrac{\text{Volume B}}{\text{Volume A}} \Rightarrow 3^3 = \dfrac{\text{Volume B}}{2\pi}$

$\Rightarrow$ Volume of B = 2π × 27 = **54π cm³**

Twice as much learning, 4 times better results, 8 times more fun...

Make sure you don't get the scale factors mixed up — try them out on this Exam Practice Question.

Q1 There are 3 stacking dolls in a set. The dolls are mathematically similar and have heights of 5 cm, 10 cm and 15 cm. The surface area of the middle doll is 80 cm², and the volume of the largest doll is 216 cm³. Find the surface area and volume of the smallest doll.   *[4 marks]*

Section Six — Shapes and Area

Revision Questions for Section Six

There are lots of opportunities to show off your artistic skills here (as long as you use them to answer the questions).
- Try these questions and tick off each one when you get it right.
- When you've done all the questions for a topic and are completely happy with it, tick off the topic.

2D Shapes (p83-85)

1) For each of the letters shown, write down how many lines of symmetry they have and their order of rotational symmetry.   H Z T N E X S
2) Write down four properties of an isosceles triangle.
3) How many pairs of equal sides does a parallelogram have? What is its order of rotational symmetry?
4) What does it mean if two shapes are congruent?
5) State the three conditions that show that two triangles are similar.
6) The shapes on the right are similar. What is the length of side x?

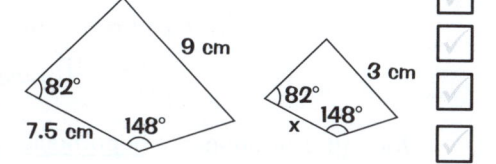

Area and Volume (p86-91)

7) What is the formula for finding the area of a parallelogram?
8) Find the area of the shape on the right. 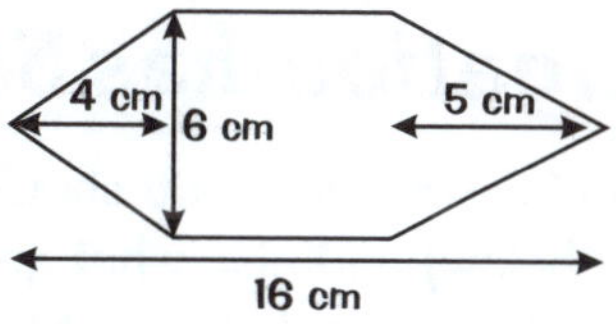
9) A square has an area of 56.25 cm². Find its perimeter.
10) A circle has diameter 16 cm. Find its exact circumference and area.
11) Find the area of the sector with radius 10 cm and angle 45° to 2 d.p.
12) On squared paper, draw the front elevation (from the direction of the arrow), side elevation and plan view of the shape on the right. 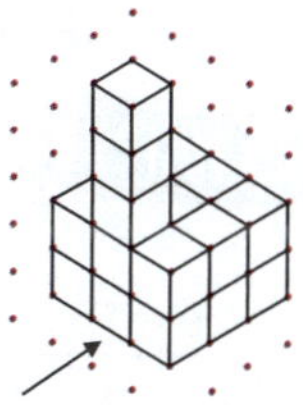
13) What is the formula for finding the surface area of a cylinder?
14) The shape on the right is made from a cylinder and a hemisphere. Find its exact surface area. 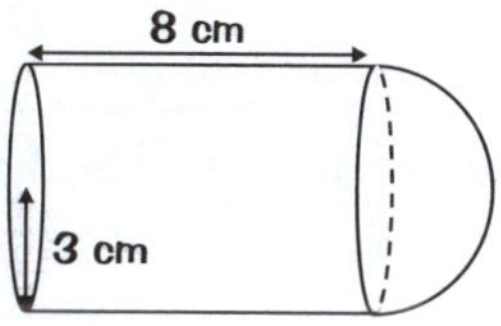
15) A pentagonal prism has a cross-sectional area of 24 cm² and a length of 15 cm. Find its volume.
16) Find the volume of the solid on the right (to 2 d.p.).

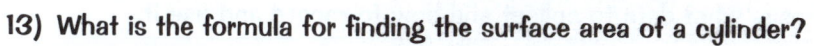

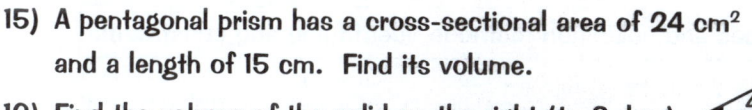

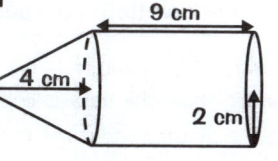

Constructions and Loci (p92-95)

17) Construct triangle XYZ, where XY = 5.6 cm, XZ = 7.2 cm and angle YXZ = 55°.
18) Construct an accurate 90° angle.
19) What shape does the locus of points that are a fixed distance from a given point make?
20) Draw a square with sides of length 6 cm and label it ABCD. Shade the region that is nearer to AB than CD and less than 4 cm from vertex A.

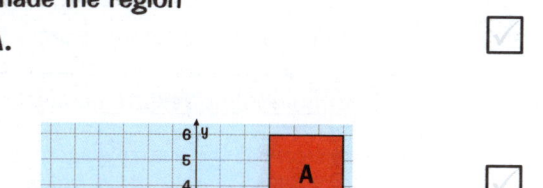

Transformations (p96-98)

21) Describe the transformation that maps:
    a) Shape A onto Shape B,   b) Shape A onto Shape C. 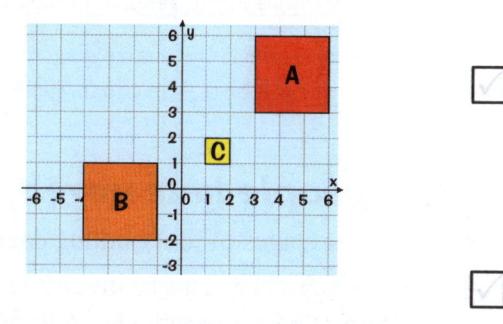
22) Carry out the following transformations on the triangle X, which has vertices (1, 1), (4, 1) and (2, 3):
    a) a rotation of 90° clockwise about (1, 1)
    b) a translation by the vector $\begin{pmatrix} -3 \\ -4 \end{pmatrix}$
    c) an enlargement of scale factor 2, centre (1, 1)
23) A shape with area 5 cm² is enlarged by a scale factor of 4. What is the area of the enlarged shape?

Section Six — Shapes and Area

Planning an Investigation

Statistics is all about <u>data</u> — you've got to <u>collect</u> it, <u>process</u> it and <u>interpret</u> it. But before you can get on with any of that, you need to know precisely what you're <u>investigating</u>. That's where a <u>hypothesis</u> comes in...

An *Investigation* Starts with a *Hypothesis*

> A HYPOTHESIS is a <u>statement</u> that might be <u>true</u> or <u>false</u>, but you haven't got enough <u>evidence</u> to support it either way yet. A hypothesis must be <u>testable</u>.

EXAMPLE: A tourist board wants to investigate whether more people go to a particular beach when the weather is warm. Suggest a suitable hypothesis for the tourist board to test.

You'd expect more people to go to the beach when it's warmer, so a <u>testable hypothesis</u> could be:
'<u>The higher the temperature, the more people go to the beach.</u>'

Once you've chosen a <u>hypothesis</u>, you should <u>plan</u> your investigation to <u>test</u> it. That means planning how you'll <u>collect</u> and <u>analyse</u> suitable <u>data</u>, and how you'll use it to draw <u>conclusions</u> about your hypothesis.

An *Investigation* has *Several Stages*

When <u>planning</u> an investigation, you should consider the <u>five stages</u> of the <u>handling data cycle</u> (see the example below) and plan what you'll do at each stage. In the exam you might be asked to give <u>examples</u> of things to include in a plan and to <u>explain</u> why they're <u>appropriate</u>.

EXAMPLE: A tourist board is planning to investigate the popularity of a particular beach. Their hypothesis is 'the higher the temperature, the more people go to the beach'. Give five examples of other details they should include in their plan, and say why each is appropriate.

1. <u>Planning</u> — choose your hypothesis, what data to collect and how to record and use it

E.g. Measure air temperature at the beach to the <u>nearest degree</u> and observe the number of people there every Saturday at the <u>same time of day</u> for a <u>year</u>, so that data is recorded for <u>all seasons</u> and is <u>consistent</u>.

2. <u>Collecting data</u> — choose data sources and collection methods, identifying any constraints

E.g. Collect your own data (<u>primary data</u>). This should be <u>reliable</u> because you can <u>control</u> how the data is collected (e.g. you can record the temperature at the same time each day).

Constraints are limitations due to availability and reliability of data, practicalities of methods, etc.

3. <u>Processing and presenting data</u> — choose diagrams and measures, considering use of technology

E.g. Put the data in a <u>spreadsheet</u>, so that a scatter diagram and calculations can be produced <u>easily</u> and <u>accurately</u>.

4. <u>Interpreting results</u> — plan analysis in order to draw conclusions and make predictions

E.g. Interpret a <u>scatter diagram</u> to see if there's a <u>relationship</u> between temperature and number of people.

5. <u>Communicating results clearly and evaluating methods</u> — being aware of the target audience

E.g. Describe what the scatter diagram shows to suit the <u>target audience</u> — this will be a <u>clear</u> visual representation of the results.

Evaluating could involve planning more analysis — e.g. looking at the summer months separately.

Most people hate novelty ringtones — a detestable hypothesis...

Knowing the stages of the handling data cycle is pretty important, so check you do with this question.

Q1 A researcher plans to investigate whether children can solve a logic puzzle faster than adults.
    a) Suggest a suitable hypothesis for the researcher to test. [1 mark]
    b) Using your hypothesis, explain three other details she could include in her plan. [3 marks]

Sampling and Data Collection

Sampling is about using what you know about smaller groups to tell you about bigger groups. Simple, or is it...

Use a *Sample* to *Find Out About* a *Population*

1) The whole group you want to find out about is called the POPULATION. It can be a group of anything — people, plants, penguins, you name it.

2) Often you can't survey the whole population, e.g. because it's too big. So you select a smaller group from the population, called a SAMPLE, instead.

3) It's really important that your sample fairly represents the WHOLE population. This allows you to apply any conclusions from your survey to the whole population. E.g. if you find that ¾ of the people in your sample like cheese, you can estimate that ¾ of the people in the whole population like cheese.

An effort to collect information about every member of a population is called a census.

For a sample to be representative, it needs to be:

> ❶ A RANDOM SAMPLE
> — which means every member of the population has an equal chance of being in it.
>
> ❷ BIG ENOUGH for the size of the population. The bigger the sample, the more reliable it should be.

Simple Random Sampling — Choosing a *Random* Sample

> TO SELECT a SIMPLE RANDOM SAMPLE...
> ❶ Assign a number to every member of the population.
> ❷ Create a list of random numbers.
> ❸ Match the random numbers to members of the population.

E.g. by using a computer, calculator or picking numbers out of a bag.

You Need to *Spot Problems* with *Sampling Methods*

A BIASED sample (or survey) is one that doesn't properly represent the whole population.

To SPOT BIAS, you need to think about:
1) WHEN, WHERE and HOW the sample is taken.
2) HOW MANY members are in it.

If certain groups are excluded, the SAMPLE ISN'T RANDOM. And that can lead to BIAS from things like age, gender, different interests, etc. If the sample is too small, it's also likely to be biased.

EXAMPLE: Samir's school has 800 pupils. Samir is interested in whether these pupils would like to have more music lessons. For his sample he selects 5 members of the school orchestra to ask. Explain why the opinions Samir collects from his sample might not represent the whole school.

The sample isn't random — only members of the orchestra are included, so it's likely to be biased in favour of more music lessons. Also, a sample of 5 is too small to represent the whole school.

When getting a sample — size matters...

Make sure you understand why samples should be representative and how to spot when they're not. Then you'll be ready to take on this Exam Practice Question.

Q1 Tina wants to find out how often people in Northern Ireland travel by train. She decides to ask 20 people waiting for trains at her local train station one morning. Comment on whether Tina can use the results of her survey to draw conclusions about the whole population. [2 marks]

Sampling and Data Collection

Stratified sampling can help to tackle bias within a sample. Read on to find out more...

Use Stratified Sampling for Different Groups

Sometimes the population can be split into groups (strata) where the members have something in common, e.g. age groups or gender. In these cases you can use STRATIFIED SAMPLING.

With this method, each group's share of the sample is calculated based on its share of the population — so bigger groups get more representation, and smaller groups get less.

To calculate the NUMBER of SAMPLE MEMBERS from EACH GROUP...
1. Find the proportion of the population contained in the group. → $\frac{\text{Number in group}}{\text{Total population}}$
2. Multiply by the sample size.

Once you've calculated the numbers, use simple random sampling within each group to create the sample.

EXAMPLE: The table on the right shows information about the students from Years 9-11 at Eastfield High School.

	Year 9	Year 10	Year 11
Boys	206	219	120
Girls	194	181	80

a) A sample of 50 students from Years 9-11 is taken, stratified by year group and gender. Calculate the number of Year 10 girls in the sample.

1) Find the proportion of students that are Year 10 girls: $\frac{181}{206 + 219 + 120 + 194 + 181 + 80} = \frac{181}{1000}$ or 0.181

2) Multiply by the sample size: $0.181 \times 50 = 9.05$

Round to the nearest whole number. → **There are 9 Year 10 girls.**

b) A second sample of 100 students from Years 9-11 is taken, stratified by year group. How many Year 11 students are in this sample?

1) Now you want the proportion of students in Year 11: $\frac{120 + 80}{1000} = \frac{2}{10}$ or 0.2

2) Multiply by the sample size: $0.2 \times 100 =$ **20 Year 11 students**

Use Sampling to Estimate Results for a Population

Once you've collected results from a sample, you can make assumptions about a whole population:

EXAMPLE: A researcher asked a randomly selected sample of 1000 Belfast residents whether they had visited the attraction Titanic Belfast. 587 said that they had. 340 000 people live in Belfast. Estimate how many of these people have visited Titanic Belfast.

Find the proportion of people in the sample that had visited Titanic Belfast. $\frac{587}{1000} = 0.587$

Then multiply by the size of the whole population. $0.587 \times 340\ 000 =$ **199 580**

There are limitations to estimating results for a whole population based on a sample — e.g. the sample could be biased or it may not be large enough to make reliable assumptions about the whole population.

Another very stratifying page...

Although stratified sampling helps to tackle bias, the process is more complicated than simple random sampling — dividing the population into groups and then sampling each group takes more time. Sigh.

Q1 A company has 10 senior managers, 22 middle managers and 68 shop-floor workers. A sample of 10 employees is to be taken, stratified by job title. How many middle managers should be in the sample? [2 marks]

Section Seven — Statistics and Probability

Sampling and Data Collection

Data you collect yourself is called primary data. If you use data that someone else has collected, e.g. you get it from a website, it's called secondary data. You need to record primary data in a way that's easy to analyse and suitable for the type of data you've got.

There are Different Types of Data

QUALITATIVE DATA is descriptive. It uses words, not numbers. E.g. pets' names — Smudge, Snowy, Dave, etc. Favourite flavours of ice cream — 'vanilla', 'caramel-marshmallow-ripple', etc.

QUANTITATIVE DATA measures quantities using numbers. E.g. heights of people, times taken to finish a race, numbers of goals scored in football matches, and so on.

There are two types of quantitative data.

DISCRETE DATA
1) It's discrete if the numbers can only take certain exact values.
2) E.g. the number of customers in a shop each day has to be a whole number — you can't have half a person.

CONTINUOUS DATA
1) If the numbers can take any value in a range, it's called continuous data.
2) E.g. heights and weights are continuous measurements.

You can Organise your Data into Classes

1) To record data in a table, you often need to group it into classes to make it more manageable. Discrete data classes should have 'gaps' between them, e.g. '0-1 goals', '2-3 goals' (jump from 1 to 2 because there are no values in between). Continuous data classes should have no 'gaps', so are often written using inequalities (see p.110).
2) Whatever the data you have, make sure none of the classes overlap and that they cover all the possible values.

When you group data you lose some accuracy because you don't know the exact values any more.

EXAMPLE: Jonty asks each person in his class 100 general knowledge questions. They score a point for each question they get right.
Design a table Jonty could use to record his data.

Include columns for: the data values, 'Tally' to count the data and 'Frequency' to show the totals.

Use non-overlapping classes — with gaps because the data's discrete.

Include classes like '...or over', '...or less' or 'other' to cover all options in a sensible number of classes.

Score	Tally	Frequency
0-19		
20-39		
40-59		
60-79		
80 or over		

Questionnaires Should be Designed Carefully

Another way to record data is to ask people to fill in a questionnaire. Your questions should be:

Watch out for response boxes that could be interpreted in different ways, that overlap, or that don't allow for all possible answers.

1) Clear and easy to understand
2) Easy to answer
3) Fair — not leading or biased

Leading questions suggest an answer.

I won't tell you what type of data it is — I'm too discrete...

You need to know what type of data you've got so you can record and display it in a suitable way.

Q1 Yu Qi asks some students how many times they went to the cinema in the last year. Say whether this data is discrete or continuous and design a table to record it in. [2 marks]

Section Seven — Statistics and Probability

Venn Diagrams

Venn diagrams are a way of displaying sets of data in intersecting circles — they're very pretty.

Show Groups on Venn Diagrams

1) On a Venn diagram, data is shown divided into groups. Each group is represented by a circle.
2) The diagram can show either the actual data values in each group, or the number of values in each group.

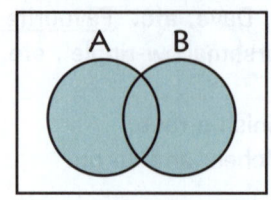

All the data values inside the circles are in either group A or group B.

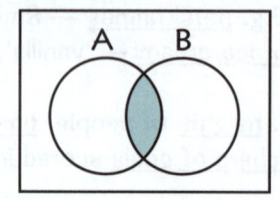

The intersection of the two circles contains all the data values in both group A and group B.

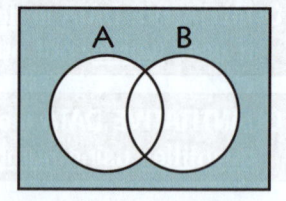

Data values that aren't in group A or group B go in the rectangle outside the circles.

EXAMPLE: In a class of 30 pupils, 8 of them like mustard, 24 of them like ketchup and 5 of them like both mustard and ketchup.

a) Complete the Venn diagram below showing this information.
Start by filling in the overlap.

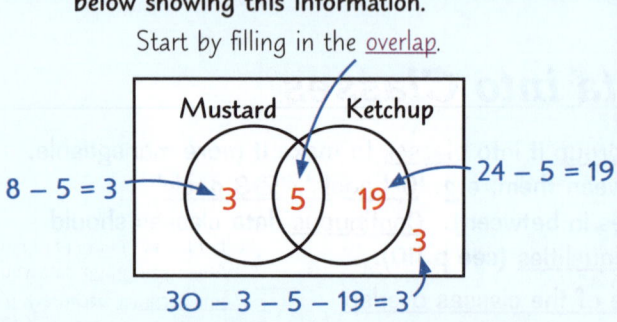

8 − 5 = 3
24 − 5 = 19
30 − 3 − 5 − 19 = 3

b) How many pupils like mustard or ketchup?
This is the number of pupils who like either just mustard, just ketchup, or both mustard and ketchup.   3 + 5 + 19 = 27

c) What fraction of the pupils like both mustard and ketchup?
5 out of 30 pupils are in the intersection. $\frac{5}{30} = \frac{1}{6}$

Venn Diagrams with Three Intersecting Circles

Venn diagrams can have three intersecting circles. The area where all three circles overlap represents the objects that are members of all three groups.

EXAMPLE: A group of 30 children in a nursery each painted a picture. They could use the colours blue, yellow and red. A Venn diagram has been started below. It is also known that 20 children used red, 10 used blue and 3 used only blue. Complete the Venn diagram.

1) 3 used only blue so 3 goes in the part of the blue circle that doesn't overlap with any others.
2) A total of 10 used blue so use this to finish the blue circle: 10 − 5 − 1 − 3 = 1
3) A total of 20 used red: 20 − 10 − 1 − 1 = 8
4) There are 30 children in total so use this to complete the diagram:
   30 − 10 − 1 − 1 − 8 − 5 − 3 = 2

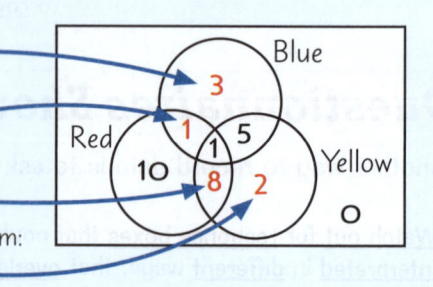

Circles keep falling on my head — it's raining Venn...

Nothing too complicated here — just make sure you check whether a question is asking about values that are in one group only, or whether you need to include the values in the intersection too.

Q1   Group J is the odd numbers, group K is the square numbers and group L is the prime numbers. Draw a Venn diagram showing the numbers 1 to 9 sorted into these groups.   *[3 marks]*

Section Seven — Statistics and Probability

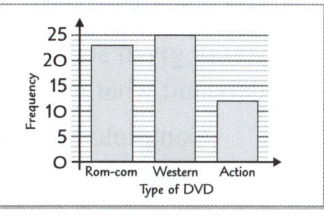

Other Charts and Graphs

Now for some more pretty maths — pie charts and flow charts. But before you dive in, take heed of this Golden Pie Chart Rule...

The TOTAL of Everything = 360°

Three More Rules for Pie Charts

1. Fraction of the total = Angle of slice ÷ 360°
2. Calculate angles using the multiplier that turns your total into 360°.
3. Calculate numbers by finding the angle for 1 thing.

EXAMPLES:

1. This pie chart shows the colour of all the cars sold by a dealer. What fraction of the cars were red?

   Fraction of red cars = $\frac{\text{angle of red cars}}{\text{angle of everything}} = \frac{72°}{360°} = \frac{1}{5}$

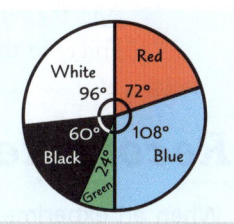

2. Draw a pie chart to show this information about the types of animal in a petting zoo.

Animal	Geese	Hamsters	Guinea pigs	Rabbits	Ducks
Number	12	20	17	15	26

   1) Find the total by adding.   12 + 20 + 17 + 15 + 26 = 90
   2) 'Everything = 360°' — so find the multiplier that turns your total into 360°.   Multiplier = 360 ÷ 90 = 4
   3) Multiply every number by 4 to get the angle for each sector.

Angle	12 × 4 = 48°	20 × 4 = 80°	17 × 4 = 68°	15 × 4 = 60°	26 × 4 = 104°

   4) Draw your pie chart accurately using a protractor.

3. The pie chart shows information about the type of animal liked most by 90 different students. Work out the number of students who liked dogs most.

   1) 'Everything = 360°', so...   →   90 students = 360°
   2) Divide by 90 to find...   →   1 student = 4°
   3) Divide the angle for dogs by the angle for 1 student to get: →   160° ÷ 4° = 40 — 40 students liked dogs most

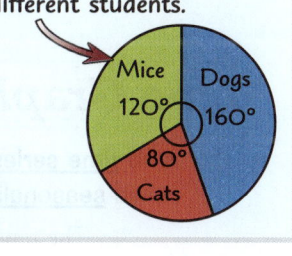

Flow Charts give you a Series of Instructions

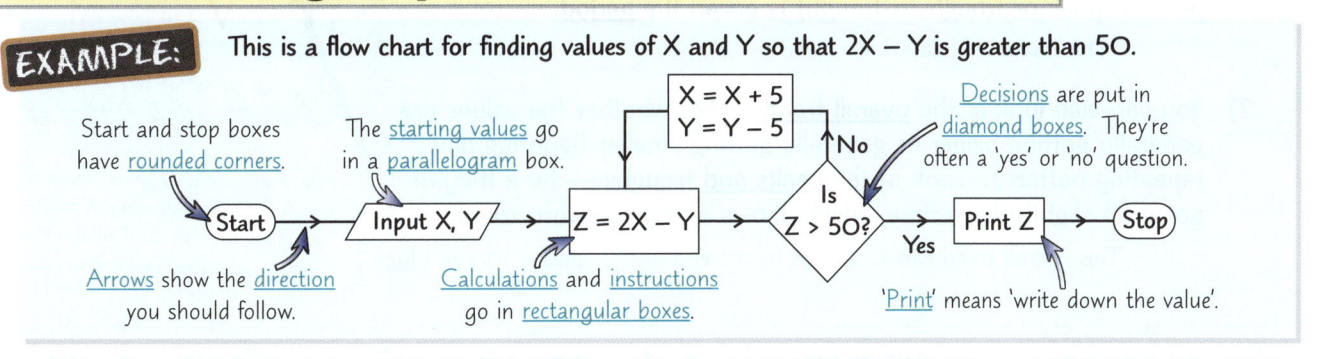

EXAMPLE: This is a flow chart for finding values of X and Y so that 2X − Y is greater than 50.

Start and stop boxes have rounded corners.
The starting values go in a parallelogram box.
Decisions are put in diamond boxes. They're often a 'yes' or 'no' question.
Arrows show the direction you should follow.
Calculations and instructions go in rectangular boxes.
'Print' means 'write down the value'.

Start → Input X, Y → Z = 2X − Y → Is Z > 50? →(No: X = X + 5, Y = Y − 5, loop back) Yes → Print Z → Stop

I like my pie charts with gravy and mushy peas...

Pie chart questions need a lot of practice. Make a start with this...

Q1 Draw an accurate pie chart to show the information about Rahul's DVD collection given in this bar chart.   [4 marks]

Section Seven — Statistics and Probability

Other Charts and Graphs

Here are <u>two-way tables</u>, <u>frequency trees</u> and <u>line graphs</u>. Make sure you can draw and/or interpret them.

Two-Way Tables Show How Many in each Category

EXAMPLE: This table shows the number of cakes and pies a bakery sold on Friday and Saturday.

a) How many pies were sold on Saturday?
Read across to 'Pies' and down to 'Saturday'.   **14 pies**

b) How many items were sold in total on Friday?
<u>Add</u> the number of <u>cakes</u> for
<u>Friday</u> to the number of <u>pies</u>.   12 + 10 = 22

	Cakes	Pies	Total
Friday	12	10	
Saturday	4	14	18
Total	16	24	40

Or you could <u>subtract</u> the <u>total</u> for Saturday from the overall total: 40 − 18 = 22.

Record Results in Frequency Trees

When an experiment has two or more steps, you can record the results using a <u>frequency tree</u>.

EXAMPLE: 120 GCSE maths students were asked if they would go on to do A-level maths.

- 45 of them said they would go on to do A-level maths.
- 30 of the students who said they would do A-level maths actually did.
- 9 of the students who said they wouldn't do A-level maths actually did.

Complete the frequency tree on the right.

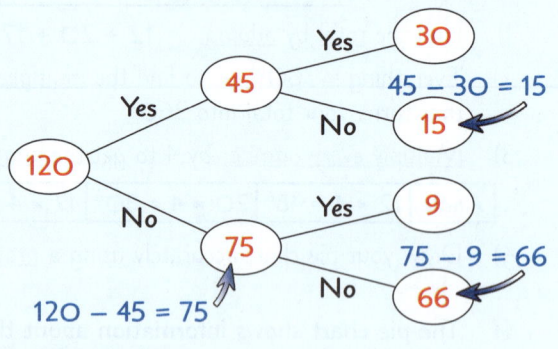

Will they take A-level maths?   Did they take A-level maths?

120 → Yes: 45 → Yes: 30, No: 15 (45 − 30 = 15)
120 → No: 75 (120 − 45 = 75) → Yes: 9, No: 66 (75 − 9 = 66)

Line Graphs can show Time Series

1) With <u>time series</u>, a basic pattern often repeats itself — this is called <u>seasonality</u> (though it doesn't have to match the seasons).

The time series plotted in <u>red</u> has a definite repeating pattern.

2) The time taken for the pattern to repeat itself (measured peak-to-peak or trough-to-trough) is called the <u>period</u>.

This pattern repeats itself <u>every four points</u>.

3) You can also look at the <u>overall trend</u> — i.e. whether the values are generally getting bigger or generally getting smaller (ignoring any repeating pattern). Look at the <u>peaks and troughs</u> — here they're going up slightly each time, which shows a slight upward trend.

This overall trend can be shown by a trend line — drawn here in <u>blue</u>.

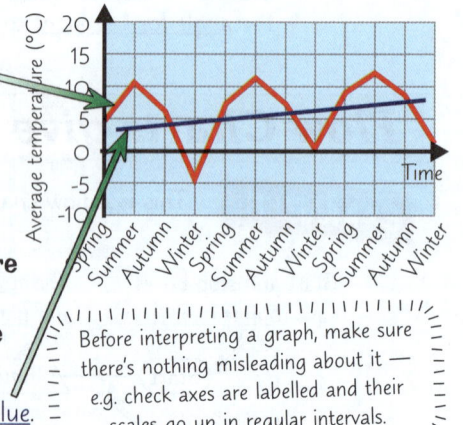

Before interpreting a graph, make sure there's nothing misleading about it — e.g. check axes are labelled and their scales go up in regular intervals.

I've seen a few programmes about herbs recently — a thyme series...

If you're given some sort of chart or graph in the exam, make sure you properly understand what it's showing before you dive in to answer the questions.

Q1 Complete the two-way table showing gender and test result.   [3 marks]

	Boy	Girl	Total
Pass	13		24
Fail		4	
Total	16		

Section Seven — Statistics and Probability

Scatter Graphs

A <u>scatter graph</u> tells you <u>how closely</u> two things are <u>related</u> — the fancy word is <u>CORRELATION</u>.

Scatter Graphs Show *Correlation*

1) If you can draw a <u>line of best fit</u> pretty close to <u>most</u> of your data points, the two things are <u>correlated</u>. If the points are <u>randomly scattered</u>, and you <u>can't draw</u> a line of best fit, then there's <u>no correlation</u>.

2) <u>Strong correlation</u> is when your points make a <u>fairly straight line</u> — this means the two things are <u>closely related</u> to each other. <u>Weak correlation</u> is when your points <u>don't line up</u> quite so nicely, but you can still draw a line of best fit through them.

3) If the points form a line sloping <u>uphill</u> from left to right, then there is <u>positive correlation</u> — both things increase or decrease <u>together</u>. If the line slopes <u>downhill</u> from left to right, then there is <u>negative correlation</u> — as one thing <u>increases</u> the other <u>decreases</u>.

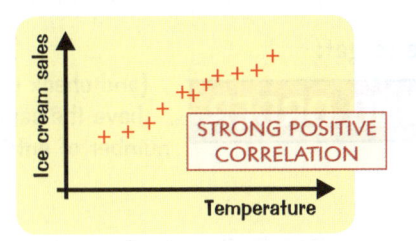

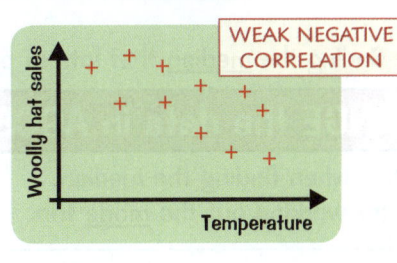

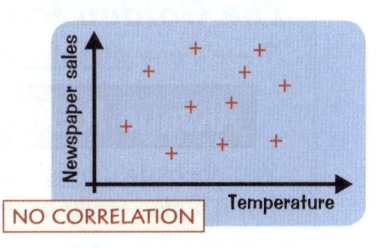

STRONG POSITIVE CORRELATION (Ice cream sales vs Temperature)

WEAK NEGATIVE CORRELATION (Woolly hat sales vs Temperature)

NO CORRELATION (Newspaper sales vs Temperature)

Use a *Line of Best Fit* to Make *Predictions*

1) You can use a <u>line of best fit</u> to make <u>estimates</u>. Predicting a value <u>within the range</u> of data you have should be <u>fairly reliable</u>, since you can see the <u>pattern</u> within this range. If you extend your line <u>outside</u> the range of data your prediction might be <u>unreliable</u>, since you're just <u>assuming the pattern continues</u>.

2) You also need to watch out for <u>outliers</u> — data points that <u>don't fit the general pattern</u>. These might be errors, but aren't necessarily. Outliers can <u>drag</u> your <u>line of best fit</u> away from the other values, so it's best to <u>ignore</u> them when you're drawing the line.

This graph shows the number of zoo visitors plotted against the outside temperature for several Sundays.

Draw a <u>line of best fit</u> to <u>estimate</u> the <u>number of visitors</u> when the temperature is <u>15 °C</u>. 2250 should be a <u>reliable</u> estimate.

Predicting <u>within</u> the range of data is called <u>interpolation</u>.

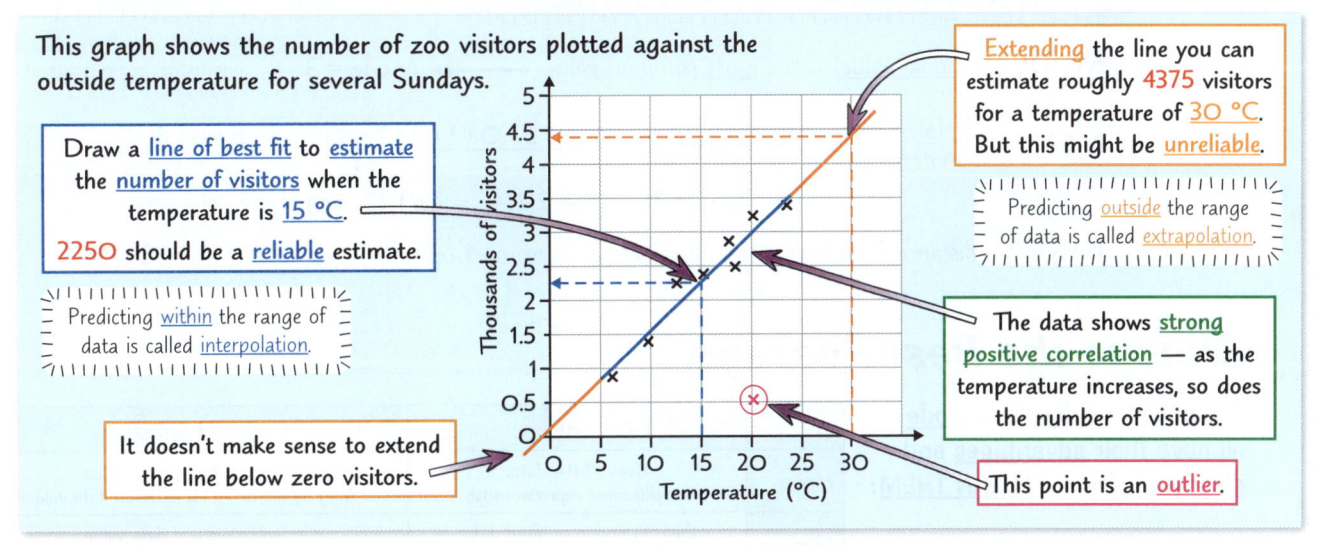

It doesn't make sense to extend the line below zero visitors.

<u>Extending</u> the line you can estimate roughly <u>4375</u> visitors for a temperature of <u>30 °C</u>. But this might be <u>unreliable</u>.

Predicting <u>outside</u> the range of data is called <u>extrapolation</u>.

The data shows <u>strong positive correlation</u> — as the temperature increases, so does the number of visitors.

This point is an <u>outlier</u>.

<u>BE CAREFUL</u> with <u>correlation</u> — if two things are correlated it <u>doesn't mean</u> that one causes the other. There could be a third factor affecting both, or it could just be a coincidence.

Relax and take a trip down Correlation Street...

Q1 This graph shows Sam's average speed on runs of different lengths.
   a) Describe the relationship between length of run and average speed. [1 mark]
   b) Circle the point that doesn't follow the trend. [1 mark]
   c) Estimate Sam's average speed for an 8-mile run. [1 mark]
   d) Comment on the reliability of your estimate in part c). [1 mark]

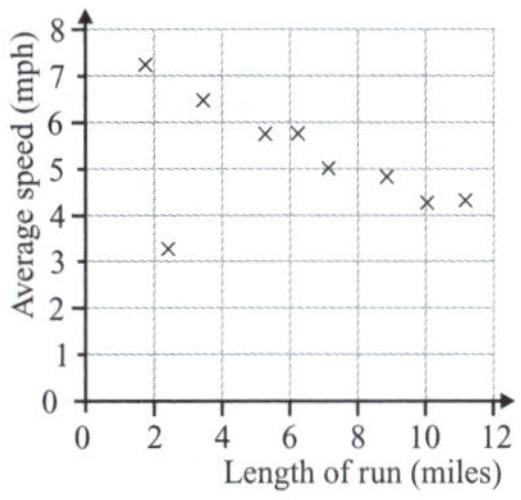

Section Seven — Statistics and Probability

Mean, Mode, Median and Range

Mean, median, mode and range pop up all the time in stats questions — make sure you know what they are.

The Four Definitions

MODE = MOST common
MEDIAN = MIDDLE value (when values are in order of size)
MEAN = TOTAL of items ÷ NUMBER of items
RANGE = Difference between highest and lowest

REMEMBER:
Mode = most (emphasise the 'mo' in each when you say them)
Median = mid (emphasise the m*d in each when you say them)
Mean is just the average, but it's mean 'cos you have to work it out.

The Golden Rule

There's one vital step for finding the median that lots of people forget:

Always REARRANGE the data in ASCENDING ORDER (and check you have the same number of entries!)

You absolutely must do this when finding the median, but it's also really useful for working out the mode too.

EXAMPLE: Find the median, mode, mean, and range of these numbers:
2, 5, 3, 2, 6, -4, 0, 9, -3, 1, 6, 3, -2, 3

The MEDIAN is the middle value (when they're arranged in order of size) — so first, rearrange the numbers.

-4, -3, -2, 0, 1, 2, (2, 3) 3, 3, 5, 6, 6, 9
← seven numbers this side   seven numbers this side →

Check that you still have the same number of entries after you've rearranged them.

When there are two middle numbers, the median is halfway between the two.

Median = 2.5

An even number of values means there will be two middle numbers.

MODE (or modal value) is the most common value. → Mode = 3

Some data sets have more than one mode, or no mode at all.

MEAN = total of items / number of items → $\frac{-4-3-2+0+1+2+2+3+3+3+5+6+6+9}{14}$

= 31 ÷ 14 = 2.214... = 2.21 (2 d.p.)

RANGE = distance from lowest to highest value, i.e. from -4 up to 9. → 9 − (−4) = 13

Choose the Best Average

The mean, median and mode all have their advantages and disadvantages — LEARN THEM:

	Advantages	Disadvantages
Mean	Uses all the data. Usually most representative.	Isn't always a data value. May be distorted by extreme data values.
Median	Easy to find in ordered data. Not distorted by extreme data values.	Isn't always a data value. Not always a good representation of the data.
Mode	Easy to find in tallied data. Always a data value (when it exists).	Doesn't always exist or sometimes more than one. Not always a good representation of the data.

The Alps — now there's a mean range...

Learn the four definitions and the extra step you have to do to find the median, then give this a go...

Q1 Find the mean, median, mode and range for these test scores: 6, 15, 12, 12, 11. [4 marks]

Q2 A set of 8 heights has a mean of 1.6 m. A new height of 1.5 m is added.
    Explain whether the mean of all 9 heights will be higher or lower than 1.6 m. [1 mark]

Section Seven — Statistics and Probability

Frequency Tables — Finding Averages

The word FREQUENCY means HOW MANY, so a frequency table is just a 'How many in each category' table. You saw how to find averages and range on p.108 — it's the same ideas here, but with the data in a table.

Find Averages from Frequency Tables

1) The MODE is just the CATEGORY with the MOST ENTRIES.
2) The RANGE is found from the extremes of the first column.
3) The MEDIAN is the CATEGORY containing the middle value.
4) To find the MEAN, you have to WORK OUT A THIRD COLUMN yourself.

The MEAN is then: **3rd Column Total ÷ 2nd Column Total**

Number of cats	Frequency
0	17
1	22
2	15
3	7

Categories / How many / Mysterious 3rd column...

EXAMPLE: Some people were asked how many sisters they have. The table opposite shows the results. Find the mode, the range, the mean and the median of the data.

Number of sisters	Frequency
0	7
1	15
2	12
3	8
4	4
5	0

1 The MODE is the category with the most entries — i.e. the one with the highest frequency:

The highest frequency is 15 for '1 sister', so MODE = 1

2 The RANGE is the difference between the highest and lowest numbers of sisters — that's 4 sisters (no one has 5 sisters) and no sisters, so:

RANGE = 4 − 0 = 4

3 To find the MEAN, add a 3rd column to the table showing 'number of sisters × frequency'. Add up these values to find the total number of sisters of all the people asked.

You can label the first column x and the frequency column f, then the third column is $f \times x$.

Number of sisters (x)	Frequency (f)	No. of sisters × Frequency ($f \times x$)
0	7	0
1	15	15
2	12	24
3	8	24
4	4	16
5	0	0
Total	46	79

MEAN = $\frac{\text{total number of sisters}}{\text{total number of people asked}} = \frac{79}{46} = 1.72$ (3 s.f.)

4 The MEDIAN is the category of the middle value. Work out its position, then count through the 2nd column to find it.

It helps to imagine the data set out in an ordered list:
0000000111111111111112222222222222333333334444
↑ median

The median is in position (n + 1) ÷ 2 = (46 + 1) ÷ 2 = 23.5 — halfway between the 23rd and 24th values. There are a total of (7 + 15) = 22 values in the first two categories, and another 12 in the third category takes you to 34. So the 23rd and 24th values must both be in the category '2 sisters', which means the MEDIAN is 2.

My table has 5 columns, 6 rows and 4 legs...

Learn the four key points about averages, then try this fella.

Q1 50 people were asked how many times a week they play sport. The table opposite shows the results.
  a) Find the median. [2 marks]
  b) Calculate the mean. [3 marks]

No. of times sport played	Frequency
0	8
1	15
2	17
3	6
4	4
5 or more	0

Section Seven — Statistics and Probability

Grouped Frequency Tables

Grouped frequency tables group together the data into classes. They look like ordinary frequency tables, but they're a slightly trickier kettle of fish...

See p.103 for grouped discrete data.

NO GAPS BETWEEN CLASSES
- Use inequality symbols to cover all possible values.
- Here, 10 would go in the 1st class, but 10.1 would go in the 2nd class.

Height (h millimetres)	Frequency
$5 < h \leq 10$	12
$10 < h \leq 15$	15

To find MID-INTERVAL VALUES:
- Add together the end values of the class and divide by 2.
- E.g. $\dfrac{5 + 10}{2} = 7.5$

Find Averages from Grouped Frequency Tables

Unlike with ordinary frequency tables, you don't know the actual data values, only the classes they're in. So you have to ESTIMATE THE MEAN, rather than calculate it exactly. Again, you do this by adding columns:

1) Add a 3RD COLUMN and enter the MID-INTERVAL VALUE for each class.
2) Add a 4TH COLUMN to show 'FREQUENCY × MID-INTERVAL VALUE' for each class.

You'll be asked to find the MODAL CLASS and the CLASS CONTAINING THE MEDIAN, not exact values.

EXAMPLE: This table shows information about the weights, in kilograms, of 60 school children.

a) Write down the modal class.
b) Write down the class containing the median.
c) Calculate an estimate for the mean weight.

Weight (w kg)	Frequency
$30 < w \leq 40$	8
$40 < w \leq 50$	16
$50 < w \leq 60$	18
$60 < w \leq 70$	12
$70 < w \leq 80$	6

a) The modal class is the one with the highest frequency.
Modal class is $50 < w \leq 60$

b) Work out the position of the median, then count through the 2nd column.
The median is in position $(n + 1) \div 2 = (60 + 1) \div 2 = 30.5$, halfway between the 30th and 31st values. Both these values are in the third class, so the class containing the median is $50 < w \leq 60$.

c) Add extra columns for 'mid-interval value' and 'frequency × mid-interval value'. Add up the values in the 4th column to estimate the total weight of the 60 children.

Weight (w kg)	Frequency (f)	Mid-interval value (x)	fx
$30 < w \leq 40$	8	35	280
$40 < w \leq 50$	16	45	720
$50 < w \leq 60$	18	55	990
$60 < w \leq 70$	12	65	780
$70 < w \leq 80$	6	75	450
Total	60	—	3220

Don't add up the mid-interval values.

Mean ≈ $\dfrac{\text{total weight}}{\text{number of children}}$ ← 4th column total / ← 2nd column total

$= \dfrac{3220}{60} = 53.7$ kg (3 s.f.)

Mid-interval value — cheap ice creams...

Q1 a) Estimate the mean of the data below. Give your answer to 3 significant figures. [4 marks]

Length (l cm)	$15.5 \leq l < 16.5$	$16.5 \leq l < 17.5$	$17.5 \leq l < 18.5$	$18.5 \leq l < 19.5$
Frequency	12	18	23	8

b) Ana says that 20% of the lengths are below 16.5 cm. Comment on her statement. [2 marks]

Section Seven — Statistics and Probability

Averages and Spread

Measures of <u>spread</u> tell you <u>how spread out</u> data is. The <u>range</u> (see page 108) is a measure of spread over all the data values. The <u>interquartile range</u> tells you the <u>spread</u> of the <u>middle 50%</u> of values.

Quartiles Divide the Data into Four Equal Groups

1) The quartiles are the <u>lower quartile Q_1</u>, the <u>median Q_2</u> and the <u>upper quartile Q_3</u>.

2) If you put the data in <u>ascending order</u>, the quartiles are <u>25%</u> (¼), <u>50%</u> (½) and <u>75%</u> (¾) of the way through the list. So if a data set has n values, you work out the <u>positions</u> of the quartiles using these <u>formulas</u>:

Q_1 position number $= (n + 1)/4$
Q_2 position number $= 2(n + 1)/4$
Q_3 position number $= 3(n + 1)/4$

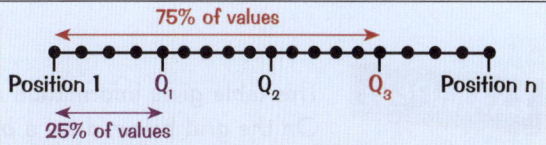

3) The <u>INTERQUARTILE RANGE</u> (IQR) is the <u>difference</u> between the <u>upper quartile</u> and the <u>lower quartile</u> and contains the <u>middle 50%</u> of values.

EXAMPLE: Here are the ages, in months, of a number of fine cheeses: 7, 12, 5, 4, 3, 9, 5, 11, 6, 5, 7
Find the interquartile range of the ages.

1) Put the data in <u>order of size</u>. → 3, 4, 5, 5, 5, 6, 7, 7, 9, 11, 12 ← <u>Check</u> you've got the <u>right</u> <u>number</u> of values — 11 ✓

2) Find Q_1 — n = 11, so Q_1 is in position $(11 + 1)/4 = 3$. So $Q_1 = \underline{5}$.

3) Find Q_3 — Q_3 is in position $3(11 + 1)/4 = 9$. So $Q_3 = \underline{9}$.

4) <u>Subtract</u> Q_1 from Q_3 — IQR $= Q_3 - Q_1 = 9 - 5 = $ **4 months**

Careful — the <u>formulas</u> tell you the <u>position</u> of the quartile, not its value.

Read Off Measures from Stem and Leaf Diagrams

An <u>ordered stem and leaf diagram</u> can be used to show a set of data in <u>order of size</u>. And that makes it easy to read off values like the <u>median</u> and <u>quartiles</u>.

EXAMPLE: Here are the scores for 15 dogs in an agility test: 26, 16, 29, 7, 12, 32, 29, 24, 13, 17, 20, 23, 24, 31, 34

a) Draw an ordered stem and leaf diagram to show the data.

1) First, put the data <u>in order</u>. → 7, 12, 13, 16, 17, 20, 23, 24, 24, 26, 29, 29, 31, 32, 34

2) <u>Group</u> the data into rows — you can group these values by '<u>number of tens</u>'.

3) Remember to include a <u>key</u>.

```
0 | 7
1 | 2 3 6 7
2 | 0 3 4 4 6 9 9
3 | 1 2 4
```

Key: 2|3 = 23

Write the <u>first digit</u> (<u>number of tens</u>) here... ...write the <u>second digit</u> for each value (<u>number of units</u>) here.

b) Find the median score and range of scores.

1) Find the <u>position</u> of the <u>middle</u> value and read off from the diagram.

Median is in position $2(n + 1)/4 = 2(15 + 1)/4 = 8$
So median score = **24**

2) The <u>range</u> is just the <u>highest minus the lowest</u>.

Range = $34 - 7 = $ **27**

Chocolate-peanut-banana butter — not your average spread...

Learn how to find quartiles and to draw and read stem and leaf diagrams. Then do this Practice Question.

Q1 a) Draw an ordered stem and leaf diagram to show: 3.0, 1.6, 1.4, 2.2, 0.7, 1.1, 2.6 [3 marks]

b) Use your diagram to find the interquartile range of the data. [3 marks]

Section Seven — Statistics and Probability

Averages and Spread

The humble box plot might not look very fancy, but it tells you lots about the spread of data.

Box Plots show the Interquartile Range as a Box

1) Box plots give a good summary of the spread of a data set — they show a few key measures, rather than all the individual data values.
2) Make sure you can draw and interpret them.

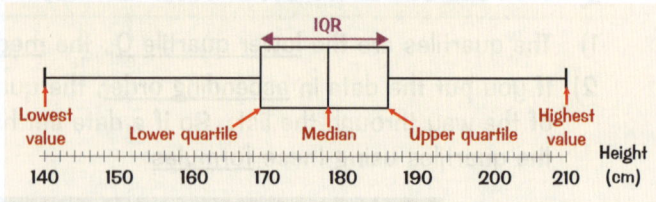

EXAMPLE: This table gives information about the numbers of rainy days last year in some cities. On the grid below, draw a box plot to show the information.

Minimum number	90
Maximum number	195
Lower quartile	130
Median	150
Upper quartile	175

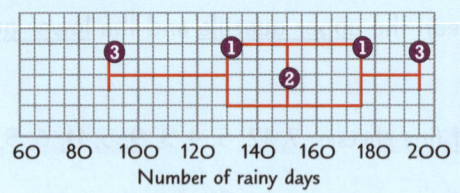

1. Mark on the quartiles and draw the box.
2. Draw a line at the median.
3. Mark on the minimum and maximum points and join them to the box with horizontal lines.

Compare Data using Averages and Spread

To compare two sets of data, you should look at:

1) **AVERAGES** — MEAN, MEDIAN or MODE

   Say which data set has the higher/lower value and what that means in the context of the data.

   You could also compare other key values like quartiles or min/max values.

2) **SPREAD** — RANGE or INTERQUARTILE RANGE

   Say which data set has the larger/smaller value. A larger spread means the values are less consistent or there is more variation in the data.

   If the data contains extreme values, it's better to use the IQR than the range.

EXAMPLE: An animal park is holding a 'guess the weight of the baby hippo' competition. These box plots show information about the weights guessed by a group of school children.

Compare the weights guessed by the boys and the girls.

1) Compare averages by looking at the median values.
   The median for the boys is higher than the median for the girls. So the boys generally guessed heavier weights.

2) Compare the spreads by working out the range and IQR for each data set:
   Boys' range = 58 − 16 = 42 and IQR = 50 − 32 = 18.
   Girls' range = 52 − 12 = 40 and IQR = 44 − 30 = 14.
   Both the range and the IQR are smaller for the girls' guesses, so there is less variation in the weights guessed by the girls.

With my cunning plot, I'll soon control all the world's boxes...

Mwahaha... Make sure you get what's going on in the examples, then do this Exam Practice Question.

Q1 Draw a box plot to represent this data: 5, 7, 12, 14, 10, 17, 22, 17, 9, 18, 12 [3 marks]

Section Seven — Statistics and Probability

Cumulative Frequency

Cumulative frequency just means adding it up as you go along — i.e. the total frequency so far.
You need to be able to draw a cumulative frequency graph and make estimates from it.

EXAMPLE: The table below shows information about the heights of a group of people.
a) Draw a cumulative frequency graph for the data.
b) Use your graph to estimate the median and interquartile range of the heights.

Height (h cm)	Frequency	Cumulative Frequency
140 < h ≤ 150	4	4
150 < h ≤ 160	9	4 + 9 = 13
160 < h ≤ 170	20	13 + 20 = 33
170 < h ≤ 180	33	33 + 33 = 66
180 < h ≤ 190	36	66 + 36 = 102
190 < h ≤ 200	15	102 + 15 = 117
200 < h ≤ 210	3	117 + 3 = 120

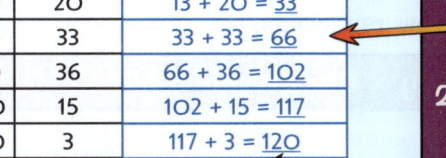

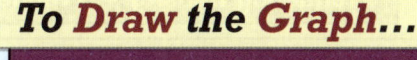

To Draw the Graph...

1) Add a 'CUMULATIVE FREQUENCY' COLUMN to the table — and fill it in with the RUNNING TOTAL of the frequency column.
2) PLOT points using the HIGHEST VALUE in each class and the CUMULATIVE FREQUENCY. (150, 4), (160, 13), etc.
3) Join the points with a smooth curve.

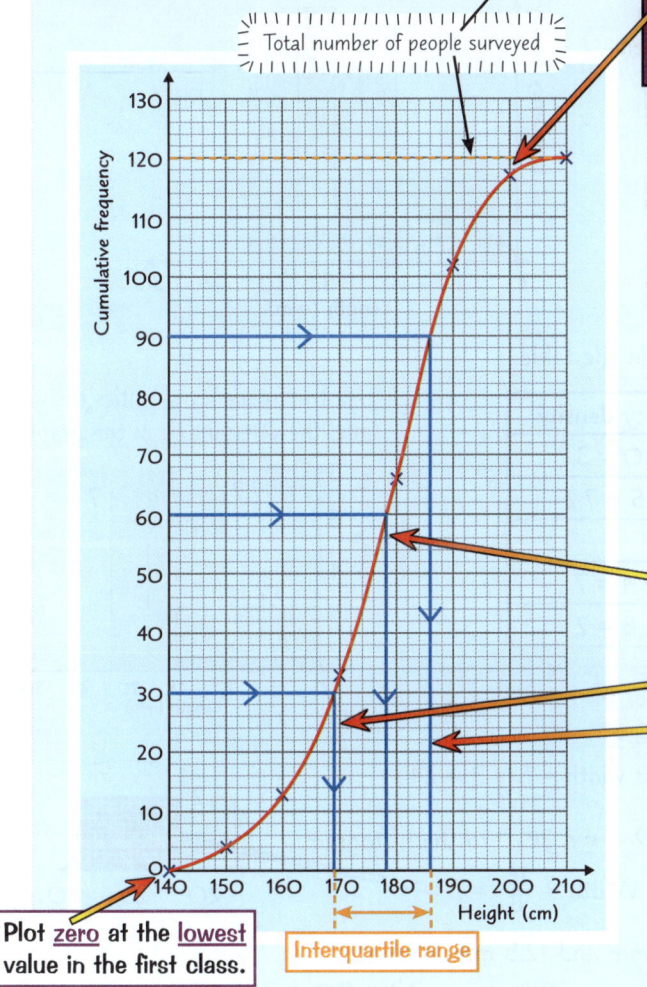

Total number of people surveyed

Plot zero at the lowest value in the first class.

Interquartile range

To Find the Vital Statistics...

1) MEDIAN — go halfway up the side, across to the curve, then down and read off the bottom scale.
2) LOWER AND UPPER QUARTILES — go ¼ and ¾ up the side, across to the curve, then down and read off the bottom scale.
3) INTERQUARTILE RANGE — the distance between the lower and upper quartiles.

1) The halfway point is at ½ × 120 = 60. Reading across and down gives a **median of 178 cm**.
2) ¼ of the way up is at ¼ × 120 = 30. Reading across and down gives a lower quartile of 169 cm.
   ¾ of the way up is at ¾ × 120 = 90. Reading across and down gives an upper quartile of 186 cm.
3) The **interquartile range = 186 − 169 = 17 cm**.

More Estimating...

To use the graph to estimate the number of values that are less than or greater than a given value:
Go along the bottom scale to the given value, up to the curve, then across to the cumulative frequency.
(See the question below for an example.)

The values you read from the graph are estimates because they're based on grouped data — you don't know how the actual data values are spread within each class.

How do you make a total run...

Time to try another lovely Exam Practice Question.

Q1 a) Draw a cumulative frequency graph for this data. [3 marks]
b) Use your diagram to estimate the percentage of fish that are longer than 50 mm. [2 marks]

Length of fish (l mm)	Frequency
0 < l ≤ 20	4
20 < l ≤ 40	11
40 < l ≤ 60	20
60 < l ≤ 80	15
80 < l ≤ 100	6

Section Seven — Statistics and Probability

M4 Histograms and Frequency Density

A histogram is just a bar chart where the bars can be of different widths. This changes them from nice, easy-to-understand diagrams into seemingly incomprehensible monsters, but they're not that bad really...

Histograms Show Frequency Density

1) The vertical axis on a histogram is always called frequency density. You work it out using this formula:

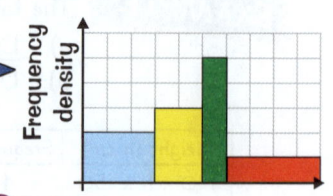

> **Frequency Density = Frequency ÷ Class Width**

Remember... 'frequency' is just another way of saying 'how much' or 'how many'.

2) You can rearrange it to work out how much a bar represents.

> **Frequency = Frequency Density × Class Width = AREA of bar**

EXAMPLE:
This table and histogram show the lengths of beetles found in a garden.

Length (mm)	Frequency
$0 < x \leq 10$	32
$10 < x \leq 15$	36
$15 < x \leq 18$	
$18 < x \leq 22$	28
$22 < x \leq 30$	16

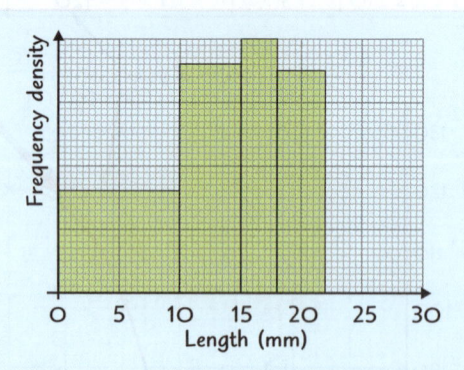

a) Use the histogram to find the missing entry in the table.

1) Add a frequency density column to the table and fill in what you can using the formula.

Frequency density
32 ÷ 10 = 3.2
36 ÷ 5 = 7.2
28 ÷ 4 = 7
16 ÷ 8 = 2

2) Use the frequency densities to label the vertical axis of the graph.

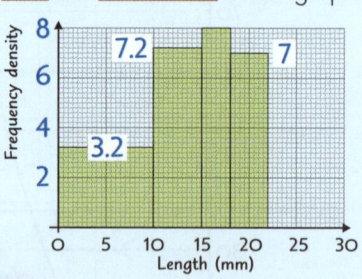

3) Now use the 3rd bar to find the frequency for the class "$15 < x \leq 18$".
Frequency density = 8 and class width = 3.
So frequency = frequency density × class width = 8 × 3 = **24**

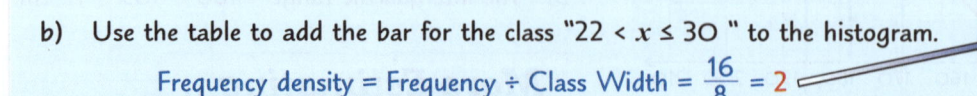

b) Use the table to add the bar for the class "$22 < x \leq 30$" to the histogram.

Frequency density = Frequency ÷ Class Width = $\frac{16}{8}$ = 2

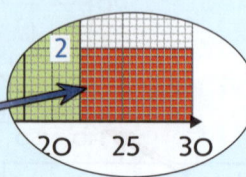

c) Estimate the number of beetles between 7.5 mm and 12.5 mm in length.
Use the formula frequency = frequency density × class width — multiply the frequency density of the class by the width of the part of that class you're interested in.

3.2 × (10 − 7.5) + 7.2 × (12.5 − 10)
= 3.2 × 2.5 + 7.2 × 2.5
= **26**

Histograms — horrid foul creatures they are...

Here's a question to make sure you've mastered the methods above...

Q1 a) This table shows information about the lengths of slugs in a garden. Draw a histogram to represent the information. **[4 marks]**

b) Estimate the number of slugs that are shorter than 70 mm. **[3 marks]**

Length (mm)	Frequency
$0 < x \leq 40$	20
$40 < x \leq 60$	45
$60 < x \leq 65$	15
$65 < x \leq 100$	70

Section Seven — Statistics and Probability

Histograms and Frequency Density

Compare Data Sets using Histograms

EXAMPLE: This histogram shows information about the times taken by a large group of children to solve a puzzle.

a) Estimate the mean time taken to solve the puzzle.

Draw a table and fill in what the graph tells you.

Time (seconds)	Frequency Density	Frequency (f)	x	fx
0 < t ≤ 20	0.25	0.25 × 20 = 5	10	50
20 < t ≤ 30	0.8	0.8 × 10 = 8	25	200
30 < t ≤ 40	1.5	1.5 × 10 = 15	35	525
40 < t ≤ 50	0.9	0.9 × 10 = 9	45	405
50 < t ≤ 80	0.1	0.1 × 30 = 3	65	195
Total	—	40	—	1375

Find the frequency in each class using:
Frequency = Frequency Density × Class Width

Add a column for the mid-interval values.

Add up the 'Frequency × mid-interval value' column to estimate the total time taken.

Number of children

Mean = $\frac{\text{total time taken}}{\text{number of children}}$ = $\frac{1375}{40}$ = 34.4 seconds (1 d.p.)

This is just like estimating the mean from a grouped frequency table (see p.110). Now you've found the frequencies, you could also find the class containing the median.

b) Write down the modal class.

Modal class is **30 < t ≤ 40** ← The modal class has the highest frequency density. It's frequency density, not frequency, because the class widths vary.

c) Estimate the range of times taken.

Highest class boundary − lowest class boundary = 80 − 0 = **80 seconds**

d) A large group of adults solve the same puzzle with a mean time of 27 seconds. Is there any evidence to support the hypothesis that children take longer to solve the puzzle than adults?

Yes, there is evidence to support this hypothesis because the mean time for the children is longer.

Large samples mean the results should represent the population.

EXAMPLE: A company makes chocolate bars and decides to change the wrappers they use.

The histograms show information on the daily sales of the chocolate bar, before and after changing the wrapper. The company claims that changing the wrapper has increased daily sales.

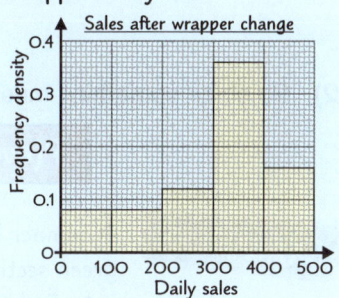

a) Is there evidence that daily sales have increased since the wrapper change?

Yes, there is evidence that daily sales have increased because there are more days with high sales values since the wrapper change than before.

Look at the shapes of the histograms — after the change, more data is on the right-hand-side (showing more days with high sales).

b) Comment on the company's claim that changing the wrapper has increased daily sales.

Changing the wrapper might have caused the increase in sales, but sales could also have been affected by other factors, e.g. pricing, advertising, economic conditions, etc.

How do you weigh a graph — in histograms...

In the exam you might have to criticise how a graph has been drawn.

Q1 Give three criticisms of the histogram opposite. [3 marks]

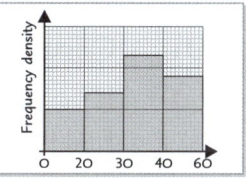

Section Seven — Statistics and Probability

Probability Basics

A lot of people reckon probability is pretty tough. But learn the basics well, and it'll all make sense.

All Probabilities are Between 0 and 1

1) Probabilities are always between 0 and 1. The higher the probability of something, the more likely it is.
2) A probability of ZERO means it will NEVER HAPPEN and a probability of ONE means it DEFINITELY WILL.

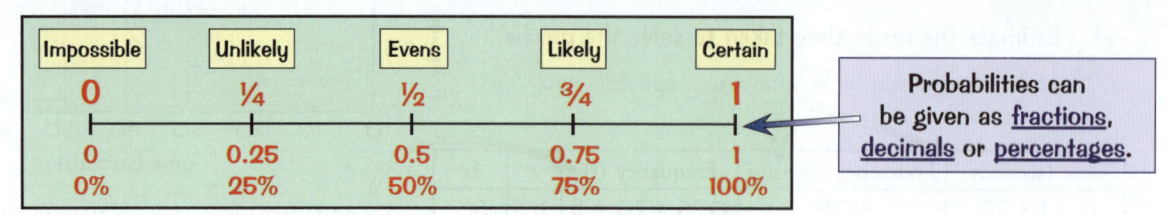

Impossible	Unlikely	Evens	Likely	Certain
0	¼	½	¾	1
0	0.25	0.5	0.75	1
0%	25%	50%	75%	100%

Probabilities can be given as fractions, decimals or percentages.

You Can Find Some Probabilities Using a Formula

Careful... this formula only works if all the possible outcomes (things that could happen) are equally likely.

$$\text{Probability} = \frac{\text{Number of ways for something to happen}}{\text{Total number of possible outcomes}}$$

Words like 'fair' and 'at random' show possible outcomes are all equally likely. 'Biased' and 'unfair' mean the opposite.

EXAMPLE: Work out the probability of randomly picking a letter 'P' from the tiles below.

APPLE PIE

1) There are 3 P's — so there are 3 different ways to 'pick a letter P'.
2) And there are 8 tiles altogether — each of these is a possible outcome.

$$\text{Probability} = \frac{\text{number of ways to pick a P}}{\text{total number of possible outcomes}} = \frac{3}{8} \text{ (or 0.375)}$$

Probabilities Add Up To 1

1) If only one possible result can happen at a time, then the probabilities of all the results add up to 1.

Probabilities always ADD UP to 1

2) So since something must either happen or not happen (i.e. only one of these can happen at a time):

P(event happens) + P(event doesn't happen) = 1

EXAMPLE: A spinner has different numbers of red, blue and green sections. Work out the value of x and use it to find the probability of spinning red or blue.

Colour	red	blue	green
Probability	$3x$	$2x$	$5x$

1) The probabilities add up to 1. $3x + 2x + 5x = 1$ so $10x = 1$ and so $x = 0.1$
2) Spinning red or blue is the same as not spinning green.
P(red or blue) = 1 − P(green)
= 1 − (5 × 0.1) = 0.5

'P(result)' just means the probability of that result.

The probability of this getting you marks in the exam = 1...

You need to know the facts in the boxes above. You also need to know how to use them.

Q1 Calculate the probability of the fair spinner on the right landing on 4. [2 marks]

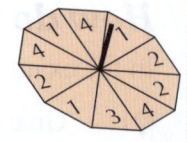

Q2 If the probability of spinning red on a spinner is $1 − 3x$, find the probability of spinning any colour except red. [1 mark]

Section Seven — Statistics and Probability

Counting Outcomes

With a lot of probability questions, a good place to start is with a list of all the possible outcomes. Once you've got a list of outcomes, the rest of the question should be straightforward.

Listing All Outcomes

A sample space diagram shows all the possible outcomes. It can be a simple list, but a two-way table works well if there are two activities going on (e.g. two coins being tossed, or a dice being thrown and a spinner being spun).

EXAMPLE: The spinners on the right are spun, and the scores added together.

a) Make a sample space diagram showing all the possible outcomes.

1) All the scores from one spinner go along the top. All the scores from the other spinner go down the side.
2) Add the two scores together to get the different possible totals (the outcomes).

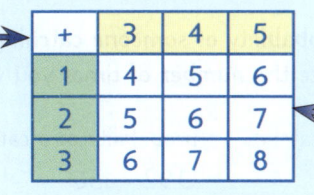

+	3	4	5
1	4	5	6
2	5	6	7
3	6	7	8

There are 9 outcomes here — even though some of the actual totals are repeated.

b) Find the probability of spinning a total of 6.

There are 9 possible outcomes altogether, and 3 ways to score 6.

$$P(\text{total} = 6) = \frac{\text{number of ways to score 6}}{\text{total number of possible outcomes}} = \frac{3}{9} = \frac{1}{3}$$

Use the Product Rule to Count Outcomes

1) Sometimes it'll be difficult to list all the outcomes (e.g. if the number of outcomes is large or if there are more than two activities going on).
2) Luckily, you can count outcomes using the product rule.

> The number of ways to carry out a combination of activities equals the number of ways to carry out each activity multiplied together.

EXAMPLE: Jason rolls four fair six-sided dice.

a) How many different ways are there to roll the four dice?
Each dice has 6 different ways that it can land (on 1, 2, 3, 4, 5 or 6).
Total number of ways of rolling four dice = 6 × 6 × 6 × 6 = **1296**

b) How many different ways are there to only get even numbers when rolling the four dice?
Each dice has 3 different ways that it can land on an even number (on 2, 4, or 6).
Number of ways of only rolling even numbers = 3 × 3 × 3 × 3 = **81**

c) What is the probability of only getting even numbers when rolling four dice?

$$P(\text{only even numbers}) = \frac{\text{number of ways to only get even numbers}}{\text{total number of ways to roll the dice}} = \frac{81}{1296} = \frac{1}{16}$$

Sample space diagrams — they're out of this world...

When you can draw a sample space diagram, probability questions are easy. If you have to use the product rule things get a bit trickier. Not to worry, have a go at these questions to see if you've got it...

Q1 Three fair coins are tossed: a) List all the possible outcomes. [1 mark]
b) Find the probability of getting exactly 2 heads. [1 mark]

Q2 Jay wants to buy a new car. The one he chooses can be automatic or manual, and comes with a choice of six colours and three different interiors. How many options does Jay have? [1 mark]

Section Seven — Statistics and Probability

Expected Frequency

You can use probabilities to work out how often you'd **expect** something to happen.

Use Probability to Find an "Expected Frequency"

1) Once you know the **probability** of something, you can **predict** how many times it will happen in a certain number of trials.

   A 'trial' could be any activity — e.g. rolling a dice.

2) For example, you can predict the number of sixes you could expect if you rolled a fair dice 20 times. This prediction is called the **expected frequency**.

> **Expected frequency = probability × number of trials**

EXAMPLE: The probability of someone catching a frisbee thrown to them is 0.92. Estimate the number of times you would expect them to catch a frisbee in 150 attempts.

Expected number of catches = probability of a catch × number of trials
= 0.92 × 150
= 138

This is an estimate. They might not catch the frisbee exactly 138 times, but the number of catches shouldn't be too different from this.

You Might Have to Find a Probability First

EXAMPLES:

1. A person spins the fair spinner on the right 200 times. How many times would you expect it to land on 5?

   1) First calculate the probability of the spinner landing on 5.

   $$P(\text{lands on 5}) = \frac{\text{ways to land on 5}}{\text{number of possible outcomes}} = \frac{1}{8}$$

   2) Then estimate the number of 5's they'll get in 200 spins.

   Expected number of 5's = P(lands on 5) × number of trials
   $$= \frac{1}{8} \times 200 = 25$$

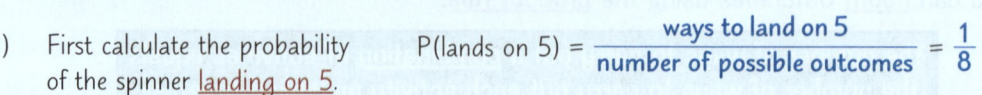

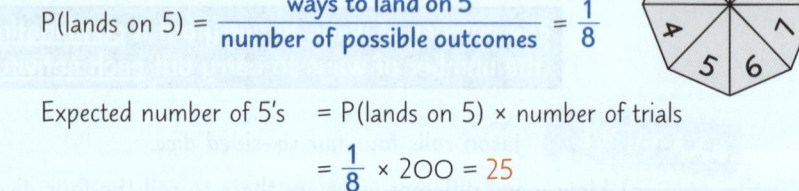

2. I buy 400 large tins of chocolates. Each tin contains 100 chocolates altogether, and 80 of these are milk chocolate. If I select one chocolate at random from each tin, how many milk chocolates would I expect to get?

   1) First calculate the probability of picking a milk chocolate from one tin.

   $$P(\text{milk chocolate from 1 tin}) = \frac{\text{number of ways to get a milk chocolate}}{\text{total number of chocolates in each tin}}$$
   $$= \frac{80}{100} = \frac{4}{5}$$

   2) Then estimate the number of milk chocolates if I pick one chocolate from each of the 400 tins.

   Expected milk chocolates = P(milk chocolate from 1 tin) × number of tins
   $$= \frac{4}{5} \times 400 = 320$$

I predict this page could earn you 3 marks in your exam...

This is why statistics is so cool — you can use it to predict the future.

Q1 A game involves throwing a fair standard dice once. The player wins if they score either a 5 or a 6. If one person plays the game 180 times, estimate the number of times they will win. *[3 marks]*

Section Seven — Statistics and Probability

Probability Experiments

The formula on page 116 only works when the outcomes are equally likely. If they're not equally likely, you can use the results from experiments to estimate the probability of each outcome.

Do the Experiment Again and Again...

You need to do an experiment over and over again and count how many times each outcome happens (its frequency). Then you can calculate the relative frequency using this formula:

$$\text{Relative frequency} = \frac{\text{Frequency}}{\text{Number of times you tried the experiment}}$$

An experiment could just mean rolling a dice.

You can use the relative frequency of a result as an estimate of its probability.

EXAMPLE: The spinner on the right was spun 100 times and the results recorded. Estimate the probability of getting each of the scores.

Score	1	2	3	4	5	6
Frequency	3	14	41	20	18	4

Divide each of the frequencies by 100 to find the relative frequencies.

Score	1	2	3	4	5	6
Relative Frequency	$\frac{3}{100}$ = 0.03	$\frac{14}{100}$ = 0.14	$\frac{41}{100}$ = 0.41	$\frac{20}{100}$ = 0.2	$\frac{18}{100}$ = 0.18	$\frac{4}{100}$ = 0.04

The MORE TIMES you do the experiment, the MORE ACCURATE your estimate of the probability should be.

E.g. if you spun the above spinner 1000 times, you'd get a better estimate of the probability for each score.

Fair or Biased?

'Fair' means all the outcomes are equally likely. If something is unfair, it's called biased.

1) If the dice/spinner/coin/etc. is fair, then the relative frequencies of the results should roughly match the probabilities you'd get using the formula on p.116.
2) If the relative frequencies are far away from those probabilities, you can say it's probably biased.

EXAMPLE: Do the above results suggest that the spinner is biased?
Yes, because the relative frequency of 3 is much higher than you'd expect, while the relative frequencies of 1 and 6 are much lower.

For a fair 6-sided spinner, you'd expect all the relative frequencies to be about 1 ÷ 6 = 0.17(ish).

This topic is tough — make sure to revise it relatively frequently...

Remember that relative frequency can only be used to estimate the probability of a result. You can increase the accuracy of your estimate by increasing the number of times you do the experiment.

Q1 This table shows how many times Jenny and Sandro got a free biscuit on their visits to a coffee shop.

	Jenny	Sandro
Visits to coffee shop	20	150
Got a free biscuit	13	117

a) All customers have the same chance of getting a free biscuit. Based on Jenny's results, estimate this probability. [2 marks]

b) Whose results will give a better estimate of the probability? Explain your answer. [1 mark]

Section Seven — Statistics and Probability

The AND / OR Rules

This page will show you how to find probabilities when <u>more than one</u> thing is happening at a time.

Combined Probability — Two or More Events

1) Always start by working out what different <u>SINGLE EVENTS</u> you're interested in.
2) Find the probability of <u>EACH</u> of these <u>SINGLE EVENTS</u>.
3) Apply the <u>AND/OR</u> rule.

And now for the rules. Say you have <u>two events</u> — call them A and B...

The AND Rule

The probability of event A <u>AND</u> event B happening is equal to the probability of event A <u>MULTIPLIED BY</u> the probability of event B.

This only works when the two events are <u>independent</u> — one event happening <u>does not affect</u> the chances of the other happening.

EXAMPLE: Dhruv picks one ball at random from each of bags X and Y. Find the probability that he picks a yellow ball from both bags.

1) The <u>single events</u> you're interested in are 'picks a yellow ball from bag X' and 'picks a yellow ball from bag Y'.
2) Find the <u>probabilities</u> of the events.
   P(Dhruv picks a yellow ball from bag X) = $\frac{4}{10}$ = 0.4
   P(Dhruv picks a yellow ball from bag Y) = $\frac{2}{8}$ = 0.25
3) Use the <u>AND rule</u>. P(Dhruv picks a yellow ball from bag X <u>AND</u> bag Y) = 0.4 × 0.25 = **0.1**

The OR Rule

The probability of <u>EITHER</u> event A <u>OR</u> event B happening is equal to the probability of event A <u>ADDED TO</u> the probability of event B.

This rule only works when the two events are <u>mutually exclusive</u> — they <u>can't both happen</u> at the same time.

EXAMPLE: A spinner with red, blue, green and yellow sections is spun — the probability of it landing on each colour is shown in the table. Find the probability of spinning either red or green.

Colour	red	blue	yellow	green
Probability	0.25	0.3	0.35	0.1

1) The <u>single events</u> you're interested in are 'lands on red' and 'lands on green'.
2) Write down the <u>probabilities</u> of the events.
   P(lands on red) = 0.25
   P(lands on green) = 0.1
3) Use the <u>OR rule</u>. P(Lands on <u>either</u> red <u>OR</u> green) = 0.25 + 0.1 = **0.35**

Learn AND remember this — OR you're in trouble...

The way to remember this is that it's the wrong way round — you'd want AND to go with '+' but it doesn't. It's 'AND with ×' and 'OR with +'. Once you've got that, try this Exam Practice Question.

Q1 Shaun is a car salesman. The probability that he sells a car on a Monday is 0.8. The probability that he sells a car on a Tuesday is 0.9.
What is the probability that he sells a car on both Monday and Tuesday? [2 marks]

Q2 a) What is the probability of spinning blue OR yellow on the spinner above? [2 marks]
b) What is the probability of spinning blue THEN green? [2 marks]

Section Seven — Statistics and Probability

Tree Diagrams

Tree diagrams can really help you work out probabilities when you have a <u>combination of events</u>.

Remember These *Four Key Tree Diagram Facts*

1) On any set of branches which meet at a point, the probabilities must <u>add up to 1</u>.

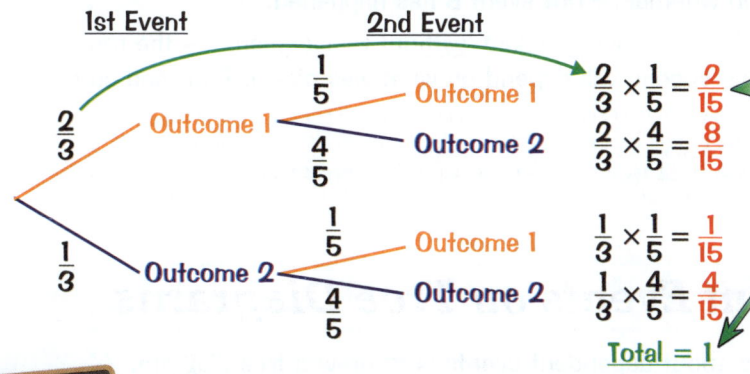

1st Event → Outcome 1 ($\frac{2}{3}$), Outcome 2 ($\frac{1}{3}$)

2nd Event from Outcome 1: Outcome 1 ($\frac{1}{5}$), Outcome 2 ($\frac{4}{5}$)
2nd Event from Outcome 2: Outcome 1 ($\frac{1}{5}$), Outcome 2 ($\frac{4}{5}$)

$\frac{2}{3} \times \frac{1}{5} = \frac{2}{15}$
$\frac{2}{3} \times \frac{4}{5} = \frac{8}{15}$
$\frac{1}{3} \times \frac{1}{5} = \frac{1}{15}$
$\frac{1}{3} \times \frac{4}{5} = \frac{4}{15}$

Total = 1

2) <u>Multiply along</u> the branches to get the <u>end probabilities</u>.

3) Check your diagram — the end probabilities must <u>add up to 1</u>.

4) To answer any question, <u>add up</u> the relevant end probabilities (see below).

EXAMPLE:

A box contains 5 red discs and 3 green discs. One disc is taken at random and its colour noted before <u>being replaced</u>. A second disc is then taken. Find the probability that both discs are the same colour.

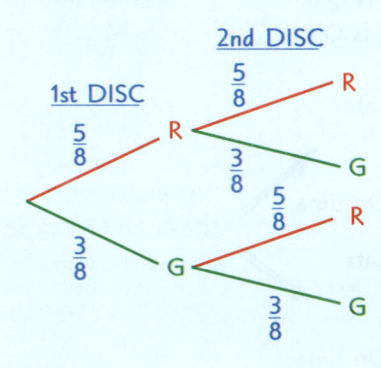

1st DISC: R ($\frac{5}{8}$), G ($\frac{3}{8}$)
2nd DISC from R: R ($\frac{5}{8}$), G ($\frac{3}{8}$)
2nd DISC from G: R ($\frac{5}{8}$), G ($\frac{3}{8}$)

The probabilities for the 1st and 2nd discs are <u>the same</u>. This is because the 1st disc is <u>replaced</u> — so the events are <u>independent</u>.

P(both discs are red) = P(R <u>and</u> R) = $\frac{5}{8} \times \frac{5}{8} = \frac{25}{64}$

P(both discs are green) = P(G <u>and</u> G) = $\frac{3}{8} \times \frac{3}{8} = \frac{9}{64}$

P(both discs are same colour) = P(R and R <u>or</u> G and G)
$= \frac{25}{64} + \frac{9}{64} = \frac{34}{64} = \frac{17}{32}$

Look Out for 'At Least' Questions

When a question asks for '<u>at least</u>' a certain number of things happening, it's usually easier to work out (<u>1 − probability of 'less than that number of things happening'</u>).

EXAMPLE:

I roll 3 fair six-sided dice. Find the probability that I roll at least 1 six.

1) Rewrite this as <u>1 minus</u> a probability.

P(at least 1 six) = 1 − P(less than 1 six)
= 1 − P(no sixes)

2) Work out <u>P(no sixes)</u>. You can use a tree diagram — don't draw the whole thing, just the part you need.

$\frac{5}{6}$ not a six → $\frac{5}{6}$ not a six → $\frac{5}{6}$ not a six

P(no sixes) = $\frac{5}{6} \times \frac{5}{6} \times \frac{5}{6} = \frac{125}{216}$

So P(at least 1 six) = $1 - \frac{125}{216} = \frac{91}{216}$

Please don't make a bad tree-based joke. Oak-ay, just this once...

How convenient — answers growing on trees. Learn the routine, and then have a go at this...

Q1   A bag contains 6 red balls and 4 black ones. If two balls are picked at random (with replacement), find the probability that they're different colours.   [3 marks]

Section Seven — Statistics and Probability

Tree Diagrams

Sometimes you have to deal with probabilities for <u>dependent events</u> — where one event affects another.

Probabilities for Dependent Events

1) If event A is <u>dependent</u> on event B, then the <u>probability</u> of event A happening will <u>change</u> based on whether or not event B has happened.
2) Keep an eye out in questions for items being picked '<u>without replacement</u>' — the probability of a particular item being picked second will depend on what was picked first, and so on.

As you saw on the previous page, if events A and B are <u>independent</u> then the probability of event A happening stays <u>fixed</u>, regardless of whether event B has happened or not.

Showing Dependent Events on Tree Diagrams

A good way to deal with questions about dependent events is to draw a tree diagram. The probabilities on a set of branches will <u>change depending</u> on the <u>previous event</u>.

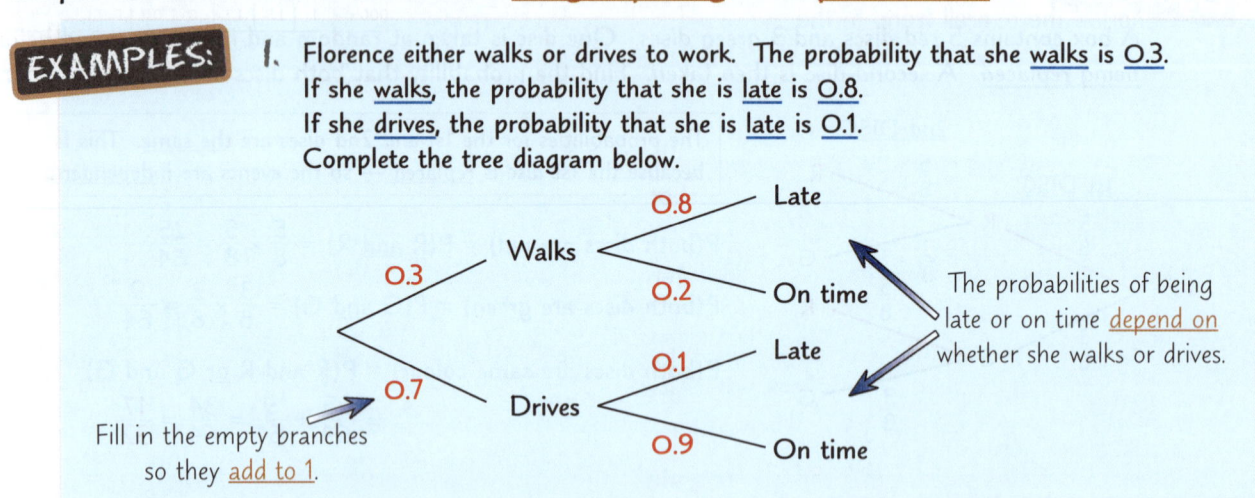

EXAMPLES:

1. Florence either walks or drives to work. The probability that she <u>walks</u> is <u>0.3</u>. If she <u>walks</u>, the probability that she is <u>late</u> is <u>0.8</u>. If she <u>drives</u>, the probability that she is <u>late</u> is <u>0.1</u>. Complete the tree diagram below.

   Fill in the empty branches so they <u>add to 1</u>.

   The probabilities of being late or on time <u>depend on</u> whether she walks or drives.

2. A box contains 5 red discs and 3 green discs. Two discs are taken at random <u>without replacement</u>. Find the probability that both discs are the same colour.

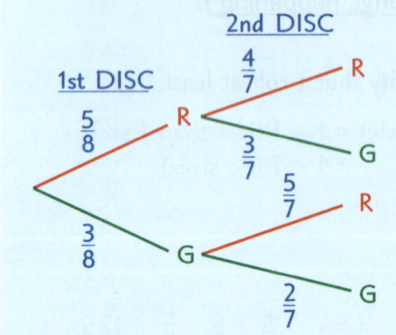

   This example was done 'with replacement' on p.121.

   The probabilities for the 2nd pick <u>depend on</u> the colour of the 1st disc picked. This is because the 1st disc is <u>not replaced</u>.

   P(both discs are red) = P(R <u>and</u> R) = $\frac{5}{8} \times \frac{4}{7} = \frac{20}{56}$

   P(both discs are green) = P(G <u>and</u> G) = $\frac{3}{8} \times \frac{2}{7} = \frac{6}{56}$

   P(both discs are same colour) = P(R and R <u>or</u> G and G)
   = $\frac{20}{56} + \frac{6}{56} = \frac{26}{56} = \frac{13}{28}$

Find the probability of laughing given that you're reading this...

With probability questions that seem quite hard, drawing a tree diagram is usually a good place to start. Try it with the (quite hard) Exam Practice Question below...

Q1 There are 21 numbers, 1-21, in a lottery draw. A machine selects the numbers randomly. Find the probability that out of the first two numbers selected:
   a) at least one is even, [3 marks]
   b) one is odd and one is even. [3 marks]

Section Seven — Statistics and Probability

Revision Questions for Section Seven

Here's the inevitable list of straight-down-the-middle questions to test how much you know.
- Try these questions and tick off each one when you get it right.
- When you've done all the questions for a topic and are completely happy with it, tick off the topic.

Sampling and Collecting Data (p100-103)

1) What is a sample and why does it need to be representative?
2) This table shows information about some students. If a stratified sample of 50 students is taken, how many boys should be in the sample?

Boys	Girls
80	120

3) Is 'eye colour' qualitative or quantitative data?

Venn Diagrams and Other Charts and Graphs (p104-107)

4) 100 people were asked whether they like tea or coffee. Half the people said they like coffee, 34 people said they like tea, 20 people said they like both.
   a) Show this information on a Venn diagram. b) What fraction of the 100 people like tea or coffee?
5) What two things could a rectangular box contain in a flow diagram?
6) a) Draw a line graph to show the time series data in this table.
   b) Describe the overall trend in the data.

Quarter	1	2	3	4	1	2	3	4
Sales (1000's)	1	1.5	1.7	3	0.7	0.9	1.2	2.2

7) Sketch graphs to show: a) weak positive correlation, b) strong negative correlation, c) no correlation.

Averages, Frequency Tables and Histograms (p108-115)

8) For this grouped frequency table showing the lengths of some pet alligators:
   a) find the modal class, b) find the class containing the median,
   c) estimate the mean.

Length (y, in m)	Frequency
$1.4 \leq y < 1.5$	4
$1.5 \leq y < 1.6$	8
$1.6 \leq y < 1.7$	5
$1.7 \leq y < 1.8$	2

9) Find the upper and lower quartiles and the interquartile range of this data:
   2, 8, 11, 15, 22, 24, 27, 30, 31, 31, 41
10) These box plots show information about how long it took someone to get to work in summer and winter one year. Compare the travel times in the two seasons.
11) Draw a cumulative frequency graph for the data in the grouped frequency table in Q8 above.
12) How do you work out what frequency a bar on a histogram represents?
13) An 800 m runner had a mean time of 147 seconds, before she increased her training hours. The histogram shows information about the times she runs after increasing her training hours. Is there any evidence that her running times have improved?

Probability (p116-122)

14) I pick a random number between 1 and 50. Find the probability that my number is a multiple of 6.
15) Describe how to use the product rule to count possible outcomes.
16) I flip a fair coin 4 times. a) Using H for heads and T for tails, list all the possible outcomes.
    b) What is the probability of getting exactly one head?
17) What are the formulas for: a) expected frequency? b) relative frequency?
18) 160 people took a 2-part test. 105 people passed the first part and of these, 60 people passed the second part. 25 people didn't pass either test.
    a) Show this information on a frequency tree. b) Find the relative frequency of each outcome.
    c) If 400 more people do the test, estimate how many of them would pass both parts.
19) I spin a fair nine-sided spinner, numbered 1-9, twice. Find P(spinning a 6 then an even number).
20) I have a standard pack of 52 playing cards. Use tree diagrams to find the probability of me:
    a) picking two cards at random and getting two kings if the first card is replaced.
    b) picking three cards at random and getting three kings if no cards are replaced.

Section Seven — Statistics and Probability

Answers

Get the full versions of these answers online
Step-by-step worked solutions to these questions, with a full mark scheme, are included as a printable PDF with your free Online Edition — you'll find more info about how to get hold of this at the front of this book.

Section One — Number

Page 2 — Types of Number and BODMAS
Q1 55

Page 3 — Multiples, Factors and Prime Factors
Q1 a) $2 \times 3^2 \times 5 \times 11$ b) $2^5 \times 5$

Page 4 — LCM and HCF
Q1 a) 36   b) 56
Q2 a) 12   b) 30

Page 6 — Fractions
Q1 a) $\frac{17}{32}$ b) $\frac{2}{3}$
    c) $6\frac{5}{27}$ d) $-3\frac{7}{12}$
Q2 6

Page 7 — Fractions, Decimals and Percentages
Q1 a) $\frac{4}{10} = \frac{2}{5}$ b) $\frac{2}{100} = \frac{1}{50}$
    c) $\frac{77}{100}$ d) $\frac{555}{1000} = \frac{111}{200}$
    e) $\frac{56}{10} = \frac{28}{5}$
Q2 a) 57%   b) $\frac{6}{25}$ c) 90%
Q3 85%

Page 8 — Fractions and Recurring Decimals
Q1 $6 \overline{)1.1^10^40^40^40^40}$ 0.16666
$1 \div 6 = 0.1666...$ so $\frac{1}{6} = 0.1\dot{6}$

Page 9 — Fractions and Recurring Decimals
Q1 $\frac{14}{111}$
Q2 Let $r = 0.\dot{0}\dot{7}$
Then $100r = 7.\dot{0}\dot{7}$
So $100r - r = 7.\dot{0}\dot{7} - 0.\dot{0}\dot{7}$
$99r = 7$
$r = \frac{7}{99}$

Page 10 — Rounding Numbers
Q1 a) 21.4 (1 d.p.)   b) 21.44 (2 d.p.)
Q2 a) 77 (2 s.f.)   b) 76.8 (3 s.f.)
    c) 76.84 (4 s.f.)

Page 11 — Estimating
Q1 a) Rounding to the nearest integer gives 6 OR rounding to 1 s.f. gives 5
    b) 11.7
    Answers in the range 11.6-11.8 would be acceptable here — the actual value is 11.66190...

Q2 a) E.g. 4000 cm³
    To get this estimate, π was rounded to 1 s.f. and the radius was rounded to the nearest 10 cm.
    b) E.g. Bigger — π is rounded down to 3, but 9 is rounded up to 10 and cubed, so the overall answer is bigger.

Page 12 — Bounds
Q1 The maximum amount is £39.37 and the minimum amount is £35.08

Page 13 — Bounds
Q1 The upper bound for $x = 216$ m to the nearest m, and the lower bound for $x = 213$ m to the nearest m
Q2 6.2 m/s to 1 decimal place

Page 15 — Standard Form
Q1 8.54×10^5
    1.8×10^{-4}
Q2 a) 2×10^{11} b) 6.47×10^{11}

Page 16 — Different Number Systems
Q1 a) 7   b) 34   c) 108
Q2 a) 10110   b) 101000   c) 111111

Page 17 — Revision Questions for Section One
Q1 a) Whole numbers — either positive or negative, or zero.
    b) Numbers that can be written as fractions.
    c) Numbers which will only divide by themselves or 1 (excluding 1 itself, which is not prime).
Q2 a) 11   b) 0.5   c) 169
Q3 Number of packs of buns = 8
    Number of packs of cheese slices = 3
    Number of packs of hot dogs = 4
Q4 a) $320 = 2^6 \times 5$
    $880 = 2^4 \times 5 \times 11$
    b) LCM $= 2^6 \times 5 \times 11 = 3520$
    HCF $= 2^4 \times 5 = 80$
Q5 Divide top and bottom by the same number till they won't go any further.
Q6 a) $8\frac{2}{9}$ b) $\frac{33}{7}$
Q7 Multiplying: Multiply top and bottom numbers separately.
    Dividing: Turn the second fraction upside down, then multiply.
    Adding/subtracting: Put fractions over a common denominator, then add/subtract the numerators.
Q8 a) $\frac{14}{99}$ b) $\frac{22}{7}$ or $3\frac{1}{7}$
    c) $\frac{11}{24}$ d) $\frac{151}{20}$ or $7\frac{11}{20}$

Q9 a) 210 kg   b) $\frac{11}{7}$
Q10 $\frac{7}{10}$
Q11 a) Divide the numerator by the denominator.
    b) Put the digits after the decimal point on the top, and a power of 10 with the same number of zeros as there were decimal places on the bottom.
Q12 a) (i) $\frac{1}{25}$ (ii) 4%
    b) (i) $\frac{13}{20}$ (ii) 0.65
Q13 Orange juice = 12.5 litres
    Lemonade = 10 litres
    Cranberry juice = 2.5 litres
Q14 Let $r = 0.5\dot{1}$
    Then $100r = 51.5\dot{1}$
    So $100r - r = 51.5\dot{1} - 0.5\dot{1}$
    $\Rightarrow 99r = 51$
    $\Rightarrow r = \frac{51}{99} = \frac{17}{33}$
Q15 a) 427.96   b) 428.0
    c) 430   d) 428.0
Q16 a) E.g. 20
    Depending on how you've rounded, you might have a different estimate — your answer should be in the range 16-20.
    b) 6.7
    Estimates between 6.6 and 6.8 are OK here — the actual value is 6.70820...
Q17 2.35 litres ≤ V < 2.45 litres
Q18 132.2425 m²
Q19 42.6 miles per gallon (3 s.f.)
Q20 310 g
Q21 1. The front number must always be between 1 and 10.
    2. The power of 10, n, is how far the decimal point moves.
    3. n is positive for big numbers, and negative for small numbers.
Q22 a) 9.7×10^5 b) 3.56×10^9
    c) 2.75×10^{-6}
Q23 $4.56 \times 10^{-3} = 0.00456$ and $2.7 \times 10^5 = 270\ 000$
Q24 a) 2×10^3 b) 2.739×10^{12}
Q25 a) 21   b) 11101

Section Two — Ratio, Proportion and Percentages

Page 18 — Ratios
Q1 a) 5:7   b) 10:3   c) 1:6
Q2 a) $\frac{3}{2}$ b) $\frac{1}{2}$

Page 19 — Ratios
Q1 a) $\frac{2}{13}$ b) 33 litres
Q2 36

Answers

Answers

Page 20 — Direct Proportion Problems
Q1 80p
Q2 £67.50
Q3 $750

Page 21 — Direct Proportion Problems
Q1 the 770 g bottle
Q2 a) E.g.

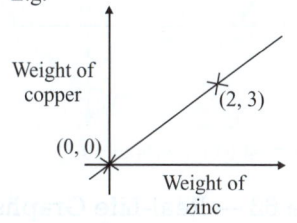

[Graph: Weight of copper (y-axis) vs Weight of zinc (x-axis), straight line through (0,0) and (2,3)]

b) The graph is a straight line through the origin.

Page 22 — Inverse Proportion Problems
Q1 1.5 hours
Q2 5 hours 20 mins

Page 23 — Harder Proportion Problems
Q1 273 m/s
Q2 $P = \dfrac{48}{Q^2}$
when $P = 8$, $Q = 2.45$ (2 d.p.)

Page 24 — Percentages
Q1 140%

Page 25 — Percentages
Q1 25% decrease
Q2 £5.49

Page 26 — Percentages
Q1 20%
Q2 £4585

Page 27 — Repeated Percentage Change
Q1 £3446.05

Page 28 — Revision Questions for Section Two
Q1 a) 9 : 11   b) 7 : 2
Q2 $\dfrac{7}{9}$
Q3 240
Q4 a) $\dfrac{1}{5}$ b) 128
Q5 Olive oil: 51 ml
Tomatoes: 1020 g
Garlic powder: 25.5 g
Onions: 204 g
Q6 £89.66

Q7 the 500 ml tin
Q8 D
Q9 a) 960   b) 3.9
Q10 $y = kx^2$
Q11 $p = 72$
Q12 0.91 Pa
Q13 a) 19   b) 39
c) 21.05%   d) 475%
Q14 % change = (change ÷ original) × 100
Q15 35% decrease
Q16 17.6 m
Q17 AER is a rate used to work out how much interest a savings account pays over a full year.
APR is a rate used to work out how much it costs you to borrow money per year.
Q18 £211 490.70
Q19 $N = N_0 \times$ (multiplier)^n
Q20 £157.37

Section Three — Algebra

Page 29 — Algebra Basics
Q1 $10x + 6y + 2$ cm

Page 30 — Multiplying Out Brackets
Q1 a) $y^2 - y - 20$
b) $4p^2 - 12p + 9$
c) $x^2 - 4xy + 4y^2$
d) $2t^2 - 5t\sqrt{2} - 6$

Page 31 — Factorising
Q1 $3y(2x + 5y)$
Q2 $(x + 4y)(x - 4y)$
Q3 $(x + \sqrt{11})(x - \sqrt{11})$
Q4 $\dfrac{6}{x + 7}$

Page 32 — Powers
Q1 a) e^{11} b) f^4
c) 1   d) $6h^7 j^2$
Q2 a) $\dfrac{1}{613}$ b) $\dfrac{1}{25}$ c) $\dfrac{27}{8}$

Page 33 — Powers and Roots
Q1 a) 5   b) $\dfrac{1}{3}$ c) 64
Q2 a) $27x^3$ b) $\sqrt[3]{x}$

Page 34 — Manipulating Surds
Q1 $13\sqrt{5}$
Q2 $4 - 2\sqrt{3}$

Page 35 — Solving Equations
Q1 $x = 2$
Q2 $y = 4$
Q3 $x = 6$

Page 36 — Solving Equations
Q1 $x = \pm 6$
Q2 $x = 8$

Page 37 — Expressions and Formulas
Q1 Noah = 13 tickets, Hellä = 26 tickets, Joe = 34 tickets
Q2 3, 15 and 30

Page 38 — Expressions, Formulas and Functions
Q1 $x = 11$
Q2 $x = 16$

Page 39 — Trial and Improvement
Q1 $x = 3.6$
Q2 $x = 5.5$

Page 40 — Rearranging Formulas
Q1 $q = 7(p - 2r)$ or $7p - 14r$
Q2 $v = u + at$

Page 41 — Rearranging Formulas
Q1 a) $y = \pm 2\sqrt{x}$ b) $y = \dfrac{xz}{x - 1}$

Page 42 — Factorising Quadratics
Q1 $(x + 5)(x - 3)$
Q2 $x = 4$ or $x = 5$

Page 43 — Factorising Quadratics
Q1 $(2x + 3)(x - 4)$
Q2 $x = \dfrac{2}{3}$ or $x = -4$
Q3 $(3x + 2)(x + 10)$
Q4 $x = -\dfrac{2}{5}$ or $x = 3$

Page 44 — The Quadratic Formula
Q1 $x = 0.39$ or -10.39
Q2 $x = \dfrac{1 \pm \sqrt{3}}{2}$

Page 45 — Algebraic Fractions
Q1 $\dfrac{2x + 19}{6}$
Q2 $\dfrac{x + 4y}{2x - y}$
Q3 $\dfrac{6x + 12}{x^2 + 5x}$

Page 46 — Algebraic Fractions
Q1 $\dfrac{5x + 11}{(x - 2)(x + 5)}$

Page 47 — Simultaneous Equations
Q1 One cup of tea costs £1.50 and one slice of cake costs £2
Q2 $x = 3, y = -1$

Page 48 — Simultaneous Equations
Q1 $x = 1, y = -1$ and $x = -4, y = 14$
Q2 $A: (0, 4)$ and $B (6, 40)$
Equally, you could have $A: (6, 40)$ and $B (0, 4)$

Answers

Page 49 — Inequalities
Q1 a) $x < 3$ **b)** $x \leq -3$
Q2 $-2 \leq x \leq 4$

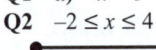

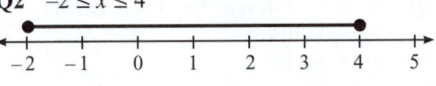

Page 50 — Graphical Inequalities
Q1 [graph showing $y = x+1$, $x = 5$, $y = -1$ with shaded region]

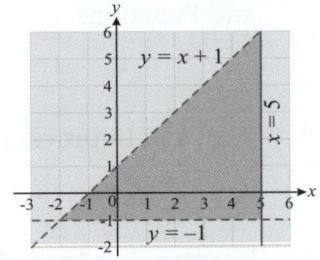

Page 51 — Sequences
Q1 Rule: multiply the previous term by 2
Next two terms: 24, 48
Rule: add 3, add 6, add 9...
Next two terms: 21, 33

Page 52 — Sequences
Q1 $n^3 + 2$
Q2 $\dfrac{n}{4n+1}$

Page 53 — Revision Questions for Section Three
Q1 $5x - 4y - 5$
Q2 a) $6x + 3$ **b)** $x^2 - x - 6$
   c) $x^2 + 10x + 25$
Q3 a) $2(2x+y)(2x-y)$
   b) $(7+9pq)(7-9pq)$
   c) $12(x+2y)(x-2y)$
Q4 a) x^9 **b)** y^2 **c)** $\dfrac{1}{z^3}$
Q5 a) 3 **b)** $\dfrac{1}{5}$ **c)** 8
Q6 a) $3\sqrt{3}$ **b)** 5
Q7 $3\sqrt{2}$
Q8 a) $x = 2$ **b)** $x = 4$ **c)** $x = \pm 8$
Q9 Tony has 37 marbles.
Q10 $6x$ cm
Q11 14
Q12 $x = 4.1$
Q13 a) $p = 4(s+1)$
   b) $p = \pm\sqrt{4v - u^2}$ **c)** $p = \dfrac{4}{3}w$
Q14 a) $x = -3$ or $x = -6$
   b) $x = -\dfrac{3}{5}$ or $x = 4$
Q15 a) $x = 1.56$ or $x = -2.56$
   b) $x = 0.27$ or $x = -1.47$
   c) $x = 1.46$ or $x = -0.46$
   d) $x = 0.44$ or $x = -3.44$
Q16 a) $\dfrac{ab}{2}$ (This is the same as $\dfrac{1}{2}ab$.)
   b) $\dfrac{c(c-1)}{d+5}$
Q17 a) $\dfrac{f - 4g}{8}$ **b)** $\dfrac{wx - yz}{wz}$
   c) $\dfrac{3x+1}{(x+3)(x-1)}$
Q18 $x = 2, y = 3$
Q19 $x = -2, y = -2$ and $x = -4, y = -8$
Q20 a) $x \geq -2$ **b)** $x < -6$ or $x > 6$

Q21 [graph showing $y = 2x - 2$, $x + y = 6$, $y = 0.5$ with shaded region]

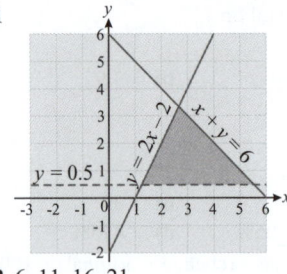

Q22 6, 11, 16, 21
Q23 a) $n^2 - 2$ **b)** $\dfrac{1}{7n - 4}$

Section Four — Graphs

Page 54 — Straight Lines and Gradients
Q1 Gradient is -5

Page 55 — Line Segments
Q1 a) $(7, 5)$ **b)** 7.21 (to 2 d.p.)

Page 56 — y = mx + c
Q1 $y = \dfrac{2}{3}x + 2$
Q2 $y = \dfrac{1}{2}x + 5$

Page 57 — Parallel and Perpendicular Lines
Q1 $y = -x + 5$
Q2 Rearrange given equations into $y = mx + c$ form to find gradients.
Gradient of line 1 = -5
Gradient of line 2 = $\dfrac{1}{5}$
$-5 \times \dfrac{1}{5} = -1$
So $y + 5x = 2$ and $5y = x + 3$ are perpendicular as their gradients multiply together to give -1.

Page 58 — Quadratic Graphs
Q1 [quadratic graph]

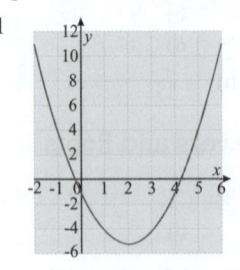

Page 59 — Harder Graphs
Q1 [graph of $y = x^3 - 4x^2 + 2$]

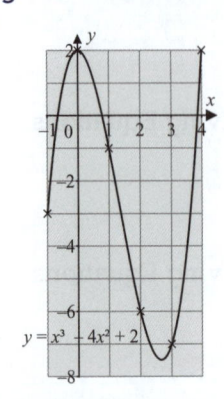

Page 60 — Harder Graphs
Q1 Radius = 13
Equation of circle is $x^2 + y^2 = 169$

Page 61 — Solving Equations Using Graphs
Q1 [quadratic graph]
$x = -3.6$ or 1.6 (both ± 0.2)

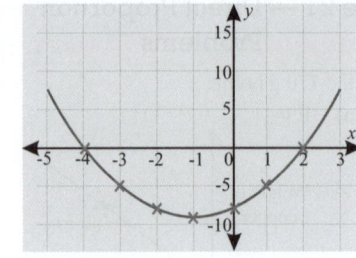

Page 62 — Real-Life Graphs
Q1 [graph of Fare (£) vs Miles]

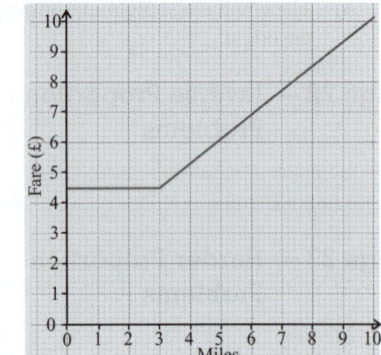

Page 63 — Distance-Time Graphs
Q1 a) 15 minutes **b)** 12 km/h

Page 64 — Gradients of Real-Life Graphs
Q1 2.3 cm per day (allow ± 0.3 cm)

Page 65 — Revision Questions for Section Four
Q1 [graph showing a) $y = -x$, b) $y = -4$, c) $x = 2$]

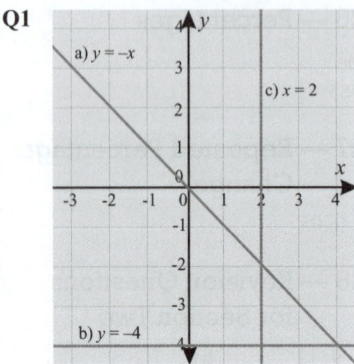

Q2 [graph showing $y = \frac{1}{2}x + 1$]

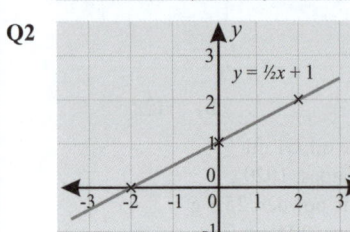

Answers

Q3 a) (1.5, 1.5)
  b) $\sqrt{74} = 8.6$ (to 1 d.p.)
Q4 $y = 2x + 10$
Q5 $y = x - 9$
Q6 a) perpendicular **b)** parallel
  c) neither
Q7 $y = -\frac{1}{2}x + 4$
Q8 a)

x	–3	–2	–1	0	1
y	–7	–9	–9	–7	–3

  b) (graph with minimum at (-1.5, -9.25))

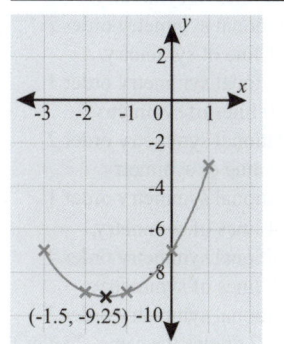

Q9 a) A graph with a "wiggle" in the middle. E.g. 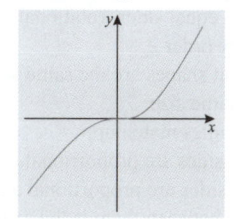
  b) A graph made up of two curves in diagonally opposite quadrants. The graph is symmetrical about the lines $y = x$ and $y = -x$. E.g. 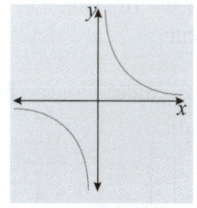
  c) A graph which curves rapidly upwards. E.g. (0, 1)
  d) A circle with radius r, centre (0, 0). E.g.

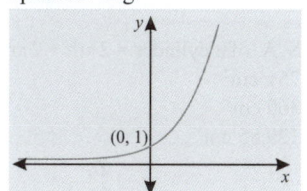

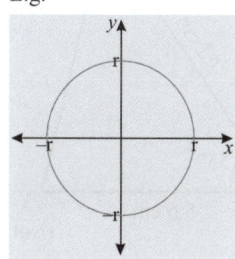

Q10 $a = 16, b = 2$

Q11 Radius is 6.32 units.
  Equation of the circle is $x^2 + y^2 = 40$
Q12 $x = 8, y = 12$
Q13 $x = 2, y = 4$ and $x = -5, y = 11$
Q14 $y = -x + 6$
Q15 (cost vs amount graph)

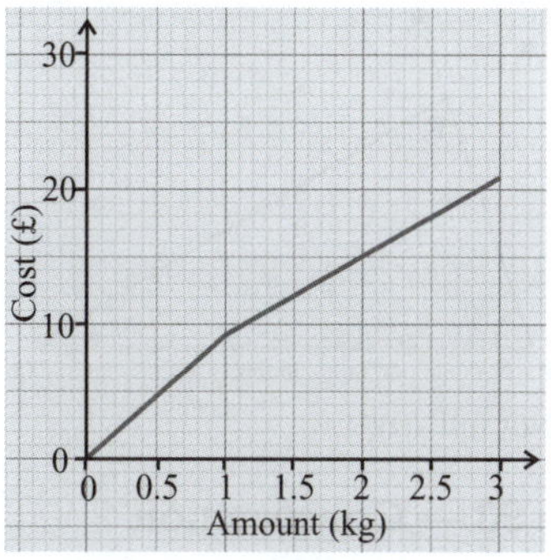

Q16 The object has stopped.
Q17 a) 14 s **b)** 16.67 (to 2 d.p.)

Section Five — Measures and Angles

Page 66 — Unit Conversions
Q1 18.08 litres (to 2 d.p.)

Page 67 — Speed, Density and Pressure
Q1 285 kg (3 s.f.)

Page 68 — Five Angle Rules
Q1 108°

Page 69 — Parallel Lines
Q1 30°

Page 70 — Geometry Problems
Q1 123°

Page 71 — Angles in Shapes
Q1 144°
Q2 pentagon
  Always read the question carefully — it asks for the name of the polygon, not just the number of sides.

Page 72 — Bearings
Q1 (diagram: Cinema × at 2.5 cm from House, bearing 35°, 1 cm = 2 miles)

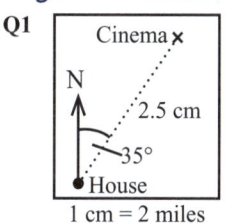

Page 74 — Circle Geometry
Q1 ABD = 63°
  ACD = 63°

Page 75 — Pythagoras' Theorem
Q1 10.3 m (1 d.p.)
Q2 3.8 m (1 d.p.)

Page 77 — Trigonometry
Q1 27.1° (1 d.p.)
  Use the trig formula triangles for questions like this.
Q2 2.97 m (3 s.f.)

Page 78 — The Sine and Cosine Rules
Q1 32.5 cm² (3 s.f.)

Page 79 — The Sine and Cosine Rules
Q1 20.5 cm (3 s.f.)
Q2 59.5° (3 s.f.)

Page 80 — 3D Pythagoras
Q1 14.8 cm (3 s.f.)

Page 81 — 3D Trigonometry
Q1 17.1° (3 s.f.)

Page 82 — Revision Questions for Section Five
Q1 a) 5600 cm³ **b)** 10.8 km/h
  c) 240 cm **d)** 12 000 000 cm³
  e) 12.8 cm² **f)** 2750 mm³
Q2 12 500 cm³
Q3 11 m²
Q4 Angles in a triangle add up to 180°.
  Angles on a straight line add up to 180°.
  Angles in a quadrilateral add up to 360°.
  Angles round a point add up to 360°.
  Isosceles triangles have 2 sides the same and 2 angles the same.
Q5 a) 154° **b)** 112° **c)** 58°
Q6 Exterior angle = 51.4° (1 d.p.)
  Sum of interior angles = 900°
Q7 Put your pencil on the diagram at the point you're going from — point A. Draw a north line at this point. Measure the angle to line AB clockwise from the north line — this is the bearing you want.
Q8 (diagram showing bearings 210° and 040°, distances 25 km (5 cm) and 20 km (4 cm))
Q9 a) 53° **b)** 69° **c)** 33°
Q10 4.72 m (3 s.f.)
Q11 (formula triangles: O/S×H, A/C×H, O/T×A)
  It's easy to write these down if you remember SOH CAH TOA.

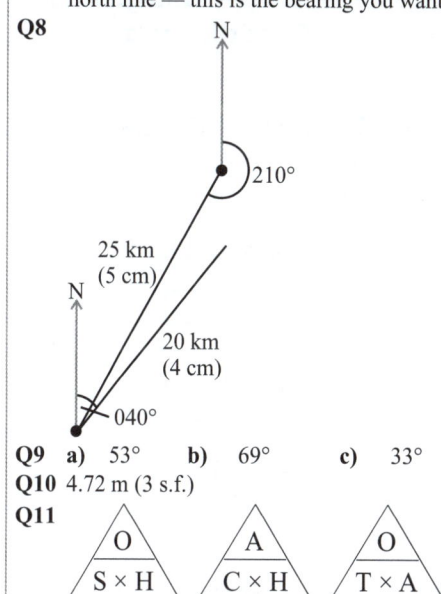

Answers

Q12 33.4° (1 d.p.)
Q13 21.5° (1 d.p.)
Q14 Sine rule: $\dfrac{a}{\sin A} = \dfrac{b}{\sin B} = \dfrac{c}{\sin C}$
Cosine rule: $a^2 = b^2 + c^2 - 2bc \cos A$
Area = $\dfrac{1}{2} ab \sin C$
Q15 1. Two angles given plus any side — use the sine rule.
2. Two sides given plus an angle not enclosed by them — use the sine rule.
3. Two sides given plus the angle enclosed by them — use the cosine rule.
4. All three sides given but no angles — use the cosine rule.
Q16 48.1 cm² (3 s.f.)
Q17 56.4° (3 s.f.)
Q18 6.84 cm (3 s.f.)
Q19 11.9 m (3 s.f.)
Q20 15.2° (3 s.f.)

Section Six — Shapes and Area

Page 83 — Properties of 2D Shapes

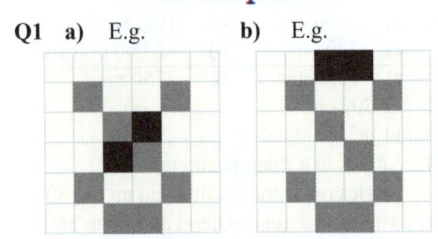

Q1 a) E.g.   b) E.g.

Page 84 — Properties of 2D Shapes

Q1 Rhombus
Rotational symmetry of order 2

Page 85 — Similar Shapes

Q1 BD = 10 cm

Page 86 — Area — Triangles and Quadrilaterals

Q1 x = 10

Page 87 — Area — Circles

Q1 a) 83.78 cm² (2 d.p.)
b) 20.94 cm (2 d.p.)

Page 88 — Plans and Elevations

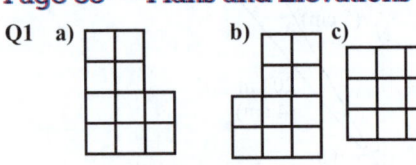

Q1 a)   b)   c)

Page 89 — 3D Shapes — Surface Area

Q1 l = 20 cm

Page 90 — 3D Shapes — Volume

Q1 h = 36 cm

Page 91 — 3D Shapes — Volume

Q1 228.81 cm³

Page 92 — Construction

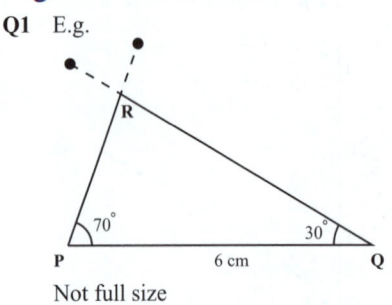

Q1 E.g.

Not full size

Page 93 — Construction

Q1 First draw a base line of 5 cm, then use compasses set to 5 cm to draw an arc from each end of the base line. Where the arcs cross is the tip of the triangle.

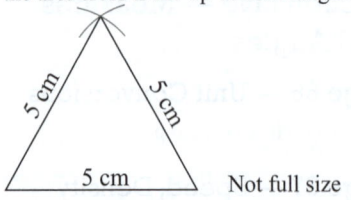

Not full size

Page 95 — Loci and Construction

Q1 Shaded area = where public can go

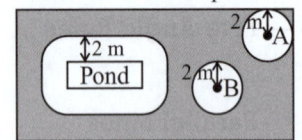

Page 96 — Translation, Rotation and Reflection

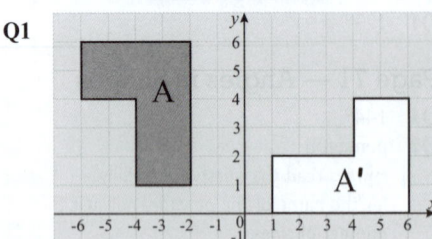

Q1

Page 97 — Enlargement

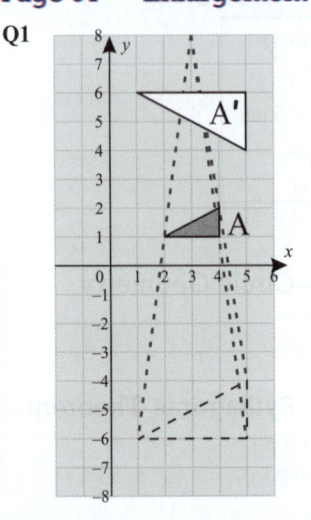

Q1

Page 98 — Enlargement — Area and Volume

Q1 Surface area = 20 cm²
Volume = 8 cm³

Page 99 — Revision Questions for Section Six

Q1 H: 2 lines of symmetry, rotational symmetry order 2
Z: 0 lines of symmetry, rotational symmetry order 2
T: 1 line of symmetry, rotational symmetry order 1
N: 0 lines of symmetry, rotational symmetry order 2
E: 1 line of symmetry, rotational symmetry order 1
×: 4 lines of symmetry, rotational symmetry order 4
S: 0 lines of symmetry, rotational symmetry order 2
Q2 E.g. 2 angles the same, 2 sides the same, 1 line of symmetry, no rotational symmetry.
Q3 2 pairs of equal sides, rotational symmetry order 2.
Q4 Congruent shapes are the same shape and the same size.
Q5 All the angles match up.
All three sides are proportional.
Any two sides are proportional and the angle between them is the same.
Q6 x = 2.5 cm
Q7 $A = b \times h_v$
Q8 69 cm²
Q9 30 cm
Q10 Circumference = 16π cm, area = 64π cm²
Q11 39.27 cm²
Q12 Front: Side: Plan:

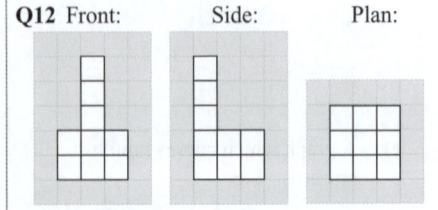

Q13 S. A. of a cylinder = $2\pi rh + 2\pi r^2$
Q14 75π cm²
Q15 360 cm³
Q16 129.85 cm³
Q17

(Not full size)

Answers

Q18 [diagram of perpendicular bisector]

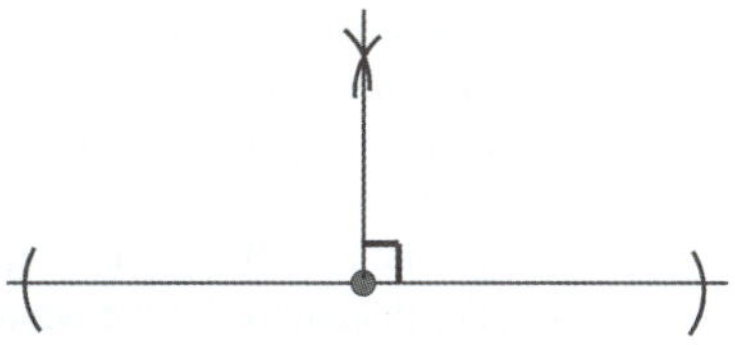

Q19 A circle

Q20 [diagram: rectangle ABCD with A 4 cm B (Not full size), 3 cm side, DC 6 cm, with shaded region]

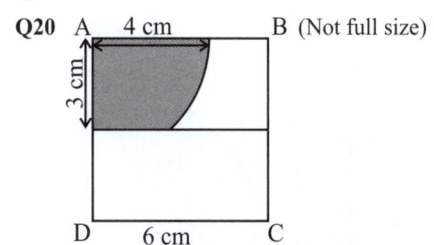

Q21 a) Translation by vector $\binom{-7}{-5}$ OR rotation 180° about point (1, 2).
b) Enlargement of scale factor $\frac{1}{3}$ and centre of enlargement (0, 0).

Q22 [diagram showing transformations on coordinate grid with shapes labelled a), b), c), X]

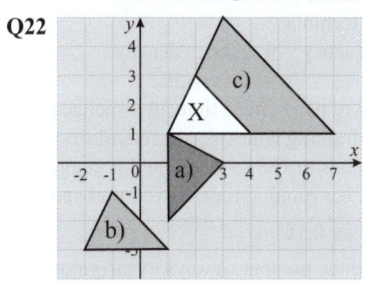

Q23 80 cm²

Section Seven — Statistics and Probability

Page 100 — Planning an Investigation

Q1 a) E.g. 'Children solve the logic puzzle faster than adults.'
b) Think about the different stages of the handling data cycle.
Collecting data:
E.g. collect primary data by doing an experiment. This data should be reliable as the researcher can measure and record the times fairly and accurately.
Processing and presenting data:
E.g. put the data into grouped frequency tables, with one for children and one for adults. Then averages, such as the mean, can be found and diagrams, such as histograms, can be drawn.
Interpreting results:
E.g. Compare the mean times for children and adults. This shows whether the children were generally faster or slower at solving the puzzle than the adults.
There are loads of things that could be included in an investigation plan — they depend on the hypothesis you've chosen.

Page 101 — Sampling and Data Collection

Q1 E.g. No, Tina can't use her results to draw conclusions about the whole population. The sample is biased because it excludes people who never use the train and most of the people included are likely to use the train regularly. The sample is also too small to represent the whole population.

Page 102 — Sampling and Data Collection

Q1 2 middle managers

Page 103 — Sampling and Data Collection

Q1 Discrete data
E.g.

Cinema visits	Tally	Frequency
0-9		
10-19		
20-29		
30-39		
40-49		
50 or over		

Page 104 — Venn Diagrams

Q1 [Venn diagram with three circles J, K, L containing: 1, 9 in J only; 4 in K only; 2 in L only; 7, 3, 5 in J∩L; 6, 8 outside]

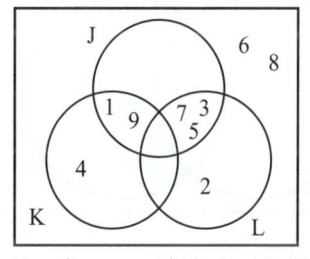

Your diagram might look a bit different — you'll get the marks as long as the data points are in the correct group. Make sure each circle is labelled with the right letter.

Page 105 — Other Charts and Graphs

Q1 [Pie chart: Action 72°, Rom Com 138°, Western 150°]

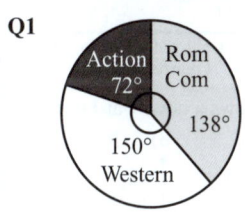

Page 106 — Other Charts and Graphs

Q1

	Boy	Girl	Total
Pass	13	11	24
Fail	3	4	7
Total	16	15	31

Page 107 — Scatter Graphs

Q1 a) There is a strong negative correlation. The longer the run, the slower Sam's speed.
b) [Scatter graph: Average speed (mph) vs Length of run (miles), with outlier circled]
c) Approximately 5 mph (±0.5 mph)
d) The estimate should be reliable because **[either]** 8 miles is within the range of the known data **[or]** the graph shows strong correlation.

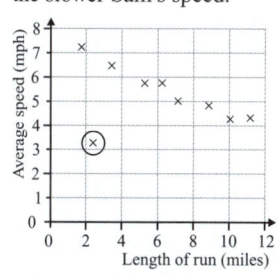

Page 108 — Mean, Mode, Median and Range

Q1 Mean = 11.2, Median = 12, Mode = 12, Range = 9
Q2 The mean of all 9 heights will be lower than 1.6 m, because the new height is lower than 1.6 m.

Page 109 — Frequency Tables — Finding Averages

Q1 a) Median = 2   b) Mean = 1.66

Page 110 — Grouped Frequency Tables

Q1 a) 17.4 cm (3 s.f.)
b) 12 out of 61 = 19.67...% of the lengths are below 16.5 cm. **[Either]** Less than 20% of the lengths are below 16.5 cm, so Ana's statement is incorrect. **[Or]** Rounding to the nearest whole percent, 20% of the lengths are below 16.5 cm, so Ana's statement is correct.

Page 111 — Averages and Spread

Q1 a)
```
0 | 7           Key: 0 | 7 = 0.7
1 | 1 4 6
2 | 2 6
3 | 0
```
b) IQR = 1.5

Page 112 — Averages and Spread

Q1 [Two box plots drawn on a number line from 0 to 25]

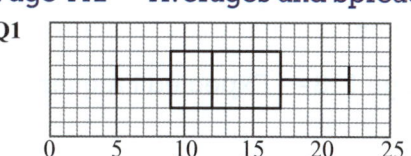

Answers

Page 113 — Cumulative Frequency

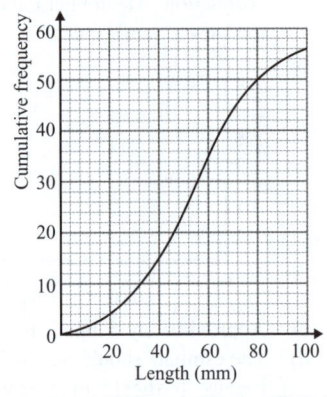

Q1 a) [Cumulative frequency graph showing an S-curve with Length (mm) on x-axis from 0 to 100 and Cumulative frequency on y-axis from 0 to 60]

b) Answer in the range 53.6 – 60.7%.

Page 114 — Histograms and Frequency Density

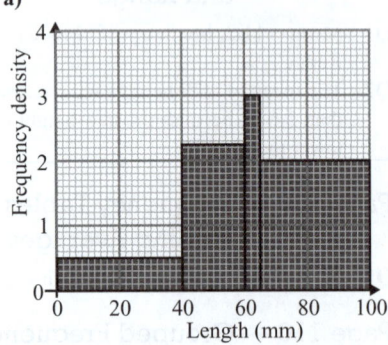

Q1 a) [Histogram with Length (mm) on x-axis from 0 to 100 and Frequency density on y-axis from 0 to 4]

b) 90 slugs

Page 115 — Histograms and Frequency Density

Q1 1) The data classes are unequal, so the columns shouldn't all be the same width.
2) The horizontal axis isn't labelled.
3) The frequency density scale isn't numbered.

Page 116 — Probability Basics

Q1 $\frac{3}{10}$ or 0.3

Q2 $3x$

Page 117 — Counting Outcomes

Q1 a) HHH, HHT, HTH, THH, TTH, THT, HTT, TTT

b) $\frac{3}{8}$ or 0.375

Q2 36

Page 118 — Expected Frequency

Q1 60 times

Page 119 — Probability Experiments

Q1 a) $\frac{13}{20} = 0.65$

b) Sandro's results are based on more visits to the coffee shop, so his results are likely to give a better estimate of the probability.

Page 120 — The AND / OR Rules

Q1 0.72
Q2 a) 0.65 **b)** 0.03

Page 121 — Tree Diagrams

Q1 $\frac{48}{100} = \frac{12}{25}$

Page 122 — Tree Diagrams

Q1 a) $\frac{310}{420} = \frac{31}{42}$ **b)** $\frac{220}{420} = \frac{11}{21}$

Page 123 — Revision Questions for Section Seven

Q1 A sample is part of a population. Samples need to be representative so that conclusions drawn from sample data can be applied to the whole population.

Q2 20

Q3 Qualitative data

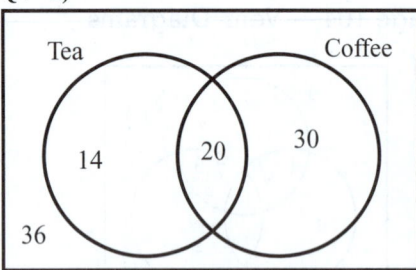

Q4 a) [Venn diagram with two circles labelled Tea and Coffee. Tea only: 14, intersection: 20, Coffee only: 30, outside: 36]

b) P(like tea or coffee) = $\frac{16}{25}$

Q5 Calculations or instructions

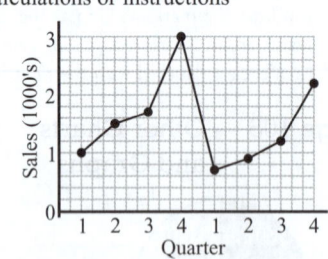

Q6 a) [Time series graph showing Sales (1000's) over Quarters 1-4 for two periods]

b) The data shows a downward trend.

Q7 a) E.g. [scatter graph] **b)** E.g. [scatter graph showing negative correlation]

c) E.g. [scatter graph]

Q8 a) $1.5 \leq y < 1.6$
b) $1.5 \leq y < 1.6$
c) 1.58 m (2 d.p.)

Q9 $Q_1 = 11$, $Q_3 = 31$, IQR = 20

Q10 The median time in winter is lower than the median time in summer, so it generally took longer to get to work in the summer.
The range and the IQR for the summer are smaller than those for the winter, so there is less variation in journey times in the summer.

Q11 [Cumulative frequency graph with Length (m) on x-axis from 1.4 to 1.8 and Cumulative frequency on y-axis from 0 to 20]

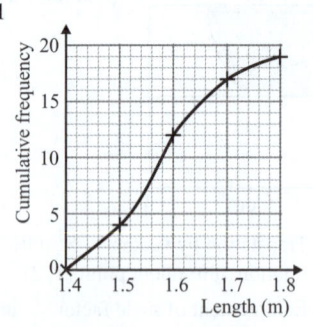

Q12 Calculate the bar's area, or use the formula:
frequency = frequency density × class width.

Q13 The runner's mean time after increasing her training hours has decreased from 147 seconds to 138 seconds, so this suggests that her running times have improved.

Q14 $\frac{4}{25}$ or 0.16

Q15 Find the number of ways to carry out each activity, then multiply all the numbers together.

Q16 a) HHHT, HHTT, HTHT, THHT, TTHT, THTT, HTTT, TTTT, HHHH, HHTH, HTHH, THHH, TTHH, THTH, HTTH, TTTH

b) $\frac{4}{16} = 0.25 = 25\%$

Q17 a) Expected frequency = probability × number of trials

b) Relative frequency = $\frac{\text{Frequency}}{\text{Number of times you tried the experiment}}$

Q18 a) [Tree diagram: Part 1 and Part 2. Total 160. Pass 105 → Pass 60, Fail 45. Fail 55 → Pass 30, Fail 25.]

b) Relative frequency of:
pass, pass = $\frac{60}{160} = \frac{3}{8}$ or 0.375
pass, fail = $\frac{45}{160} = \frac{9}{32}$ or 0.28125
fail, pass = $\frac{30}{160} = \frac{3}{16}$ or 0.1875
fail, fail = $\frac{25}{160} = \frac{5}{32}$ or 0.15625

c) 150

Q19 P(a 6 then an even number) = $\frac{4}{81}$

Q20 a) P(2 Kings) = $\frac{1}{169}$

b) P(3 Kings) = $\frac{1}{5525}$

Index

2D shapes 83, 84
3D shapes 89-91

A

AER (Annual Equivalent Rate) 26
algebra 29-52
algebraic fractions 46
AND rule 120
angles
   angle rules 68, 70
   around parallel lines 69
   exterior angles 71
   interior angles 71
   of depression 77
   of elevation 77
   three letter notation 70
APR (Annual Percentage Rate) 26
arcs 87
area 98
   converting area 66
   of a circle 87
   of a triangle 78, 86
   of quadrilaterals 86
averages 108, 112

B

bacon and eggs 64
bearings 72
best buy questions 21
bias 101, 119
binary numbers 16
BODMAS 2
bounds 12, 13
box plots 112
brackets 30

C

calculators 15, 18, 75, 76
chords 73, 87
circles 60, 73, 74, 87
   arcs 87
   circle theorems 73, 74
   equation of a circle 60
   sectors 87
compasses 93, 94
compound decay 27, 60
compound growth 27, 60
cones 89, 90
congruent shapes 85, 96
construction 92, 93, 95
   of perpendiculars 93
   of triangles 92, 93
continuous data 103
conversion graphs 62
correlation 107
cosine rule 78, 79
cubic graphs 59
cumulative frequency 113
cylinders 89, 90

D

data classes 103, 110
data collection 101
decimal places 10
decimals 7
   recurring decimals 7-9
   terminating decimals 7, 8
density 67
difference of two squares (D.O.T.S.) 31
direct proportion 20, 21
   algebraic problems 23
   golden rule 20
   graphs 21
discrete data 103
distance-time graphs 63

E

edges 89
elevations 88
enlargements 97, 98
equations
   of graphs 56-60
   rearranging 35
   solving 35-37
   solving using graphs 61
estimating 11
   rate at a point 64
   square roots 11
exchange rates 20
expanding brackets 30
expected frequency 118
exponential graphs 60
expressions
   forming 37, 38
   simplifying 29

F

faces 89
factorising 31
   quadratics 42, 43
factors 3
   factor trees 3
   prime factors 3
fair 119
flow charts 105
formula triangles 67, 76
formulas 37, 38, 40, 41
   rearranging formulas 40, 41
fractions 5-9, 18
   algebraic fractions 45, 46
   improper fractions 5
frequency 109
   cumulative frequency graphs 113
   expected frequency 118
   relative frequency 119
frequency density 114, 115
frequency tables 109
   grouped frequency tables 110
frequency trees 106

frustums 91
functions 38
   function machines 38

G

Gorgonzola 9
gradients 54, 63, 64
   of parallel lines 57
   of perpendicular lines 57
graphs
   conversion 62
   cubic 59
   cumulative frequency 113
   direct proportion 21
   distance-time 63
   exponential 60
   inequalities 50
   line 106
   quadratic 58
   reciprocal 59
   solving equations 61
   straight-line 54-57

H

handling data cycle 100
HCF (Highest Common Factor) 4
histograms 114, 115
hypothesis 100

I

identities 30
imperial units 66
inequalities 49, 50
   graphical inequalities 50
   number lines 49
inequality symbols 110
integers 2
interest 26, 27
   compound interest 27
   simple interest 26
interquartile range 111-113
inverse proportion 22, 23
   algebraic problems 23
   graphs 22
investigations 100
irrational numbers 2
irregular polygons 83
isosceles triangles 68

K

kites 84

Index

L
LCM (Least Common Multiple) 4
line graphs 106
line segments 55
line symmetry 83, 84
lines of best fit 107
loci 94, 95
lower bounds 12, 13

M
maximum values 12, 13
mean 108-110, 112
median 108, 109, 112
metric units 66
midpoints 55
minimum values 12, 13
mixed numbers 5
modal class 110
mode 108, 109, 112
multiples 3
mushy peas 105

N
negative numbers 29
north line 72
nth term formula 51
number lines 49

O
OR rule 120

P
parallel lines 57, 69
parallelograms 84
percentages 7, 24-27
  finding the original value 25
  percentage change 25
perimeter 98
perpendicular bisectors 94
perpendicular lines 57
pie charts 105
plans 88
polygons 71, 83
populations 101, 102
powers 32, 33
  fractional powers 33
  negative powers 32
  power rules 32
pressure 67
primary data 103
prime factors 3
prime numbers 3
prisms 90
probability 116-122
  combined probability 120
  dependent events 122
  probability experiments 119

product rule 117
proportional division 19
protractors 92
Pythagoras' theorem 55, 75
  3D 80

Q
quadratic equations 42-44
quadratic formula 44
quadratic graphs 58
quadrilaterals 68, 84, 86
qualitative data 103
quantitative data 103
quartiles 111-113
questionnaires 103

R
range 108, 109, 112
rates 64
rational numbers 2
ratios 18, 19
  converting to fractions 18
  proportional division 19
  scaling up ratios 19
real-life graphs 62
reciprocal graphs 59
reciprocals 2
rectangles 84
recurring decimals 7-9
reflections 96
regular polygons 83
relative frequency 119
rhombuses 84
roots 11, 33
rotational symmetry 83, 84
rotations 96
rounding 10

S
sample space diagrams 117
sampling 101
  simple random sampling 101, 102
  stratified sampling 102
scale drawings 72
scale factors 97, 98
scatter graphs 107
secondary data 103
segments 87
sequences 51, 52
  linear 51
  non-linear 52
shapes 83
significant figures 10
similar shapes 85, 97
simple interest 26
simplifying expressions 29
simultaneous equations 47, 48
sine rule 78, 79

speed 67
spheres 89, 90
squares 84
standard form 14, 15
stem and leaf diagrams 111
straight-line graphs 54-57
  equations 54, 56
stratified sampling 102
surds 2, 34
surface area 89, 98
  of a cone 89
  of a cylinder 89
  of a sphere 89
symmetry 83
  line symmetry 83, 84
  rotational symmetry 83, 84

T
tables of values 54
tangents 64, 87
  equation of a tangent 60
terms 29
time series 106
translations 96
trapeziums 84
tree diagrams 121, 122
trial and improvement 39
triangles 68, 76-79, 84-86
  construction 92, 93
  equilateral 84
  isosceles 84
  right-angled 84
  scalene 84
  similar 85
triangular numbers 51
trigonometry 76-79, 81
  3D 81
  formulas 76
two-way tables 106, 117

U
units 66
upper bounds 12, 13

V
Venn diagrams 104
vertices 89
volume 98
  converting volume 66
  of a cone 90
  of a cylinder 90
  of a frustum 91
  of a prism 90
  of a sphere 90